FNB

THE NEW CRITICAL IDIOM

SERIES EDITOR: JOHN DRAKAKIS, UNIVERSITY OF STIRLING

The New Critical Idiom is an invaluable series of introductory guides to today's critical terminology. Each book:

- provides a handy, explanatory guide to the use (and abuse) of the term;
- offers an original and distinctive overview by a leading literary and cultural critic;
- relates the term to the larger field of cultural representation.

With a strong emphasis on clarity, lively debate and the widest possible breadth of examples, *The New Critical Idiom* is an indispensable approach to key topics in literary studies.

Also available in this series:

GOTHIC

Second edition
Fred Botting

Routledge
Taylor & Francis Group

LONDON AND NEW YORK

First published 2014
by Routledge
2 Park Square, Milton Park, Abingdon, Oxon OX14 4RN

and by Routledge
711 Third Avenue, New York, NY 10017

Routledge is an imprint of the Taylor & Francis Group, an informa business

British Library Cataloguing in Publication Data
A catalogue record for this book is available from the British Library

Library of Congress Cataloging in Publication Data
Botting, Fred.
Gothic / Fred Botting. – 2nd edition.
pages cm. – (THE NEW CRITICAL IDIOM)
Includes bibliographical references and index.
1. Horror tales, English–History and criticism–Theory, etc. 2. Horror tales, American–History and criticism–Theory, etc. 3. Gothic revival (Literature)–English-speaking countries. 4. Literary form. I. Title.
PR830.T3B68 2013
823'.0872909–dc23
2013015355

ISBN: 978-0-415-83171-0 (hbk)
ISBN: 978-0-415-83172-7 (pbk)
ISBN: 978-0-203-48771-6 (ebk)

Typeset in Garamond
by Cenveo Publisher Services
Printed and bound by CPI Group (UK) Ltd, Croydon, CR0 4YY

CONTENTS

SERIES EDITOR'S PREFACE

The New Critical Idiom is a series of introductory books which seeks to extend the lexicon of literary terms, in order to address the radical changes which have taken place in the study of literature during the last decades of the twentieth century. The aim is to provide clear, well-illustrated accounts of the full range of terminology currently in use, and to evolve histories of its changing usage.

The current state of the discipline of literary studies is one where there is considerable debate concerning basic questions of terminology. This involves, among other things, the boundaries which distinguish the literary from the non-literary; the position of literature within the larger sphere of culture; the relationship between literatures of different cultures; and questions concerning the relation of literary to other cultural forms within the context of interdisciplinary studies.

It is clear that the field of literary criticism and theory is a dynamic and heterogeneous one. The present need is for individual volumes on terms which combine clarity of exposition with an adventurousness of perspective and a breadth of application. Each volume will contain as part of its apparatus some indication of the direction in which the definition of particular terms is likely to move, as well as expanding the disciplinary boundaries within which some of these terms have been traditionally contained. This will involve some re-situation of terms within the larger field of cultural representation, and will introduce examples from the area of film and the modern media in addition to examples from a variety of literary texts.

ACKNOWLEDGEMENTS

Many people – too many to mention by name – have contributed over the years to the development of both editions of this book. At the start of research, members of the Centre for Critical and Cultural Theory and the Department of English at Cardiff University offered great support and advice. Later, colleagues, friends and students at various institutions – the universities of Lancaster, Keele and Kingston in particular – provided numerous suggestions and insights, as did a host of researchers involved in the friendly meetings of the International Gothic Association. Staff and postgraduates at Stirling University, too, were particularly helpful in the process of rethinking and revising the book. One person, however, should be thanked by name: John Drakakis. Not only has he overseen the production of both editions, but he has done so with the kind of critical attention and care that is rare these days.

1

INTRODUCTION
NEGATIVE AESTHETICS

Transgression, then, is not related to the limit as black to white, the prohibited to the lawful, the outside to the inside, or as the open area of a building to its enclosed spaces. Rather, their relationship takes the forms of a spiral which no simple infraction can exhaust. Perhaps it is like a flash of lightning in the night which, from the beginning of time, gives a dense and black intensity to the night it denies, which lights up the night from the inside, from top to bottom, and yet owes to the dark the stark clarity of it manifestation, its harrowing and poised singularity; the flash loses itself in this space it marks with its sovereignty and becomes silent now that it has given a name to obscurity.

(Michel Foucault, 'Preface to Transgression', p. 35)

DARKNESS

A negative aesthetics informs gothic texts. First produced in the middle of the eighteenth century, a period when the Enlightenment was establishing itself as the dominant way of ordering the world, gothic tales were set in the Middle, or 'Dark', Ages. Darkness – an absence of the light associated with sense, security and knowledge – characterises the looks, moods, atmospheres and connotations of the genre. Gothic texts are, overtly but ambiguously, not rational, depicting disturbances of sanity and security, from superstitious belief in ghosts and demons, displays of uncontrolled passion, violent emotion or flights of fancy to portrayals of perversion and obsession. Moreover, if knowledge is associated with rational procedures of enquiry and understanding based on natural, empirical reality, then gothic styles disturb the borders of knowing and conjure up obscure otherworldly phenomena or the 'dark arts', alchemical, arcane and occult forms normally characterised as delusion, apparition, deception. Not tied to a natural order of things as defined by realism, gothic flights of imagination suggest supernatural possibility, mystery, magic, wonder and monstrosity.

Gothic texts are not good in moral, aesthetic or social terms. Their concern is with vice: protagonists are selfish or evil; adventures involve decadence or crime. Their effects, aesthetically and socially, are also replete with a range of negative features: not beautiful, they display no harmony or proportion. Ill-formed, obscure, ugly, gloomy and utterly antipathetic to effects of love, admiration or gentle delight, gothic texts register revulsion, abhorrence, fear, disgust and terror. Invoking ideas and objects of displeasure, gothic texts were invariably considered to be of little artistic merit, crude, formulaic productions for vulgar, uncultivated tastes. They were also considered anti-social in content and function, failing to encourage the acquisition of virtuous attitudes and corrupting readers' powers of discrimination with idle fantasies, seducing them from paths of filial obedience, respect, prudence, modesty and social duty. Definitively negative, gothic fictions appear distinctly anti-modern in their use of the customs, costumes and codes of chivalry associated with feudal power: the gallantry and romanticism of knights, ladies and martial honour also evoked an era of barbarism, ignorance, tyranny and superstition.

Yet there is a paradox in the appeal to the past. Though 'gothic' calls up feudal associations, medieval styles of architecture and a notoriously fierce Germanic tribe, or grouping of tribes ('the Goths'), all antithetical to models of order established by the Roman empire, the invocation occurs in the middle of an eighteenth century in which the promotion of reason, science, commerce and bourgeois values was in the ascendancy and in the process of transforming patterns of knowledge (empiricism rather than religion), production (commerce and manufacture rather than agriculture), social organisation (city rather than country) and political power (representative democracy rather than monarchy). The past with which gothic writing engages and which it constructs is shaped by the changing times in which it is composed: the definition of Enlightenment and reason, it seems, requires carefully constructed antitheses, the obscurity of figures of feudal darkness and barbarism providing the negative against which it can assume positive value.

The interplay of light and dark, positive and negative, is evident in the conventions, settings, characters, devices and effects specific to gothic texts. Historical settings allow a movement from and back to a rational present: more than a flight of nostalgic retrospection or an escape from the dullness of a present without chivalry, magic or adventure, the movement does not long for terrifying and arbitrary aristocratic power, religious superstition or supernatural events but juxtaposes terrors of the negative with an order authorised by reason and morality. Romance, imagined in the darkness of history, encourages and assuages threats to propriety, domesticity and social duty. The movement remains sensitive to other times and places and thus retains traces of instability where further disorientations, ambivalence and dislocations can arise. Returns of the past, in an opposing direction, involve the very characteristics – superstition, tyranny, violence – supposedly banished by the light of reason. In more psychological renderings, ghostly recurrences manifest an unease and instability in the imagined unity of self, home or society, hauntings that suggest loss or guilt or threat. Generations are subject to the crossing of temporal lines: an ancestor's crime threatens a family's status; immature desires upset social mores; an old misdeed tarnishes paternal respectability. In seeing one time and its values cross into another, both periods are disturbed. The dispatching of unwanted ideas and attitudes into an imagined past does not guarantee they have been overcome. Savage and primitive energies, archaic and immature, link different historical and individual ages, marking out the other side, the unconscious, as it were, of both cultural and personal development.

Physical locations and settings manifest disturbance and ambivalence in spatial terms as movements between inside and out: the castles, abbeys and ruins at the centre of many early gothic fictions, while recalling feudal times and power, transfer these institutions to zones outside a rational culture in which, in actuality (aristocracy, monarchy, church), they still exist. Not only places of defence, but also of incarceration and power, they are located in isolated spots, areas beyond reason, law and civilised authority, where there is no protection from terror or persecution and where, inside, creaking doors, dark corridors and dank dungeons stimulate irrational fancies and fears. Power, property and paternal lineage combine in the image of the castle. But these sites are often tempered with decay: deserted, haunted and in ruins, like the feudal institutions they incarnate, their hold on and in the present, like their spectral tenants and aristocratic owners, apparently on the wane. With another staple edifice – the isolated house or mansion – there is a similar conjunction of family line, social status and physical property. Conjoining ideas of home and prison, protection and fear, old buildings in gothic fiction are never secure or free from shadows, disorientation or danger. Nature is also divided between domesticated and dangerous forms. Landscapes stress isolation and wilderness, evoking vulnerability, exposure and insecurity. Mountains are craggy, inaccessible and intimidating; forests shadowy, impenetrable; moors windswept, bleak and cold. Nature appears hostile, untamed and threatening: again, darkness, obscurity and barely contained malevolent energy reinforce atmospheres of disorientation and fear.

The sense of power and persecution beyond reason or morality is played out in the two central figures of the narratives: a young female heroine and an older male villain. The latter, beyond law, reason or social restraint gives free reign to cruel, selfish desires and ambitions and violent moods and intentions. His object, the body or wealth of the heroine, registers danger in a series of frights and flights. Prey to imagined as well as actual dangers, quick to lose rational control and give way, or faint, in fear of bandits, murderers, ghosts where there may be none, heroines enjoy an unusual, if daunting, degree of independence, often drawn by misunderstanding and curiosity into situations that lead to a sense of powerlessness and persecution. Her vulnerability and his violence play out the lawlessness and insecurity manifested in settings and landscapes. Their distance from social and familial bonds is simultaneously the locus of adventurous, romantic independence and physical danger: she may be active but is alone, with nowhere to turn, without protection and security; he, outside social scrutiny, is able to act out all manner of unacceptable wishes unchecked. Both heroines and villains, whether the latter are gentlemen, scientists, outcasts or criminals, are placed in situations where the suspension of normal rules leads to tension and ambivalence: to be independent of social and domestic regulation (also double-faceted like castles or monasteries) can be pleasurable, dangerous, exciting and frightening.

Movements across time and place are double (desired and feared; frightening and comforting) because they are bound up with figures and conventions – mirrors, portraits, ghosts, hallucinations, doubles, misread manuscripts – that link a sense of reality (or unreality) to structures of fiction: tensions between perception and misperception, understanding and misreading, fancy and realism, provide the condition and problem of gothic texts. The devices and techniques employed heighten ambivalence and ambiguity, suggesting opposed ways of understanding events as supernatural occurrences or venally materialistic plots, imagined or actual. Sudden encounters with moving statues or portraits, with skeletons, reproductions of corpses, bloody daggers or bleeding nuns may cause the direct frights and shocks that lead to screams, flight or fainting, or make the heart beat faster, the skin crawl or hair rise, but the macabre repertoire of terror is designed to have disturbing effects on characters' – and readers' – imaginations, prolonging the interplay of anticipation and apprehension: the darkness and decay of ruins, the flickering of candles, the drafts that cause curtains to move, the creaks and echoes of underground chambers all conspire to stimulate superstitious fancy, mystery and suspense. Fragments of letters, torn testimonies, mouldy manuscripts, bloody daggers, intimate dreadful secrets; mysterious doors and hidden passageways encourage desire as well as trepidation: despite the encroachment of horror, a wish to know presses curious heroines forward. The use of obscurity, the interplay of light and shadow, and the partial visibility of objects, in semi-darkness, through veils, or behind screens, has a similar effect on the imagination: denying a clearly visible and safe picture of the world, disorientation elicits anxiety or extends a stimulating or scary sense of mystery and the unknown. Narratives operate in the same way to delimit the scope of reason and knowledge by framing events from partial perspectives: the rattling of chains is attributed to the presence of a ghost, not the suffering of a long-term prisoner. Reasons and explanations, if they come at all, arrive late and only after a range of apprehensive or expectant projections have been elicited: fear and anxiety about the balance of human faculties and borders of everyday life are provoked in the process of making what is perceived, imagined, real or true both shadowy and threatening. Indeed, sense, in terms of what is perceived and what is understood, is suspended, often to the point of total loss – of consciousness, self-control or sanity.

Knowledge and understanding do not constitute the primary aim of gothic texts: what counts is the production of affects and emotions, often extreme and negative: fear, anxiety, terror, horror, disgust and revulsion are staple emotional responses. Less intense, but still negative, affects instilled by bleak landscapes include feelings of melancholic gloom, loneliness and loss. These quieter emotions are punctuated by bursts of destructive rage or anger, cruel cries of villainous satisfaction or expostulations of awe and wonder. The negative aspect of intense emotions is not simply a sign of the loss or absence of rational judgement. Reason is overwhelmed by feeling and passion, and signalled as a horrified, paralysing encounter with something unspeakable, an obscure presence too great to comprehend evoking an excess of feeling or registering an experience too intense for words. Negative aesthetics, in these terms, is double: deficiency, the absence, exclusion or negation of knowledge, facts or things; and excess, an overflow of words, feelings, ideas, imagining. Its countervailing and contradictory force leaves sense without easy reconciliation to a single and familiar framework. One might lose reason and the clearly demarcated sense of self and world it sustains, but the loss might also entail the excitement of shedding the restraints of reason and being invigorated by passion.

NEGATIVITY

Aesthetic theories, the idea of the sublime notably, emerging in the eighteenth century and informing the revival of gothic and romantic cultural forms, offer ways to grasp the appeal of particular types of artistic and affective negativity. In *The Critique of Aesthetic Judgement* (1790), the German philosopher Immanuel Kant described the sublime as a 'negative pleasure' (p. 91). In *A Philosophical Enquiry into the Origin of Our Ideas of the Sublime and the Beautiful* (1757), the English philosopher, Edmund Burke, also discussed the apparently contradictory effects of the sublime in terms of the way it combined delight and horror, pleasure and terror. In contrast to beauty, which formed the standard and ideal of artistic creation and involved a pleasing balance between harmonious natural forms and subjective feelings of love and tenderness, the sublime resulted from a disrupted sense of order and a discombobulation of reason, imagination and feeling: intensities, magnitudes and violent contrasts overwhelmed mental faculties – evoking terror, awe, wonder – and threatened the eclipse of any subjective unity. In the face of too much feeling or imagination, however, a sense of self (in Burke) or higher rational power (in Kant) is recovered in the move from an experience of threatened limitations to a reinvigorated idea of mental capacities: a shocking or thrilling experience glimpsing the loss, absence and negation of subjectivity, objects and order is turned round. It is a dynamic process that involves both loss and recovery. Since objects are kept at an aesthetic distance, at least when it comes to terror (horror signals an excessive proximity and indistinctness of negative, overpowering things), and located in the mind, the experience is intense but subjective: the imaginary quality of the sublime allows for both terror and pleasure.

A negative aspect to pleasure is also noted by the psychoanalyst Sigmund Freud. Two notions Freud proposes in 'The Uncanny' (1919) and *Beyond the Pleasure Principle* (1922) are illuminating. The former, which examines belief in animated objects, ghosts, fear of premature burial and notions of the double, manifests the breakdown of a sense of subjective unity in the face of unconscious and external disturbances: what seemed familiar and comfortable is threatened by the return of known but hidden fears, ideas and wishes, disclosing how much a sense of self depends on early development as well as a secure anchorage in social structures. When inanimate objects like statues or portraits start to move, or when machines or corpses come alive, the contours of the world in which one defines oneself seem to have changed radically to suggest that, in horror, reality's frames have ceded to supernatural forces or to powers of hallucination or unconscious desire. Strangeness lies within as much as without. Freud's writings on the pleasure principle discuss how negative experiences are made bearable through processes of repetition: psychic organisation requires balance and pleasure signals the release of tension and the return to equilibrium. Events and emotions that over-stimulate the mind (from childhood development to shell-shock) are first experienced negatively and passively: a mother leaves a child in distress; trauma leaves the mind blank. By repeating the negative experience, however, the individual is able to move from a position of passive victim to someone who has, at least imaginatively, taken an active role in producing and expelling the disturbance. Like the sublime, the experience of loss and negativity which is initially overpowering is reconfigured through an imaginative and active process.

The dynamic processes involved in gothic negativity can be seen in patterns of transgression, excess and monstrosity. From medieval morality plays, which put figures of vice on stage so that their deformities would be visible and repellent, monsters fulfil a cautionary function: they make negative attributes visible in order that they can be seen for what they are and be condemned or destroyed. Aesthetically unappealing, monsters serve a useful social and regulative function distinguishing norms and values from deviant and immoral figures and practices. They give shape, moreover, to obscure fears or anxieties, or contain an amorphous and unpresentable threat in a single image. But only as long as the boundaries separating virtue and vice, good and evil remain clearly delineated. In the context of monstrosity, the role of transgression, and the limits and excesses that it makes manifest, concerns both the delineation of boundaries and the mechanisms – the norms, taboos, prohibitions – that keep them in place. Like the relation between prohibition and desire, transgression involves a crossing of limits or breaking of taboos and rules. Telling a gothic heroine not to do something is often enough to make her wish to do it, the prohibition an incitement to curiosity and desire. The result is not simply punishment for breaking an injunction: desire is often heightened and given more intense significance due to the weight of the initial sanction. Transgression, too, brings out the importance of limits in the act of exceeding them: one becomes more keenly aware of boundaries and taboos, both of their existence and the consequences of breaking them. Crossing boundaries, however, demonstrates the protection they offer. The excesses of gothic fictions, involving the breaking of codes of law or knowledge, disobeying paternal injunctions, indulging immoral desires and appetites, displays transgression and brings norms and limits more sharply into focus. Transgression and excess, the excitement they generate, can also be enjoyed as ends in themselves. But if borders and norms are not clear or too weak, the intensity is also diminished.

Gothic texts operate ambivalently: the dynamic inter-relation of limit and transgression, prohibition and desire suggests that norms, limits, boundaries and foundations are neither natural nor absolutely fixed or stable despite the fears they engender. Crossing a boundary, for all the tension released, shows that it is neither impermeable nor unchangeable. Universal or natural guarantees seem to vanish; norms are sustained only by the conjoined and opposed forces of limit and transgression. Supposedly unchanging laws are opened up: life and death, for Victor Frankenstein, are sites of scientific transformation and the release of monstrous energies; for ghosts and vampires, too, death is not a final limit. Nature, then, is both necessary, part of the make-up of acculturated humanity, but also (in the shape of diverse, multiple and excessive cosmic, planetary and bodily energies) monstrous, alien to civilisation and rationality. Human nature, too, becomes divided. Frankenstein's monster says as much when he reflects on humans being composed of noble and base elements, compounds of both good and evil, of individual pleasure and social pressures, like Dr Jekyll. Norm and monster, self and shadow, one is inseparable from the other.

Alterity constitutes an important and complex notion in relation to monstrosity and transgression. Transgressors move beyond norms and regulations, thereby challenging their value, authority and permanence. Monsters combine negative features that oppose (and define) norms, conventions and values; they suggest an excess or absence beyond those structures and bear the weight of projections and emotions (revulsion, horror, disgust) that result. Monsters such as vampires, talking bodies, or ghosts are thus constructions indicating how cultures need to invent or imagine others in order to maintain limits. They are pushed in disgust to the other side of the imaginary fence that keeps norm and deviance apart. It requires a repeated effort of constructing and casting out figures of fear and anxiety. Alterity, ambivalence, anxiety are thus both outside and within. When it comes to making monsters and identifying others, the dangers of blurring lines of demarcation, of losing distinction and separation, of dissolving values, meanings and identities require vigilant and vigorous attention. At issue is never just the existence, form or face of others since these features change according to alterations of history, culture and political power. Alterity involves structural relationships: the maintenance of orders based on patterns of exclusion requires hierarchies of difference to maintain divisions. Others are often acceptable, though derogated and degraded, if they remain in a designated and subordinate position: monstrosity marks a refusal to stay in an allotted place, a destabilisation of power relations. Vampires (threatening to invade London from the East) provided a monstrous form for late Victorian fears sustaining colonialism and empire. Associated with magic, primitive violence and sexual corruption, these figures evince standard characteristics of imperialist and Orientalist ideology in the eyes of which members of colonised cultures lack civilisation (remaining too bound to savage rituals and practices), lack reason (or are too invested in superstitious or magical ideas), lack intelligence (or possess too much diabolical cunning), lack moral discipline (or show too much belief), all of which supposedly justifies exploitation. If they remained in their subordinate place, these figures would be no more than exotic spectacles, curiosities for Western eyes to enjoy as entertainment. But they turn their attentions towards Western culture: what is then depicted as an invasion, disease or contamination of body, mind and culture (that is, not so different from practices of colonisation) also discloses insecurities within the home culture.

The construction of feminine sexuality as monstrous follows a similar and ambivalent pattern. Defined as other to man, women are subordinated to a regime of ideas, values and practices (patriarchy) in which their position is demarcated and authorised by 'nature' as different from and less than males in terms of rational powers, moral character, physical strength. Though idealised romantically in terms of beauty or domestically in terms of maternal affections, female alterity (despite powerful counter-arguments for equal rights being made since the late eighteenth century) is linked to over-sensitivity, decorativeness, nature and commodities and held in place through figures of monstrosity. Displaying and even enjoying arbitrary male power in the persecution of women, abuses like enforced marriage, sequestration of self and property or threats of violation, murder or imprisonment remain recurrent, apparent and abhorrent issues in gothic fictions. Pleasure and fear accompany stories of women being chased along dark corridors and fictions rarely endorse an unequivocally emancipatory message. At times seeming to license male fantasy salivating over the images of defenceless and vulnerable femininity, thereby replicating the position of villains, fictions also disclose a range of injustices inflicted on women. Homes and families do seem constraining when one is obliged to be demure and subservient or to accept someone one has not met as husband just because he is wealthy or well-connected, or see a future breeding sons and heirs. And worse, paternal authority is clearly neither protective nor beneficent when one's fratricidal uncle or married father-in-law will stop at nothing to possess one's hand or body.

Much gothic fiction, however, was produced by women, some earning a degree of economic independence, and the focus on heroines able to be physically and romantically active outside domestic spheres hints at different cultural horizons for women, if only imaginatively. Yet there is also conservatism in evidence: in taking heroines on often dangerous journeys outside the home, romances show readers the terrors of inhabiting a world without male protection. The axis of patriarchal persecution–protection is set against a romantic horizon of freedom. Too much independence in fiction, many critics complained, might lead to actual excesses, provoking all sorts of domestic and filial revolts. Though the question of female sexuality returns in diverse forms and in different periods of gothic production as an object for (monstrous) male enjoyment or site of social control, it retains the potential of monstrosity, of bodily pleasures, desires, energies that exceed prescription and containment, that remain double: ideal and frightening, comforting and horrific.

TRANSFORMATIONS

Gothic texts are not realistic. Emerging in the eighteenth century, gothic fiction develops in relation to the romance and the novel. The latter, sometimes referred to as the 'modern romance', privileges realism, probability and morality in its representations of facets of eighteenth-century life. Romances, in contrast, delivered tales of love and adventures that, as their name suggests, returned to courtly tales of knights and castles, and included supernatural, fantastic mysteries and mythical creatures, from dragons to goblins and fairies. The gothic tale set out to combine both types of writing, though the combination of romance with characters imbued with more contemporary rational attitudes was not always critically successful. Since the eighteenth century the development of gothic fictions has involved similarly inter-generic patterns, adding a darker aspect to more acceptable literary forms. In criticism of the early nineteenth century, gothic writing is sometimes referred to as 'dark Romanticism'. Many Romantic writers were careful to maintain a critical distance, for example, William Wordsworth, Samuel Taylor Coleridge and Kant all bemoaned the crude taste for popular fiction. None-the-less, Romanticism did share an aesthetic history with gothic fiction (interests in the sublime, in dramatic and medieval literary styles, and romance itself), and a 'darker side' can be found in concerns with creative consciousness: rebellious and freethinking, the solitary visionary can become alienated and outcast; the self can be split in two, its double becoming a figure of imagination or fantasy separated from reality and acceptable models of existence.

If Romanticism sees gothic metaphors change to address psychological and imaginative limits, the genre alters again in relation to Victorian writing and culture: romance persists in stories of young women, sullen masters and old houses on moors (rather than castles in the Apennines) and ghosts signify dubious class origins or family secrets. But an age of industrial prosperity and scientific advancement brings new concerns: the growth of cities delivers a new darkness of poverty and crime and the boundaries crossed by science transform the understanding of humanity's place in the natural world, theories of evolution raising the spectre of regression (the 'descent' of man) alongside questions of faith and material progress. While religious ideas were threatened by science, technology, curiously, became attached to a world of spirits: new media with seemingly magical powers, like photography, telegraphy, electricity, provided ways to test or support public interest in spirits and psychic phenomena. The growth of imperialism also encountered a number of supra-rational or otherworldly powers, the spoils of colonialism delivering more than was bargained for. By the end of the century, figures of regression, threats from colonised lands, internal issues of sexual, moral and cultural degeneration, and a host of psychic and scientific experimentation, saw a return to familiar gothic monsters (vampires, ghosts and doubles) and a range of new figures, composites for the sexual, racial, class and cultural anxieties of the times.

The first decades of the twentieth century, preoccupied by the speed of technological and economic development, seemed to have little time for monsters. The all-too-real horrors of World War I pushed fantastic terrors aside. None-the-less, scientific innovation, mechanisation and the rapidity of urban and economic life seemed to render things and selves less substantial: a sense of ghostliness pervaded the times and the techniques of innovative literary presentation. New media extended the popular shelf-life of gothic fiction: cinema relished stories of ghosts, vampires and doubles that offered metaphors of its own technological magic. Animating unreal things and extracting hallucinatory powers, the black and white world of the screen made the shadowplay, terror and disorientation of gothic aesthetics its own and called it 'horror'. Other developments saw generic combinations of romance, mystery and adventure diverge in different popular genres and media: science, horror and weird fiction, comic books, tales of fantasy, women's romances. Given such generic diffusion, it is surprising that, after World War II, there is anything left that is specifically gothic. Yet, familiar rather than frightening, or as relics of all sorts of stiff and dusty Victorian attitudes being swept aside in the white light and heat of technological, economic and social transformation, gothic forms and figures begin to tell different stories in contexts of sexual, national and social liberation: their monstrous displays of power and persecution provide images of the artifices and illegitimacy of patriarchy, social conformism, racism, imperialism. Negatives of the grand narratives that shaped modernity, gothic forms are reinvented for postmodern interrogations as well as for the accompanying freedoms of consumerist, corporate, creative and post-industrial orders. New biotechnological innovations need new Frankensteins, new media require new ghosts. Women's writing re-examines gothic images of femininity and masculinity to challenge the constraining artifice of sexual and social categories, liberating sexual difference from normative constraints. Monsters not only display alterity, but also demonstrate – and criticise – the cultural practices of making others, interrogating the legitimacy of condemnation, prejudice and exclusion: their position moves from eliciting pity, sympathy and fear to demanding admiration for defiance and insubordination. Exploding patterns of limit and transgression, norm and heterogeneity, monsters become aligned with performances and techniques of subversion. Identity, like text and history rendered plural and playful, is a matter of political choice or lifestyle, a consumer culture in which vampires predominate as singular aesthetes or fabulous rebels. At the same time, technological innovations in medicine, media and surveillance provide hitherto unimaginable powers of control along with the means to transform irreversibly cellular, organic and planetary bodies, the shadow cast on humanity and its habitat offers new darker global horizons for fictional speculations.

Postmodernism, emerging as a global aesthetic style at the end of the 1970s and associated with the wider transformations of modernity, seems particularly hospitable to the resuscitation of gothic forms and figures. Its aesthetic reflexivity, enjoyment of fabrication, simulation and doubling parallels the gothic genre's consciousness of textual artifice, its playful use of narrative and social conventions, its camp constructions of the past and its evocation of striking affects. But postmodern challenges to social and cultural authority have implications for the genre: not only do they facilitate its diffusion in various forms and media, they also signal a new context in which meanings and affects change. The negative aesthetics historically linked to gothic forms alters: prohibition cedes to pastiche and play, and signs of negativity or transgression become reassessed as attractive, acceptable commodities. With genre, familiarity and repetition are necessary, but too much repetition breeds over-familiarity: a little bit of excess or difference is required. If features of gothic excess include transgression or disturbing effects, over-familiarity will diminish a capacity to cross borders or produce terror or horror. Yet genre and its formal restrictions are also at issue in contemporary diffusions: hybrid mixtures of style, mode, zone and mood emerge too quickly for any attempt at classification. When and where does a gothic genre stop and others, such as magical realism, dark romance, science fiction, fantasy, occult, horror, cyberpunk, splatterpunk, steampunk, neo-Victorian, body horror, slasher or weird fiction begin? Is gothic just one mode, mood or inflection among others? Can its particular dark atmospheres, its estranging effects and its in-human monsters remain distinctive or useful in processes of composing, classifying and comprehending contemporary texts?

CRITICISM

It is no accident that academic studies of gothic forms burgeoned in the wake of postmodernist critical challenges to ideas of literary value, canon and approach. Before the later twentieth century most criticism of the genre, tacitly or not, shared the views of eighteenth-century and Romantic commentators in derogating gothic fictions as minor, low, popular and formulaic productions. In periods advocating the greatness of literary tradition and vision, or analysing the complex ironies of style and form, gothic writing did not qualify as Literature and hence warranted scant attention. At best, and often well informed in terms of scholarship, criticism echoed eighteenth-century antiquarianism in exploring the dusty byways of literary and cultural history: gothic, as a word, a style or a revival, was a footnote to understanding the broader context of Romanticism. This strand, in which gothic forms are examined in terms of established literary-historical periods, genres and national traditions, continues to shape much contemporary scholarship.

Aesthetic values and canons are not innocent since selection involves exclusion, with value often occluding prejudice or political agenda. Feminist critical interventions, notably, observed the absence of women writers from reading lists, criticised the patriarchal assumptions and ideologies at work and promoted the cultural significance of representations of female experience and sexual difference in a range of texts by women. 'Female Gothic' drew out particularities of women's experience, suffering and oppression under patriarchy and enabled a range of reinterpretations of women's gothic writing that explored, exposed and exploded the limitations of patriarchal representations of gender and sexuality. Re-examinations of the historical conditions and political implications of gothic writing also involved negotiating matters of class oppression. Karl Marx, in *Capital* (1867), used the metaphor of the vampire to describe how capitalism exploits living human labour. Marxist criticism, noting the historical conditions of cultural and economic production, traces contradictions and class antagonisms in which gothic figures like monsters appeared as exploited yet resistant bodies of dehumanising

systems, signalling tensions in the ideological fabric that natur-
alises a bourgeois view of the world.

The movement from oppression to repression marked another
influential, and perhaps the most extensive, orientation of gothic
criticism: psychoanalysis. Influenced by German Romanticism,
the work of Sigmund Freud with its focus on the entanglement of
fear and desire, on 'dark continents' of female sexuality and the
unconscious, the return of buried, anti-social wishes, on dreams,
hysteria and phobias often reads like a gothic novel. Stressing the
role of politics and history in the shaping of cultural and individual identity, these approaches were supplemented by criticism
that attended more closely to the interaction of language, discourse and power in the construction and performance of conventions, values and norms. Texts were embedded in social
exchange, generating and receiving meanings through the circulation of partial and practically effective forms of knowledge.
They were subject to reinterpretation under changing conditions.
Deconstruction, tracing gothic attention to textual form, tracked
uncertainties through figures of the spectre: haunting signalled
the division and multiplication of meanings, absences interrupt-
ing presence. Historicism unpicked the imbrications of gothic
metaphors and moods in other texts such as medical or legal
documents. Performative analyses of cultural power and resistance
bear heavily on readings of gothic fiction's capacity to engage
with sexual meanings and norms.

Gothic fiction's engagement with cultural and inter-cultural
concerns, particularly at the end of the nineteenth century, has
proved amenable to Orientalist, colonial and post-colonial critical
modes, both in the analysis of the effects and horrors of imperialist practices, ideology and racist representation and in responses
that interrogate the contradictions of those representations in
disclosing the limitations and aberrations of dominant positions.
'Civilisation' is neither natural nor universal: it is a Western
construct often maintained in fear of the very cultures it exploits
and misconstrues. Its encounters with alterity see a fantasy of
mastery breaking down. The experience of colonisation, moreover,
receives gothic treatment. The movement from one culture to
encounters with new landscapes and peoples leaves colonists

caught between worlds: haunted by past traditions, disturbed by strange environments, customs and beliefs, their responses to colonial situations are sometimes fearful, callous or violent, and provide cause for melancholy, guilt or shame. Imposing a Euro-centric view on a new culture is not without tension or resistance, indeed subjugation, banishment, enforced assimilation, slavery, genocide can be its very real consequences. The recipients of the process who see native traditions, beliefs and peoples erased by the colonial subjugation find a mode of registering and resisting cultural dispossession in ghostly and ghastly images, often appropriating the metaphors of coloniser as figures of their own haunting. Haunting, engaging a sense of loss and dislocation, of history, culture, identity and autonomy also tells the suppressed stories of colonisation, of its terrors, trauma and violence, and offers a path, in the telling, to recovery.

Gothic figures, from opposed positions, thus become subject to criticism that engages with both colonial and post-colonial experience. In presenting complex and conflicted cultural his-tories, moreover, gothic writing has found itself increasingly involved in redefinitions of the development of particular national literatures, articulating the different geographies, languages, beliefs and myths that, after political independence is achieved, come to compose a country's new make-up. Concerns with national difference are already evident in early gothic fiction, given that many writers came from Scottish, Irish and Welsh backgrounds. Current patterns, such as 'Australian Gothic' or 'Canadian Gothic', also register the various specific cultural effects of British imperialism. In this volume, the history of gothic forms in the USA sketches one version of how a national literature develops in relation to and beyond its (European) influences, to trace the specific locations, cultures and historical exigencies through which it presses forward. US cultural history also points towards a transformation in the use of gothic images across the world: in the forefront of world economic transformation (con-sumerism, media and culture industries notably), US models have established post- or multinational structures in which corpora-tions, commodities, finance, scientific innovation proceed very rapidly and without the checks of national borders. In this spread

of information, money, images, both Western and Eastern countries – particularly those, like Japan and Korea, combining rapid
industrial and post-industrial development with diverse local
cultural traditions – have produced distinctive but highly effective gothic tales, images and media that deal with the 'new dark
age' associated with the 'new world order'. What does it mean to
live in a world of pervasive media and virtual technologies; in a
global, inter-connected and fragile financial network; in a threatened ecology; or among porous national borders and widespread
yet localised political conflicts? What has very recently been
termed 'globalgothic' is a mode of criticism that tries to engage
the very different senses of self, world and culture which global
transformation instantiates. There is occasion, it seems, to be
anxious and seek figures that give form to fear. The shape of
monsters to come, however, remains unclear. Patterns of criticism
may be more predictable, almost mimicking the vast inter-connected network circumscribing creative and critical industries,
with gothic figures of monstrosity and spectrality spreading from
literary, cultural and media forms to haunt other fields, periods
and histories and extending and revising the specific nature and
role of gothic modes (Shakespeare has recently been re-re-invented
as gothic) in the manner of many generic, sub-generic and medial
transformations and re-contextualisations. Demands that critics be
'research experts' may further encourage specialisations focused on
highly discrete concerns with a 'darkening' of diverse genres,
cultural phenomena, topics or themes. Further multiplications of
association, significance and context may occur, with 'gothic', as a
noun and as an adjective, doing and being done to in equal
measure, all testing the ability of critical approaches to frame or,
even, gauge the significance of the word.

2

GOTHIC ORIGINS

Lust, murder, incest, and every atrocity that can disgrace human nature, brought together, without the apology of probability, or even possibility for their introduction. To make amends, the moral is general and very practical; it is, 'not to deal in witchcraft and magic because the devil will have you at last!!' We are sorry to observe that good talents have been misapplied in the production of this monster.

(*The British Critic* 7, June 1796, p. 677)

Morality and monstrosity were two of the hallmarks of eighteenth-century aesthetic judgement. The lack of the former and abundance of the latter, in the eyes of the reviewer for *The British Critic* (1796), distinguished M.G. Lewis' *The Monk* as a particularly deserving object of critical vitriol. The review is not extraordinary either in the tone it adopts or in the terms it employs, though *The Monk* achieved special notoriety. While a few writers now established as founders of the gothic tradition – Horace Walpole and Ann Radcliffe particularly – received both critical and popular approbation, they were in the minority. Between 1790 and 1810 critics were almost univocal in their condemnation of what was seen as an unending torrent of popular trashy novels. Intensified by fears of radicalism and revolution, the challenge to aesthetic values was framed in terms of social transgression: virtue, propriety and domestic order were considered to be under threat. However, the basis for rejections of gothic novels had been laid much earlier in the century. The values that gave shape and direction to the Enlightenment, dominated as it was by writings from Greek and Roman culture, privileged forms of cultural or artistic production that attended to classical rules: buildings, works of art, gardens, landscapes and written texts had to conform to precepts of uniformity, proportion and order. Aesthetic objects were praised for their harmony and texts were designed to foster appreciation on these terms, to instruct rather than entertain, to inculcate a sense of morality and rational understanding and thus help readers discriminate between virtues and vices. Taste, judgement and value were predicated on ideas of cultivation and civilised behaviour and linked to public and domestic duty, harmony and propriety. The dominance of classical values produced a national past that was distinct from the cultivation, rationality and maturity of an enlightened age. This past was called 'Gothic', a general and derogatory term for the Middle Ages which conjured up ideas of barbarous customs and practices, of superstition, ignorance, extravagant fancies and natural wildness. Manifestations of the gothic past – buildings, ruins, songs and romances – were treated as products of uncultivated if not childish minds. But characteristics like extravagance, superstition, fancy and wildness which were initially considered in negative terms became associated, in the course of the eighteenth century, with a more expansive and imaginative potential for aesthetic production.

Gothic productions never completely lost their earlier, negative connotations to become fully assimilated within the bounds of proper literature: implicated in a major shift in cultural attitudes, they harboured a disturbing ambivalence which disclosed the instability not only of modes of representation but also of the structures that held those representations in place. Throughout the century important social, economic and political changes began to prise apart the bonds linking individuals to an ordered social world. Urbanisation, industrialisation, revolution were the principal signs of change. Enlightenment rationalism displaced religion as the authoritative mode of explaining the universe and altered conceptions of the relations between individuals and natural, supernatural and social worlds. Gothic works and their disturbing ambivalence can thus be seen as effects of fear and anxiety, as attempts to account for or deal with the uncertainty of these shifts. They are also attempts to explain what the Enlightenment left unexplained, efforts to reconstruct the divine mysteries that reason had begun to dismantle, to recuperate pasts and histories that offered a permanence and unity beyond the scope of rational and moral order. In this respect the past labelled gothic was a site of struggle between enlightened forces of progress and more conservative impulses to retain continuity. The contest for a coherent and stable account of the past, however, was not resolved. The complex and often contradictory attempts either to make the past barbaric in contrast to an enlightened present or to find in it a continuity that gave English culture a stable history had the effect of bringing to the fore and transforming the way in which both past and present depended on modes of representation.

The various developments in aesthetic practice that paved the way for gothic fiction are themselves accompanied by similar concerns about the nature and effects of representation. Romances, the tales of magical occurrences and exotic adventures that drew on the customs and superstitions of the Middle Ages, met, from the late seventeenth century on, with general disapproval. Graveyard poetry, rejecting human vices and vanities through an insistence on mortality, encouraged an interest in ruins, tombs and nocturnal gloom as the frontiers that opened on to an eternal afterlife. The taste for the sublime that dominated eighteenth-century aesthetic enquiries also offered intimations of infinity beyond the limits of any rational framework. Natural and artistic objects were seen to evoke emotional effects like terror and wonder which marked an indistinct sense of an immensity that exceeded human comprehension and elevated human sensibility. The effusive and imaginative descriptions of objects both natural and supernatural that were recovered by scholars collecting the songs and ballads of medieval culture provided the examples of a romantic and sublime way of writing. Similarly, medieval architecture, with its cathedrals, castles and ruins, became a worthy model for evocations of sublimity.

The gothic novel owes much to these developments. The marvellous incidents and chivalric customs of romances, the descriptions of wild and elemental natural settings, the gloom of graveyard and ruin, the scale and permanence of the architecture, the terror and wonder of the sublime, all become important features of the eighteenth-century gothic novel. Similarly, the emphasis on the limits of the neo-classical aesthetic project that occurs in reappraisals of romances, ruins and sublimity provides an important stimulus to the imaginative aspirations of gothic fiction.

ROMANCE AND NOVEL

In discussions of eighteenth-century fiction, the term 'Gothic romance' is more applicable than 'Gothic novel' as it highlights the link between medieval narratives of love, chivalry and adventure, imported from France from the late seventeenth century onwards, and the tales that in the later eighteenth century were classified as 'Gothic'. Neo-classical criticism throughout the eighteenth century found much to disapprove of, often without any attempt at formal discrimination, in novels and romances. Works of fiction were subjected to general condemnation as wildly fanciful pieces of folly that served no useful or moral purpose.

In a review of Smollett's *Peregrine Pickle* (1751), John Cleland, complained:

> Serious and useful works are scarce read, and hardly any thing of morality goes down, unless ticketed with the label of amusement. Hence that flood of novels, tales, romances, and other monsters of the imagination, which have been either wretchedly translated, or even more unhappily imitated, from the French, whose literary levity we have not been ashamed to adopt, and to encourage the propagation of so depraved a taste.
>
> (Williams, p. 161)

Instead, the precepts of classical writers like Horace and Plutarch are recommended. Writing from life is considered the morally instructive way to ward off 'monsters of the imagination', providing guidance in the ways of the world rather than extravagant excursions of the imagination:

> For as the matter of them is taken chiefly from nature, from adventures, real or imaginary, but familiar, practical and probable to be met with in the course of common life, they may serve as pilot's charts, or maps of those parts of the world, which every one may chance to travel through; and in this light they are public benefits. Whereas romances and novels which turn upon characters out of nature, monsters of perfection, feats of chivalry, fairy-enchantments, and the whole train of the marvellously absurd, transport the reader unprofitably into the clouds, where he is sure to find no solid footing, or into those wilds of fancy, which go for ever out of the way of all human paths.
>
> (Williams, p. 161)

It was not only the failure to attend to rules of imitation that proved to be an object of critical concern. The straying of fancy from the paths of nature demonstrated more than a depraved taste: it was also believed to exert a corrupting influence on the morals of readers. Complaining at the 'deluge of familiar romances', T. Row observed in the *Gentleman's Magazine* (1767): 'Tis not only a most unprofitable way of spending time, but extremely prejudicial to their morals, many a young person being entirely corrupted by the giddy and fantastical notions of love and gallantry, imbibed from thence' (Williams, p. 272). The danger of moral degeneration became the principal reason for the general condemnation of romances, tales and novels.

Despite the prevailing indiscriminate dismissal of romances and novels, attempts were made to distinguish between modes of fictional writing and to admit a few examples of the latter within the parameters of acceptability. James Beattie's 'On Fable and Romance' (1783) draws clear distinctions between medieval romances and novels. The essay argues that Cervantes' *Don Quixote* signals the end of the old medieval romance and the emergence of the modern romance or novel: 'Fiction henceforth divested herself of her gigantick size, tremendous aspect, and frantick demeanour; and, descending to the level of common life, conversed with man as his equal, and as a polite and cheerful companion.' From Cervantes, writers learnt 'to avoid extravagance, and imitate nature' by adhering to rules of probability (Williams, p. 320). Novels are divided into serious and comic forms. Included, with some approval, in these categories are works by writers who are now regarded as the instigators of the eighteenth-century novel: Defoe, Richardson, Fielding and Smollett. However, Beattie's essay concludes on a cautionary and, by 1783, conventional note, describing romances as 'a dangerous recreation' of which a few 'may be friendly to good taste and good morals' while the majority 'tend to corrupt the heart, and stimulate the passions'. 'A habit of reading them', Beattie continues, 'breeds a dislike to history, and all the substantial parts of knowledge; withdraws the attention from nature, and truth; and fills the mind with extravagant thoughts, and too often with criminal propensities' (Williams, p. 327). Beattie's warning about romances echoes the distinctions that grounded eighteenth-century criticism: in the maintenance of morality, propriety and virtue, truth, reason, knowledge and taste should always be elevated above fiction, passion, ignorance and depravity.

In *The Rambler* (1750), Samuel Johnson differentiated between romances and novels in similar terms. But he was also keen to stress the moral usefulness of the latter. Romances were described as wildly extravagant and fanciful tales of knights, giants, fabulous entities and marvellous incidents. Novels were privileged as instructive observations on the living world. It was, however, more than accurate imitation of nature or polite society that separated good writing from bad. For Johnson, the 'familiar histories' offered by novels possessed the capacity to educate readers, to convey with greater efficiency a knowledge of virtue and vice. The realism of novels, moreover, was required to be selective: imitations of nature and life were to be chosen on the basis of their propriety and not be coloured by passion or wickedness. Novels ought to highlight virtue and elicit a reader's abhorrence at depictions of vice. The reason for the representation of vice is made clear in lines from Pope's *Essay on Man* (1734): 'Vice is a monster of so frightful mien/As, to be hated, needs but to be seen' (ll. 217–18).

Representations of vice as a monster conformed to an important strategy of defining the limits of propriety. The term monster also applied in aesthetic judgements to works that were unnatural and deformed, which deviated either from the regularity attributed to life and nature or from the symmetry and proportion valued in any form of representation. Thus it was less a matter of concern that monsters were represented and more a question of the manner in which they were represented and of the effects of those representations. Romances were easily categorised as examples of childish fancy, trivial and incredible tales of ignorance and superstition. Their effects, however, remained a concern. In encouraging readers' credulity and imagination, and in blurring the boundaries between supernatural and illusory dimensions and natural and real worlds, romances loosened the moral and rational structures that ordered everyday life. By displaying monsters in too attractive a light, vice rather than virtue might be promoted. For, if fiction, as Johnson maintained, should establish and reproduce moral and proper ideas of conduct, it could also become a manual of misconduct.

Fiction was thus recognised as a powerful but ambivalent form of social education. The insistence on distinctions between romances and novels forms part of a wider process of teaching readers proper moral and rational understanding. Distinguishing between good and bad modes of writing was more than a merely aesthetic enterprise: it marked an attempt to supplement an assumed inability on the part of romances and their growing readership to discriminate between virtue and vice, and thus to forestall their seduction along fictional paths that stimulated anti-social passions and corrupt behaviour. The difficulty of policing these boundaries is emphasised by repeated critical fears about the dangers of transgression. Even the clear classifications proposed by Beattie and Johnson fell foul of the way in which their terms were framed. Beattie's essay on medieval romances and the novel form describes another type as a 'strange mixture' of the two. As examples, Beattie cites texts by the late seventeenth-century French writer Madeleine de Scudery which he goes on to describe:

> In them, all facts and characters, real and fabulous; and systems of policy and manners, the Greek, the Roman, the Feudal, and the modern, are jumbled together and confounded: as if a painter should represent Julius Caesar drinking tea with Queen Elizabeth, Jupiter, and Dulcinea del Toboso, and having on his head the laurel wreathe of antient Rome, a suit of Gothick armour on his shoulders, laced ruffles at his wrist, a pipe of tobacco In his mouth, and a pistol and tomahawk stuck in his belt.
>
> (Williams, p. 320)

The diversity of events, styles, settings and characters composing this strange assemblage engage in an extravagant refusal to respect boundaries of fact and fiction and reproduce imitations of nature and life. As a result they are rejected as 'intolerably tedious' and 'unspeakably absurd'. These romances, however, are the forerunners of the strange mixture of forms that appeared as gothic tales later in the century. Indeed, while at Eton, Horace Walpole described the effects of his predilection for romances in a letter to George Montagu (6 May 1736): 'As I got farther into Virgil and Clelia, I found myself transported from Arcadia, to the garden of Italy, and saw Windsor Castle in no other view than the *capitoli immobile saxum*'.

The word 'romance' had come to signify more recent productions as well as medieval narratives. Charlotte Lennox's novel *The Female Quixote* (1752) satirised romance reading by presenting a heroine who interprets every event as though it were part of some great romantic adventure. Despite critical and novelistic attempts to sustain distinctions, fiction continued to upset conventions of reading and codes of behaviour. Even forceful attempts, like Johnson's, to mark out the useful and moral aspects from the wasteful and corrupting potential of fiction encountered the destabilising pleasures of writing. In her *The Progress of Romance* (1785), Clara Reeve, herself a writer of gothic and historical romances, outlined in very Johnsonian terms a definition of romance and novel while acknowledging the seductive power of fiction:

> The Romance is an heroic fable, which treats of fabulous persons and things. – The Novel is a picture of real life and manners, and of the times in which it is written. The Romance in lofty and elevated language, describes what never happened or is likely to happen. – The Novel gives a familiar relation of such things, as pass every day before our eyes, such as may happen to our friend, or to ourselves; and the perfection of it, is to represent every scene, in so easy and natural a manner, and to make them appear so probable, as to deceive us into a persuasion (at least while we are reading) that all is real, until we are affected by the joys or distresses, of the persons in the story, as if they were our own.

(I, p. 111)

In deceiving readers with persuasively real representations of events and characters, novels work in an opposite manner to romances. The concern about the effects of fiction becomes paramount in eighteenth-century criticism. That these are representations is not at issue. What are more important are the values reproduced as natural or real rather than the actual form of nature or everyday life. Fiction becomes distinctly, though ambivalently, ideological. Able to reproduce a set of dominant ideas about the relationship of individuals to their social and natural world, all narratives were acknowledged, if only at times tacitly, to possess the capacity to order or subvert manners, morals and perceptions.

In the response to gothic architecture, too, the operations of enlightenment ideology are apparent. Privileging uniformity and proportion over scale and extravagance, eighteenth-century critics classified any deviations from symmetrical structure as the deformities exhibited by the absence of taste of a barbaric age. Neve's *Complete Builder's Guide* (1703) dismisses medieval edifices as 'massive, cumbersome and unwieldy'. In contrast Elizabethan imitations of gothic structure were characterised by their 'affected lightness, Delicacy, and over-rich, even whimsical Decorations' (Clark, pp. 50–51). As in criticism of romances, chronological differences tended to be elided so any constructions that were wastefully over-ornamented or unwieldy and cumbersome were described as gothic. Comparisons between gothic and classical architecture served only to display the superiority of the latter. Joseph Addison praised the great and amazing form of the Pantheon in Rome and contrasted it with the meanness he found in gothic cathedrals; Alexander Gerard, in his *Essay on Taste* (1764), denied gothic structures any claim to beauty because they lacked proportion and simplicity (Monk, pp. 34–35). Lord Kames, in his *Elements of Criticism* (1762), clearly states prevailing attitudes towards beautiful form: 'Viewing any body as a whole, the beauty of its figure arises from regularity and simplicity; viewing the parts in relation to each other, uniformity, proportion and order, contribute to its beauty' (p. 85).

The insistence on neo-classical rules of composition manifests the importance attached to the manner in which eighteenth-century culture constructed and reproduced its own idea of itself. Architecture told the story of its development and represented its values; it was interpreted accordingly. Some of Kames' apparently inconsequential speculations on the appropriate architectural style of ruins indicate a certain investment in distancing the enlightened present from a gothic past: 'Whether should a ruin be in the gothic or Grecian form? In the former, I think; because it exhibits the triumph of time over strength; a melancholy but not unpleasant thought: a Grecian ruin suggests rather the triumph of barbarity over taste; a gloomy and discouraging thought' (p. 430). This somewhat fastidious way of accounting for appropriate tastes displays a serious effort to privilege classical cultivation over the barbarity of the past. Any deviation from the standards of the present, any sign of imperfection, irregularity and disorder, Kames later insists, is painfully disagreeable and excites a sense of horror at its monstrosity (p. 450). But deviations are also monstrous in that they offer a lesson in what is not proper. Anna Barbauld's 'On Monastic Institutions' describes her 'secret triumph' at seeing the ruins of an old abbey. The ruins stand as testaments to the ascendancy of knowledge and reason and also, since they were of an old Catholic institution destroyed during the Reformation, Protestantism. 'Always considered as the haunts of ignorance and superstition' by Barbauld, the ruins mark the ascendancy of neo-classical over gothic values (p. 195).

RUINS, GRAVEYARDS AND THE POETRY OF THE PAST

Ruins and other forms of gothic architecture assumed a different and positive significance in the course of the eighteenth century. The gothic revival marked a major change in attitudes towards medieval styles. Though an increasing number of buildings in this style were commissioned, it was literary works that provided the impulse for the new taste. Antiquarianism, the vogue for the Graveyard school of poetry and intense interest in the sublime were significant features of the cultural environment that nurtured the gothic revival. While the gothic past continued to be constructed as the subordinated and distanced antithesis to Enlightenment culture, the events, settings, figures and images began to be considered on their own merits. Gothic style became the shadow that haunted neo-classical values, running parallel and counter to its ideas of symmetrical form, reason, knowledge and propriety.

Shadows, indeed, were among the foremost characteristics of gothic works. They marked the limits necessary to the constitution of an enlightened world and delineated the limitations of neo-classical perceptions. Darkness, metaphorically, threatened the light of reason with what it did not know. Gloom cast perceptions of formal order and unified design into obscurity; its uncertainty generated both a sense of mystery and passions and emotions alien to reason. Night gave free reign to imagination's unnatural and marvellous creatures, while ruins testified to a temporality that exceeded rational understanding and human finitude. These were the thoughts conjured up by Graveyard poets.

Graveyard poetry was popular in the first half of the eighteenth century. Its principal poetic objects, other than graves and churchyards, were night, ruins, death and ghosts, everything, indeed, that was excluded by rational culture. It did not, however, celebrate these features idly. Robert Blair's 'The Grave'

(1743) revels in images of death and encourages readers to think about the horrors of the grave, of night and ghosts not in morbid fascination but rather as a warning to the godless. For Blair death is a 'gloomy path' (l. 687) that leads from earth to heaven. To contemplate death and its accompanying signs is to recognise the transience of physical things and pleasures: 'How shocking must thy Summons be, O Death!/To him that is at Ease in his possessions' (ll. 350–51). Death lays waste to material human aspirations:

> Soon, very soon, thy firmest Footing fails;
> And down dropp't into that darksome Place,
> Where nor Device, nor knowledge ever came.
>
> (ll. 294–96)

But it also elevates one's considerations to higher, spiritual objects and ends:

> Thrice welcome Death!
> That after many a painful bleeding Step
> Conducts us to our Home, and lands us safe
> On the long-wish'd for Shore.
>
> (ll. 706–9)

Death, as leveller of earthly desires and ambitions, demands religious faith and hope in order to pave the way for souls to ascend to heaven.

As a poem imbued with the sentiments of the Evangelical revival taking place in the eighteenth century, 'The Grave' enjoyed a long life in print as required reading for the spiritually minded. Edward Young's *Night Thoughts* (1749–51) also received such acclaim. This much longer poem develops evangelical themes, but in a more extravagant fashion. In *Night Thoughts* the contemplation of death and decay serves to encourage speculations on the life to come. Fears of mortality and associated superstitions are unwarranted if one has faith. Confronting and overcoming the limits of material existence, *Night Thoughts* is organised by a play of images which double the significance of life and death, light and dark. For Young, the life of the body entombs the soul in darkness, while death and darkness enable the apprehension of a transcendent and immanent brilliance. It is for these reasons that night and darkness are so valued:

> Darkness has more Divinity for me,
> It strikes Thought inward, it drives back the Soul
> To settle on Herself, our Point supreme!
>
> (V, ll. 128–30)

Darkness enables a person to perceive the soul within and expands the mind by producing a consciousness of its own potential for divinity.

Although *Night Thoughts* alters the significance of Enlightenment metaphors of light and dark and goes beyond the limits of rationality and empirical knowledge in its efforts to inspire the individual imagination with a sense of religious mystery and wonder, its role as a moral text was beyond question. In many ways, the poem's warnings against corruption, depravity and atheism as well as many of its images of Divinity as a mighty mind distinguish it as a product of its age. Like other poems of its kind, *Night Thoughts* criticises ignorance and superstition. Thomas Parnell's 'Night-piece on Death' (1722), Nathaniel Cotton's 'Night-piece' (1751) and John Cunningham's 'The Contemplatist' (1762) all emphasise that the leveller, death, is not to be feared. Without fear, the spectres and ghosts that haunt superstitious minds disappear. In the face of death, moreover, science remains impotent and blind. Graveyard poetry, its injunctions to nocturnal speculation on human finitude and the vanity of earthly ambitions, uses tombs, ruins, decay and ghosts as a mode of moral instruction rather than excitement.

The attractions of darkness, however, and the power of the images and visions it engendered were not lost on other poets associated with the melancholy evocations of the Graveyard school. William Collins' 'Ode to Fear' (1746) describes the fanciful and shadowy shapes, the monsters, giants and phantoms that the emotion produces. These figures testify less to the power of the grave in elevating thought to spiritual matters and more to the power of imagination:

> Dark power, with shuddering meek submitted thought,
> Be mine, to read the visions old,
> Which thy awakening bards have told.
>
> (ll. 51–53)

Fear and the supernatural figures it conjures up are one of the 'divine emotions' that poets and bards of earlier ages were able to produce. To these the ode appeals for an imaginative power, a sense of nature and a capacity to evoke feelings unavailable in neo-classical compositions. The growing importance of older forms of writing is further manifested in lines from Joseph Warton's 'The Enthusiast' (1740): 'What are the lays of artful Addison,/Coldly correct, to Shakespear's warblings wild?' (ll. 166–67). Or, in the words of Joseph Warton's brother, Thomas, in his 'The Pleasures of Melancholy' (1745), 'But let the sacred genius of the night/Such mystic visions send, as Spenser saw' (ll. 62–63).

Shakespeare and Spenser were considered to be the inheritors of a tradition of romantic writing that harked back to the Middle Ages. Like the songs of bards and minstrels, the emotional power of their descriptions of nature as well as visionary images were held up as examples of a more imaginative form of literary creation. Wildness of natural scenery, marvellous figures and lyrical style became signs of a re-evaluation of writing which privileged inventiveness and imagination over imitation and morality. 'The Pleasures of Melancholy', like many Graveyard poems, dwells on darkness, ghosts and tombs, but not in order to raise thoughts to heaven. The thoughts that it encourages are on the visionary and mystical power of writing, not to produce moral understanding, but to evoke intense feelings. This power, moreover, is linked, in the many images of storms, rocks and caverns to a dark and wild nature.

These departures from classical rules of imitation and creativity were supported by the work of antiquarians in their reassessments of old texts. Thomas Warton was himself a major figure in this process. His *History of English Poetry* (1774–81) traces the origins of romantic fiction to Arabia. From there it had started its migration across Europe during the period of the Crusades. Other scholars queried the idea of the Eastern origins of romances and preferred to identify the beginnings of romance among the Celtic, Saxon and Norse tribes of northern Europe. Of this opinion was Thomas Percy who, in his *Reliques of Ancient English Poetry* (1765), published a collection of romantic songs and ballads. Other collections, or – in the case of Macpherson's 'Ossian' poems (1762) – fabrications, established the popularity of 'the rude songs of ancient minstrels', as Percy's dedication to the *Reliques* put it. These 'barbarous productions of unpolished ages' were held up for approval 'not as the labours of art, but as the effusions of nature, showing the first efforts of ancient genius'. While the precise origins of romances remained a matter of scholarly dispute, their importance lay chiefly in the fact that they were not classical. Moreover, the recovery and validation of romances enabled certain neo-classical prejudices to be challenged. Thomas Warton wrote of how gothic romances, though shaken by classical fictions, maintained their ground:

> the daring machineries of giants, dragons and enchanted castles, borrowed from the magic storehouse of Boiardo, Ariosto and Tasso, began to be employed by the epic muse. These ornaments have been censured by the bigotry of precise and servile critics, as abounding in whimsical absurdities, and as unwarrantable deviations from the practice of Homer and Virgil.
>
> (IV, p. 360)

Such strong criticisms questioned the limits of neo-classical aesthetic values by developing, on the basis of romantic texts, different ideas about art, originality and nature.

In his *Letters on Chivalry and Romance* (1762), Richard Hurd criticises the vehemence of neo-classical prejudices. The *Letters* argue that romances are derived from societies structured by chivalry and feudal customs. The argument, however, does not make its case with an analysis of medieval romances but focuses on writings that draw heavily upon them for their poetical effect.

These writers, Hurd states, included Ariosto, Tasso, Spenser, Shakespeare and Milton, and

> were seduced by these barbarities of their forefathers; were even charmed by the gothic Romances. Was this caprice and absurdity in them? Or, may there not be something in the gothic Romance peculiarly suited to the views of a genius, and to the ends of poetry? And may not the philosophic moderns have gone too far, in their perpetual ridicule and contempt of it?
>
> (p. 4)

Invoking the acknowledged literary value associated with these writers, Hurd is able to defend the gothic tradition against biases of eighteenth-century judgement. The gothic influence is, moreover, bound up with the genius of these poets, making a significant contribution to the imaginative power of their poetry: Hurd contends that Spenser and Milton 'When most inflamed', poetically speaking, were 'more particularly rapt with the gothic fables of chivalry' (p. 55).

The *Letters on Chivalry and Romance* not only challenge the prejudices of neo-classical criticism, they also begin a process of re-evaluation. Cultural productions, Hurd insists in an important displacement of neo-classical dominance, demand consideration on their own terms:

> When an architect examines a gothic structure by Grecian rules, he finds nothing but deformity. But the gothic architecture has its own rules, by which when it comes to be examined, it is seen to have its merit, as well as the Grecian.
>
> (p. 61)

Given the importance of classical forms of reason, knowledge, imitation and morality in eighteenth-century judgements, Hurd presents a significant challenge to models of criticism. Hurd's *Letters*, however, do more than interrogate the homogeneity and consequent exclusiveness of neo-classical hierarchies of taste: towards the end of the work these hierarchies undergo a process of inversion. Hurd attacks, as a 'trite maxim' of bad criticism, the view that poets must imitate nature. Poetical truth, he argues, lies beyond the bounds of a natural order. Instead, poetry should indulge imagination and range in marvellous, magical and extraordinary worlds, worlds that are associated with forms of nature that evoke a sense of wonder (pp. 91–94).

THE SUBLIME

Hurd's argument in favour of judging cultural productions according to the rules employed in their composition, and his case for a very different set of poetic values in which imagination and genius come to the fore and nature becomes the source of inspiration, emerge from changing attitudes regarding the relationship of art and nature. Natural scenery, for example, was being perceived differently. Mountains, once considered as ugly blemishes, deformities disfiguring the proportions of a world that ideally should be uniform, flat and symmetrical, began to be seen with eyes pleased by their irregularity, diversity and scale. The pleasure arose from the range of intense and uplifting emotions that mountainous scenery evoked in the viewer. Wonder, awe, horror and joy were the emotions believed to expand or elevate the soul and the imagination with a sense of power and infinity. Mountains were the foremost objects of the natural sublime.

No topic of aesthetic enquiry in the eighteenth century generated greater interest than the sublime. De Boileau's translation of Longinus on sublimity in the late seventeenth century inspired a host of writings examining the nature, objects and effects of the sublime, among the most influential of which was Edmund Burke's *A Philosophical Enquiry into the Origin of Our Ideas of the Sublime and the Beautiful* (1757). For Burke, beautiful objects were characterised by their smallness, smoothness, delicacy and gradual variation. They evoked love and tenderness in contrast to the sublime which produced awe and terror. Objects which evoked sublime emotions were vast, magnificent and obscure. Loudness and sudden contrasts, like the play of light and dark in buildings, contributed to the sense of extension and infinity associated with the sublime. While beauty could be contained within the individual's gaze or comprehension, sublimity presented an excess that could not be processed by a rational mind. This excess, which confronted the individual subject with the thought of its own extinction, derived from emotions which, Burke argued, pertained to self-preservation and produced a frisson of delight and horror, tranquillity and terror.

The terror was akin to the sense of wonderment and awe accompanying religious experience. Sublimity offered intimations of a great, if not divine, power. This power was experienced in many objects and not only in the grandeur of natural landscape. Gothic romances and poetry, which drew on the wildness and grandeur of nature for their inspiration, partook of the sublime. The awful obscurity of the settings of Graveyard poetry elevate the mind to ideas of wonder and divinity, while similar settings of poems by Collins and the Wartons attribute a sacred, visionary and sublime power to the supernatural evocations of ancient bards as well as to the wildness of nature. Hugh Blair, in his *Lectures on Rhetoric and Belles Lettres* (1783), identifies gothic architecture as a source of the sublime: 'A gothic cathedral raises ideas of grandeur in our minds, by its size, its height, its awful obscurity, its strength, its antiquity, and its durability' (p. 59). The irregularity, ornamentation, immensity of gothic buildings overwhelmed the gaze with a vastness that suggested divinity and infinity. Age and durability also evoked sublimity for an essayist writing 'On the Pleasure Arising from the Sight of Ruins or Ancient Structures' in the *European Magazine* (1795): 'No one of the least sentiment or imagination can look upon an old or ruined edifice without feeling sublime emotions; a thousand ideas croud upon his mind, and fill him with awful astonishment' (Monk, p. 141).

The interest in the sublime is crucial in the reappraisal of medieval artefacts. Implicated in the transformation of ideas concerning nature and its relation to art, both gothic and sublime objects also participated in a transformation of notions of individuality, of the mind's relation to itself as well as to natural, cultural and metaphysical worlds. John Baillie's *An Essay on the Sublime* (1747) gives a powerful account of what the sublime meant for an individual's sense of self:

> Hence comes the Name of Sublime to everything which thus raises
> the Mind to fits of Greatness and disposes it to soar above her
> Mother Earth; Hence arises that Exultation and Pride which the Mind
> ever feels from the Consciousness of its own Vastness – That Object
> only can be justly called Sublime, which in some degree disposes the
> Mind to this Enlargement of itself, and gives her a lofty Conception of
> her own Powers.
>
> (p. 4)

The vastness that had been glimpsed in the natural sublime
became the mirror of the immensity of the human mind. Elevating and expanding mental powers to an almost divine extent
signified the displacement of religious authority and mystery by
the sublimity of nature and the human imagination. Sacred
nature, glimpsed in sublime settings and evoked by old poetry
and buildings, ceded to the genius and creative power of a sacred
self. By means of natural and cultural objects of sublimity the
human mind began its transcendence. In its imaginary ascendancy over nature, it discovered a grander scale and a new sense of
power and freedom for itself.

This sense of freedom was neither purely subjective nor simply a
matter of exceeding previous aesthetic forms. Freedom, in a political sense, was evoked in the process of recovering old texts,
themselves markers of a history in which endured a different idea
of nation and culture. It was a culture, if not entirely indigenous to
Britain, distinguished from those of Greece or Rome and possessed
of a history which had the permanence identified in gothic architecture. Moreover, it was a culture believed to foster a love of liberty and democracy. Paul-Henri Mallett's Preface to his 1755
account of the early history of the Germanic tribes, translated by
Percy as *Northern Antiquities* (1770), outlines these aspects of gothic
culture. It was among the nations of northern Europe and Scandi-
navia that European hatred of slavery and tyranny originated:

> is it not well known that the most flourishing and celebrated states of
> Europe owe originally to the northern nations, whatever liberty they
> now enjoy, either in their constitution, or in the spirit of their gov-
> ernment? For although the gothic form of government has been

almost every where altered or abolished, have we not retained, in most things, the opinions, the customs, the manners which that government had a tendency to produce? Is not this, in fact, the principal source of that courage, of that aversion to slavery, of that empire of honour which characterize in general the European nations; and of that moderation, of that easiness of access, and peculiar attention to the rights of humanity, which so happily distinguish our sovereigns from the inaccessible and superb tyrants of Asia?

(pp. 57–58)

Asia was not the only locus of tyranny. Closer to home was the tyranny that attended the decline of the Roman Empire, which became a site of despotism, degradation and barbarity and was itself overthrown by the Germanic tribes.

The significance of gothic culture was cited in British political discussions from the mid-seventeenth century. Parliaments and the legal system, it was believed, were derived from gothic institutions and peoples who were free and democratic. The word was employed loosely, embracing Celtic and Germanic tribes. The native culture that it referred to was one composed of those indigenous peoples and invaders whose occupation preceded the invasions of the Romans. Any relics of a non-Roman past were taken as evidence of a native and enduring tradition of independence. In 1739 one contributor to *Common Sense* wrote:

Methinks there was something respectable in those old hospitable Gothick halls, hung round with the Helmets, Breast-plates, and Swords of our Ancestors; I entered them with a Constitutional Sort of Reverence and look'd upon those arms with Gratitude, as the Terror of former Ministers, and the Check of Kings.

(Kliger, p. 27)

Like the durability of gothic buildings, these relics are reminders of the 'noble Strength and Simplicity' of the gothic Constitution. The hierarchical relation of the meanings of 'Gothic' and 'Roman' was far less clear than eighteenth-century critics made out: privileged meanings of 'Gothic' or 'classical' alternated, polarised by the political positions of Whig or Tory that employed the terms.

The word 'Gothic' was thus implicated in an ongoing political struggle over meanings. In the mid-eighteenth century the tyranny of Rome signified more than a period in early European history. After the Reformation, Protestantism constructed Roman Catholicism as a breeding-ground of despotism and superstition. The resistance to the imposition of classical aesthetic values also vindicates an enduring idea of British national culture as free, natural and imaginative. But 'Gothic' was also a term of abuse in other political positions. In the contest for the meaning of 'Gothic' more than a single word was at stake. At issue were the differently constructed and valued meanings of the Enlightenment, culture, nation and government as well as contingent, but no less contentious, significances of the family, nature, individuality and representation.

3

GOTHIC FORMS

Take – An old castle, half of it ruinous.
A long gallery, with a great many doors, some secret ones.
Three murdered bodies, quite fresh.
As many skeletons, in chests and presses ...
Mix them together, in the form of three volumes, to be taken
at any of the watering-places before going to bed.

(Anon., 'Terrorist Novel Writing', p. 229)

Other staple gothic ingredients could be added to the recipe
offered by an anonymous critic in an essay entitled 'Terrorist
Novel Writing' (1797): dark subterranean vaults, decaying
abbeys, gloomy forests, jagged mountains and wild scenery
inhabited by bandits, persecuted heroines, orphans and malevolent aristocrats. The atmosphere of gloom and mystery populated
by threatening figures was designed to quicken readers' pulses in
terrified expectation. Shocks, supernatural incidents and superstitious beliefs set out to promote a sense of sublime awe and
wonder which entwined with fear and elevated imaginations.
Though many devices and settings were repeated, they were
inflected differently. A hybrid form from its inception, the gothic

blend of medieval and historical romance with the novel of life and manners was framed in supernatural, sentimental or sensational terms. The consistency of the genre relied on the settings, devices and events. While their project was the production of terror, their repeated use turned them into rather hackneyed conventions and then into objects of satire. Sublime aspirations often veered towards the ridiculous. Detailing the absurdities, confusions and silly artifices of gothic novels, satirical judgements regarded them negatively for their failure as representations of human life and manners and their lack of moral instruction. Like romances before them, gothic novels were irrational, improper and immoral wastes of time. Worse, however, they were popular. T.J. Matthias observes in *The Pursuits of Literature* (1796): 'The spirit of enquiry which he [Horace Walpole] introduced was rather frivolous, though pleasing, and his Otranto Ghosts have propagated their species with unequalled fecundity. The spawn is in every novel shop' (p. 422). Horace Walpole's *The Castle of Otranto* (1764) was recognised as the origin of this new, popular and prodigious species of writing.

Though providing the blueprint for a new mode of writing, the framework that was established by *The Castle of Otranto* underwent a number of significant changes in the hands of later writers, under pressure from different historical circumstances. The relative consistency of gothic settings and plots, in conjunction with the romance tradition from which they drew, enabled the gothic novel to be recognisable as a distinct type of fiction. Framed as another manifestation of the romance form or as a pastiche of the productions of uncivilised ages, gothic novels could be readily criticised by the literary establishment: ridicule serves to reinforce social and literary values while simultaneously acknowledging some degree of anxiety. Indeed, the increasing popularity of the genre exacerbated the neo-classical fear that all romances and novels could produce anti-social effects and lead to social disintegration. Despite being associated with literary and moral impropriety, many gothic novels set out to vindicate morality, virtue and reason. They were thus caught between their avowedly moral and conventional projects and the unacceptably unrealistic mode of representation they employed. This tension produced

ambivalence within novels themselves as well as in critical recep-
tions. It also contributed to the subsequent changes in narrative
strategy and setting.

While ambivalence characterises both the structure of gothic
narratives and their relation to the literary codes of the time, it
cannot be restricted to the sphere of literature itself. What literature was, its nature and function, was undergoing significant
revision. This can be seen in the shifting attitude to non-classical
texts, in the way 'Gothic' began to be positively associated with
nature, feeling and the expansiveness of the individual imagination. Fiction was becoming less a mode of moral instruction, a
guide to proper behaviour, a way of representing society as natural, unified and rational, and more an invitation to pleasure and
excitement, a way of cultivating individual emotions detached
from the obligations of the everyday world. While it freed writers
from neo-classical conventions, it also imaginarily liberated readers from social constraints.

Changing ideas of literature were evident in wider shifts in
modes of literary production and consumption. Markets for and
access to texts of all kinds were expanding as a result of cheaper
printing processes and the emergence of circulating libraries. The
growing reading public included larger numbers of readers from
the middle class, especially women, and reflected a change in the
distribution of power and wealth from an aristocratic and landed
minority to those whose interests lay in a mercantile economy.
Writing, too, was becoming less a pursuit associated with those
who could afford leisure and more a professional activity. Needing
to sell their work, writers were increasingly dependent on the
market that consumed fiction. The popularity of the gothic novel
highlights the way that the control of literary production was
shifting away from the guardians of taste and towards the reading
public itself, much to the chagrin of those interested in maintaining an exclusive set of literary values. Women constituted an
important part of this market, and not only as avid consumers of
fiction: an increasing proportion of novels were written by
women, often in order to maintain themselves and their families.

These shifts in the class and gender composition of readers are
linked to social and political changes as well as economic ones.

Industrialisation, urbanisation and the shifts of political power manifested in the American Revolution's rejection of imperialism (1776), and the French Revolution's overthrow of absolutist monarchy (1789), constitute large signals of changing notions of government, social organisation and independence. All areas of British society seemed unstable, as were its ways of representing and regulating itself according to rational and moral principles. While much gothic fiction can be seen as a way of imagining an order based on divine or metaphysical principles that had been displaced by Enlightenment rationality, a way of conserving justice, privilege and familial and social hierarchies, its concern with modes of representing such an order required that it exceed the boundaries of reason and propriety. In this context gothic fiction blurs rather than reinforces social boundaries, interrogating, rather than restoring, any imagined continuity between past and present, nature and culture, reason and passion, individuality, family and society.

THE CASTLE OF OTRANTO

Many of the main ingredients of the genre that came to be known as the gothic novel can be found in Horace Walpole's *The Castle of Otranto*. While other novels, like Tobias Smollett's *The Adventures of Ferdinand Count Fathom* (1753), used feudal customs and settings or characters, it was Walpole's text that condensed features from old poetry, drama and romance and provided the model for future developments. In the preface to the second edition of *The Castle of Otranto*, Horace Walpole both situated the novel in relation to romances and novels and justified its project in terms of the move away from neo-classical aesthetic values. The novel, he states, 'was an attempt to blend the two kinds of romance, the ancient and the modern' (p. 7). The mixing of medieval romance and realistic novel tries to overcome the perceived limitations of both: the latter's insistence on realistic representation of nature and life cramps the imagination while the former is too unnatural and improbable. Wanting to let fancy roam freely in 'the boundless realms of invention' and create 'more interesting situations', Walpole also states his intention to preserve rules of probability and have his characters 'think, speak and act, as it might be supposed mere men and women would do in extraordinary positions' (pp. 7–8). The story, however, inclines more to the presentation of marvellous events than to human characterisation and realistic action.

In the second preface Walpole appeals to new ideas about writing. Inspiration, individual artistic genius and imaginative freedom overstep the boundaries of neo-classical taste. The originality and genius of Shakespeare legitimates imaginative licence as well as being cited as a major influence on the novel's dramatic and melodramatic contrasts of figures, pace, dialogue, settings and use of supernatural events. Despite these justifications for his 'new species of romance', the preface, written in the third person and acknowledging authorship, tries to obviate suspicions of impropriety. Novels and romances were far from being completely acceptable pastimes for a member of polite society. Indeed, it was only the success of the first edition of the novel, published anonymously, that led to Walpole's admission of authorship.

For the development of the gothic novel, the significance of anonymous publication is more than the recognition of impropriety associated with authorial disavowal. The first edition had a preface that became a crucial device in gothic narratives: it was itself a fiction, a fiction, moreover, with pretensions to historical authenticity and veracity. The antiquarian tones of the preface declare *The Castle of Otranto* to be a translation of a medieval Italian story printed in 1529 and written at the time of the Crusades. Everything, from the gothic script in which it is printed to the feudal customs and miraculous incidents it presents, conspires to give it an air of truth as a production of the barbarous and superstitious dark ages. Its moral, questionable to the eighteenth-century 'translator' – that 'the sins of the fathers are visited on their children' – also establishes a foundation for later stories. Doubting whether 'ambition curbed its appetite of dominion from the dread of so remote a punishment', the 'translator' judges an avowedly superstitious past in the terms of his present. The historical distance that is opened up by the device of the discovered manuscript returns readers to the neo-classical strictures and produces an uncomfortable interplay between past and present that both displaces and invokes contemporary aesthetic and social concerns. Historical distance also acknowledges cultural difference: English Protestant culture is distinguished from the southern European, and thus Catholic, background which is constructed as both exotic and superstitious, fascinating but extreme in its aesthetic and religious sentiments.

The Castle of Otranto tells the story of Manfred, prince of Otranto by virtue of his grandfather's usurpation of the rightful owner, Alphonso, and his attempts to secure his lineage. His sickly son is crushed by a gigantic helmet on the day of his wedding to Isabella, daughter of another noble. The helmet comes from the statue of the original owner. Against all reason, the credulous followers of Manfred blame and imprison a young peasant, Theodore, for its miraculous transportation. Ambitious and unscrupulous as he is, Manfred decides that, though already married, he will have to wed Isabella in order to produce an heir. Repulsed by his advances, Isabella is saved by the sighing portrait of Manfred's grandfather. She flees from the castle, helped by a recently escaped Theodore, through subterranean vaults. The youth, however, is recaptured. At the same time, servants are terrified by the sight of a giant in armour and Manfred, jealous of an imagined attachment between Theodore and Isabella, threatens his life. A friar, Jerome, intercedes, and discovers the youth to be his long-lost son.

A troop of knights arrive at the castle carrying a gigantic sword (which matches the helmet) and the colours of Isabella's family. Suspicious of Manfred, the knights join the search for her. In the meantime, Theodore is helped to escape by Mathilda, Manfred's rejected daughter, and flees through the castle vaults to encounter Isabella among a labyrinth of caverns. There, to defend her honour, he defeats a knight in combat and discovers him to be Isabella's father, Frederic. Back at the castle, the conjugal problems are still unresolved. Theodore is attracted by Mathilda, as is Frederic. At the mention of this amorous interest, blood runs from the nose of Alphonso's statue. Manfred, finding the lovers in the chapel and believing Mathilda to be Isabella, stabs her in a fit of passion. His guilt and his forebears' guilt is discovered, Jerome and Theodore are revealed to be the true heirs to Otranto and, with a clap of thunder and a clanking of ghostly chains, the castle crumbles to ruin. The guilty die or incarcerate themselves in convents and proper lineage is restored with a warning about human vanities and with the eventual marriage of Theodore and Isabella.

While *The Castle of Otranto* sets out the features and themes for use in all later gothic texts, it does so in a rather ambivalent way. The aristocratic order of primogeniture, property and patriarchy that it restores with such speed, and so many convolutions, stretches the bounds of credulity and reduces the basis of feudal society to a few of its more extravagant customs. Even as it associates virtue and character with breeding (Theodore is never anything but a knight in peasant's clothes) and seems to naturalise patriarchal and aristocratic values within a wider metaphysical order governed by supernatural manifestations of an eternal law, its mode of representation undercuts these links. Supernatural manifestations guarantee the restitution of an old order but present it as a law at once violent and sublime, disproportionate and just, and founded as much on superstition as on power. Despite the comedy of the servants' superstitious fears, superstition is encouraged by the irrational and anti-Enlightenment manifestation of gigantic and supernatural justice.

The novel's style stimulates emotional effects rather than rational understanding, thereby emulating the vicious passions of the selfish and ambitious villain. The frenetic pace of the text is, in part, an effect of excitement and irrationality. In a letter to the Reverend William Cole (9 March 1765), Walpole describes how his own gothic mansion and its decorations contributed to the dream he offers as the origin of the story. These factors centre the interest of the story on marvellous and disturbing events and on the terrors they produce instead of the moral resolution they deliver. The style of writing itself works against reason and propriety and led critics of the time to baulk at its absurdities, lack of morality and false taste. The story's pretence to historical veracity exposed the artifice of its representations for a neo-classically informed audience. Extravagant depictions of passion and incredible events, the thinness of its cautionary ending, so the 'translator' notes in the first preface, leaves an eighteenth-century reader suspicious of its supposed morality. But the contrast of distinct aesthetic impulses positions the text between serious purpose or subversive play. Its evocations of terror and superstition can be seen to advocate a sense of awe at supernatural power and its restitution of justice, or can render such a notion of justice comic, suggesting that the orders which depend on such superstitious notions are quaintly unrealistic. If ideals of chivalrous virtue and honour depend on spectral appearances and supernatural wrath to preserve them then they, like the castle itself, may be destined for ruin. Chivalry and honour, indeed, are like ghostly incarnations of an old order that have no place in the enlightened eighteenth century. Mere superstitions, these ideals, while underpinning aristocratic and patriarchal culture, have no power against the cunning and tyranny of the selfish and ambitious individual. Virtue, too, is helpless in the face of tyrannical fathers interested only in the preservation of a law of primogeniture. Confronted with indifference, forced marriage and death, their lot, it seems, is to suffer and be sacrificed to the persecutions of patriarchal power with only the occasional knight fighting for their honour. Indeed, the predominance of arms and armour presents a culture founded on a violence that is constructed as both metaphysical and individual. But it is not, in eighteenth-century terms, natural.

In this respect, *The Castle of Otranto* seems to reinforce eighteenth-century values, distinguishing a barbaric past from the enlightened present. None-the-less, eighteenth-century culture still depended on notions of virtue and honour. Nor did it witness the total disappearance of an aristocratic order, of which Walpole, later to become Earl of Orford, was a part. From the position offered by the second preface, however, with its avocation of imagination and original genius and its privileging of individualist values, the novel appears as a text that examines the limitations of reason, virtue and honour in the regulation of the passions, ambitions and violence underlying patriarchal and family orders. Despite their significant inter-relation, distinctions between terms and values are left unresolved. *The Castle of Otranto* displays the tensions and contradictions traversing eighteenth-century society's representations of itself. It was ambivalently received by reviewers in the 1760s. For one, not knowing whether the translator 'speaks seriously or ironically', the absurdity of its contents and wretchedness of its conclusion were not sufficiently compensated for by the 'well marked' characters and the 'spirit and propriety of the narrative'. For another, the gothic machinery is entertaining, the language is accurate and its representations of character, manners and humanity 'indicate the keenest penetration'. Its 'principal defect', however, is its lack of any moral but the 'very useless' one concerning the sins of the father. In contrast to reviews that noticed, and approved of, eighteenth-century shapings of character, another reviewer criticised 'the foibles of a supposed antiquity' and went on to declare that 'it is, indeed, more than strange, that an Author, of a refined and polished genius, should be an advocate for re-establishing the barbarous superstitions of gothic devilism!' (McNutt, pp. 163–64).

The ambivalent reactions produced by *The Castle of Otranto* partake of a wider ambivalence concerning the eighteenth century's relation to its gothic past and its changing present. The function of literature in representing a rational and natural social order and guiding readers in proper modes of conduct and discrimination is also questioned: in failing to offer an overriding and convincing position, *The Castle of Otranto* leaves readers unsure of its moral purpose. Its uncertain tone and style, between seriousness and irony, is perhaps the novel's cardinal sin and one that is visited in various forms on its literary offspring. Rending the correspondence of representation and reality, gothic fancy and invention were able to construct other worlds that dislocated boundaries between fact and fiction, history and contemporaneity, reality and fantasy. The loosening of rational and moral rules for writing facilitated by the idea of the individual imagination, and the indulgence of emotions and pleasures, also entailed evocations of anxiety – evinced by figures of darkness and power – that any form of justice or order, whether natural, human or supernatural, had itself become spectral.

EARLY REVISIONS

Walpole's excessive use of supernatural and irrational impulses, however, was tempered in subsequent gothic works. In 1777, *The Champion of Virtue. A Gothic Story* was published anonymously in the guise of a translated old manuscript. This device acknowledges the influence of *The Castle of Otranto*. In 1778 the preface to the second edition, in which Clara Reeve declared her authorship and changed the title to *The Old English Baron*, outlined criticisms of Walpole's text. Its ability to engage the reader's sympathy is praised but 'the machinery is so violent, that it destroys the effect it is intended to excite' (p. 4). As a result the novel exceeds the limits of probability and credibility, disappointing instead of interesting readers: 'when your expectation is wound up to the highest pitch, these circumstances take it down with a witness, destroy the work of the imagination, and instead of attention, excite laughter' (p. 5). In the light of these criticisms *The Old English Baron* attempts to reduce the ambivalent effects of gothic fiction, and restore a balance between marvellous and supernatural incident and the natural life and manners of eighteenth-century realism.

Ghostly machinations are kept to a minimum and, though the customs and settings of feudal times are invoked, they are contained by eighteenth-century sentiments. One contemporary critic observed that the book's claim to gothic status arose primarily from the architectural descriptions (McNutt, p. 171). Although other critics gave relatively favourable reviews of the novel, Walpole was less than impressed by its claims to be a gothic story: 'Have you seen "The Old English Baron"', he wrote in a letter to Reverend William Mason (8 April 1778), 'a gothic story, professedly written in imitation of Otranto, but reduced to reason and probability? It is so probable that any trial for murder at the Old Bailey would make a more interesting story!' For Walpole, Reeve's text elided the excitements of a very different past by framing it too heavily in the terms of a neo-classical present. *The Old English Baron* establishes a historical continuity maintained by the imposition of eighteenth-century rules and morality. Differences between Walpole and Reeve, moreover, implied disagreements that were not solely concerned with the purpose and place of literature. Unlike the aristocrat, Walpole, Reeve came from an educated middle-class background, her father a curate in Ipswich. This social position is reflected in the novel's highlighting of gentility and merit, dissociated from social position. The hero's virtues, for instance, are not solely related to his high birth, since he was raised by a peasant family. His courage, kindness and generosity of spirit qualify him as one deserving of his advantages rather than merely inheriting them. Gothic devices and setting are subordinated to the social and domestic proprieties of the emerging middle class of the eighteenth century.

Set during the reign of Henry VI, the novel tells the story of a foundling, Edmund, ostensibly peasant of birth, who distinguishes himself in social and military skills. He is steward to the sons of Baron Fitz-Owen whose family inhabit a castle owned by a relation, Lord Lovel. The castle has a decayed set of apartments that have been mysteriously locked for years. Edmund's past is linked to these apartments. After his talents have excited rivalries in the Baron's family, he is sent to the apartments to spend the night. There, groans and strange lights lead to a dream in which he sees a knight in armour and a lady who address him as their child. Consequently, Edmund attempts to discover the truth of his parentage, gathered from diverse local anecdotes. After a feudal combat, the sins of Lord Lovel are brought to light and Edmund is established as the rightful heir to the castle and estates. Propriety as well as property is restored. The usurper is punished and Edmund is allowed to marry the Baron's daughter, thus harmonising family relations. Morality, too, is restored: 'All these, when together, furnish a striking lesson to posterity, of the over-ruling hand of Providence, and the certainty of RETRIBUTION' (p. 153). Not only do virtue, morality, social and domestic harmony prevail, they are, so the cautionary ending declares, divinely sanctioned and protected.

Though it reduces the incidence and effects of supernatural powers, the story none-the-less invokes heavenly might as a guarantee of the tale's moral. While its subjects are aristocratic and its world is feudal, the story keeps superstition in check with its emphasis on virtuous character, individual merit, human vanities and domestic order. Returned to a distinctly eighteenth-century framework, the fiction absorbs and rewrites the past in a manner which privileges the neo-classical present. In this respect, the relationship between history and fiction highlighted by gothic tales is more complicated than the novel's preface acknowledges: 'history represents human nature as it is in real life' while 'romance displays only the amiable side of the picture' (p. 3). Unlike Walpole's version of a wild and irrational feudal past, Reeve's romance renders history itself as an amiable picture of eighteenth-century nature and life which in turn discloses them as somewhat unreal. Disturbing the boundaries between past and present, however, became an inevitable feature of gothic fiction, even though the manner in which the two were articulated differed from writer to writer. History, like nature, the supernatural and the passions of individuals, became a contradictory site for both imaginative speculation and moral imposition.

In Sophia Lee's *The Recess* (1783–85) the interweaving of history and gothic romance is complicated further. The novel situates its fictional heroines in a world populated by real figures and events from the Elizabethan age. Sir Philip Sidney, Sir Francis Drake, the Earl of Leicester as well as Elizabeth I all appear. Spicing fiction with fact, however, did not lend the tale greater veracity. For one critic it detracted from the narrative. History was employed 'too lavishly', leaving the mind 'ever divided and distracted when the fact so little accords with the fiction, and Romance and History are at perpetual variance with one another' (*The Recess*, Introduction, p. xxiii). Romance, however, to use Reeve's distinction, does not win out in painting the real life of history in an amiable light. The novel's melancholic and gloomy tones were at odds with the romance form. Historical accuracy, indeed, is not a primary concern of the novel in which fictional licence freely alters events and their chronology. In many ways it serves as the backdrop for the representation of eighteenth-century concerns. Critics noted the novel's 'neglect of the peculiar manners of the age' while appreciating it as an instructive and interesting text (Introduction, pp. xxi–xxii). Gothic elements feature as part of the wider plot of a historical narrative that owes much to the extravagant composition of seventeenth-century

French romances. Ruins, underground vaults and heroines' terrified flights are blended with romantic adventures ranging over a
wide geographical area. Picturesque descriptions of natural scenery and accounts of domestic happiness, sufferings and tensions,
however, maintain a thoroughly eighteenth-century perspective.

The use of history in *The Recess* introduced some important new
directions for the gothic model derived from Walpole. Like
Reeve, it reduced the incidence of the supernatural and also gave
new impetus to the historical romance, a form in which the past
is liberally recomposed in fictional narrative. Unlike both Reeve
and Walpole, however, the action of the novel centres on the lives
of two women. They are the daughters of Mary Queen of Scots
who have to be hidden from society and the court of Elizabeth in
order not to suffer the same fate as their mother. They grow up in
secret in the subterranean chambers of a ruined abbey. The novel
charts their entry into the world under assumed names and their
marriages to Lord Leicester and the Earl of Essex. Society and
marriage offer only brief moments of happiness until the secret of
their identity is disclosed. The disclosure leads to the death of one
sister and the flight of the other, powerless against the political
intrigues and violent passions of the Elizabethan world.

The world at large presents the greatest terrors for the young
heroines. Rather than the imaginary threats of supernatural
powers it is the accounts of pursuit and persecution by noblemen,
female courtiers and hired bandits that constitute the major
instances of fear. In contrast, domesticity, represented by the
sentimental attachments of the sisters in their hidden, underground habitation, offers love and security. However, the novel
suggests that there is no refuge in secrecy, hidden recesses or
domesticity itself. The outside world invades this sphere, turning
a refuge into a place of menace. Its focus on female virtue and
domesticity is not idealised: virtuous women continually confront
suffering and persecution, their ideals leaving them both powerless and unrewarded. Neither virtue nor the security of domestic
space forms an adequate defence and itself becomes a prison rather
than a refuge, a physical and ideological confinement in a system
of values that privileges the male and active world beyond the
family. At the same time romances marked a putative and

contradictory attempt to offer access to worlds other than the home which circumscribed real life and horizons of the majority of middle-class women. At home they could read tales that, while reinforcing ideals of female virtue and propriety, offered some escape from domestic confinement through fictional adventures even if, in the fictions, the impulse came from external violence. Foregrounding confinement, virtue in suffering, and a threatening external world, fiction none-the-less attempted to articulate the contradictory requirements of propriety and excitement. The resulting ambivalence only entwines the realms of women's reality and fantasy. The novel, by a successful writer and headmistress of a girls' school in Bath, is traversed by these contradictory impulses: the moral and social imperative to inculcate female virtues and domestic values conflicts with the fact that working in the world involves some transgression of the accepted role for women. In locating problems in ideals of female virtue and domesticity *The Recess* establishes an important direction for the gothic novel.

Neither virtue nor propriety were a particular concern of William Beckford's *Vathek*, published in French in 1782 and translated into English in 1786. Frequently cited as a gothic novel, *Vathek* remains distinct from the genre, though its influence can be traced in later and more obviously gothic texts. One of the main connections is that its author, the extremely wealthy Beckford, built an extravagant and costly gothic building, Fonthill Abbey. Like Walpole and his gothic mansion at Strawberry Hill, he cited the intricate and sublime architecture of Fonthill as a source of inspiration for his novel, comparing it to the hall of Eblis in *Vathek*. There are many evocations of sublimity in its descriptions of nature and supernatural excess; its hero-villain, Caliph Vathek, is an Eastern tyrant whose violent actions and passionate temper instils terror and horror among his subjects. Vathek is also a sensualist, building great palaces in order to indulge his carnal pleasures. Adept in the arts of astrology and magic, the Caliph fervently pursues forbidden knowledge, until he is finally damned.

Though many antiquarians believed that the romance tradition originated in Arab or Eastern countries, *Vathek* invokes another mode of eighteenth-century writing. Translations of Arabian stories led to a vogue for Oriental tales and a love of the exotic. The East constituted another space in which the expanding imagination could freely roam. Indulgence in descriptions of excessive passion, irrational violence, magical events and sensual pleasure was acceptable, as many critics of *Vathek* seemed to agree, because they demonstrated the disastrous consequences of those forms of behaviour. *Vathek*'s ending aligns itself with this code: describing how Vathek will wander eternity in anguish, the concluding moral declares that 'such was, and should be, the punishment of unrestrained passions and atrocious deeds!' (p. 120). Ironically, and perhaps as a satire on eighteenth-century Orientalism, this warning against excess comes at the end of a story that has flagrantly indulged all sorts of formal, imaginative and descriptive excess.

The ending, like the uncomfortable identification with the hero-villain throughout the tale, refuses to affirm any stable boundary line between good and evil. Vathek is the villain and also the victim of his ambitions and passions. Like Faust, having over-indulged a quest for knowledge and power, he incurs damnation at the hands of a violent supernatural order. The moral tone of the ending, as in *The Castle of Otranto*, remains unconvincing. Like Walpole's novel, *Vathek* makes no concessions to reason or probability, indulging in the imaginative pleasures of supernatural and fantastic events for the sublime emotions they produce rather than the morals they present.

In the connections and contrasts manifested in the writings of Walpole and Beckford, on the one hand, and Reeve and Lee on the other, two of the major strands of gothic fiction are displayed. Despite differences of historical and geographical setting, the male writers of gothic, of a more aristocratic class position, lean towards representations of irrationality and the supernatural, exercising the privileges and freedoms conferred by gender and class position. The female writers, usually more solidly middle-class in origin, remain more concerned with the limits of eighteenth-century virtues, careful to interrogate rather than overstep the boundaries of domestic propriety which, because of their gender, were more critically maintained. Though darkness, ruin, superstition and human passion are objects of fascination and sublimity in both strands, their significance and effect is shaped by the very different ends of the narratives. The gothic fictions that dominated the 1790s introduced certain changes into the genre but the basic pattern of the narratives, as well as the conventional settings, can be directly identified with these two strategies of indulging or rationalising imaginative excess.

4

GOTHIC WRITING IN THE 1790s

Perhaps at this point we ought to analyze these new novels in which sorcery and phantasmagoria constitute practically the entire merit: foremost among them I would place *The Monk*, which is superior in all respects to the strange flights of Mrs Radcliffe's brilliant imagination. But this would take us too far afield. Let us concur that this kind of fiction, whatever one may think of it, is assuredly not without merit: 'twas the inevitable result of the revolutionary shocks which all Europe has suffered.

(Marquis de Sade, 'Reflections on the Novel', pp. 108–9)

A period when the largest number of gothic works were produced and consumed, the 1790s was very much the decade that defined the terms of gothic production. Terror was the order of the day. Gothic stories littered literary magazines, three- and four-volume novels filled the shelves of circulating libraries and, in their cheap card covers, found their way into servants' quarters as well as drawing rooms. Though the startling gothic machinery of *The Castle of Otranto* was cranked up in every text, there were significant shifts in emphasis. These tended to follow the lines laid down by Reeve and Lee in framing the past in terms of a rational and moral present. Eighteenth-century values were never far from the surface in these tales of other times. Terror, moreover, had an over-whelming political significance in the period. The decade of the French Revolution saw the most violent of challenges to monarchical order: heads rolled and blood washed the streets. In Britain, the Revolution and the political radicalism it inspired were represented as a tide of destruction threatening the complete dissolution of the social order. In gothic images of violence and excessive passion, in villainous threats to proper domestic structures, a significant overlap in literary and political metaphors of fear and anxiety occurs, metaphors implying how much a culture sensed itself to be under attack both from within, in the dissemination of radical ideas, and from without, in the shape of revolutionary mobs across the Channel.

ANN RADCLIFFE

The most successful of gothic writers was undoubtedly Ann Radcliffe, a woman whose uneventful life in many ways mirrored that of her middle-class audience. Married to a lawyer who became the editor of a literary magazine, she appears to have spent most of her time at their home in Bath. Her novels were enormously popular and, unusually, also received critical approbation. An index of her popularity can be seen in the amounts she was paid by booksellers: *The Mysteries of Udolpho* (1794) and *The Italian* (1797) earned her the then huge sums of £500 and £600. Radcliffe's success can also be measured by the many imitations of her work. Well into the nineteenth century books were produced using her narrative techniques, and even parts of her titles. Like Sophia Lee, Radcliffe chose virtuous young women as heroines of novels set in the Middle Ages or the Renaissance. Like Walpole, her geographical settings were usually in southern European countries, Italy and France in particular, continuing the association of Catholicism with superstition, arbitrary power and passionate extremes. The physical settings, too, were suitably gothic: isolated and ruined castles and abbeys, old chateaux with secret vaults and passage-ways, dark forests and spectacular mountain regions populated by bandits and robbers. Radcliffe's heroines

suffer repeated pursuit and incarceration at the hands of malevolent and ambitious aristocrats and monks. Orphans separated
from protective domestic structures, these heroines journey
through mysterious, threatening environments composed of an
unholy mixture of social corruption, natural decay and imagined
supernatural power. At the end virtue has, of course, been preserved and domestic harmony reaffirmed. The tales are all framed
as lessons in virtue and faith in a guiding providential hand.

Where Radcliffe's tales differ significantly from previous gothic
texts is in their production and development of terrifying scenes
and mysterious occurrences. In response to the strange noises and
spectral figures that inhabit the dark world of ruins, castles and
forests, the heroines conjure up images of ghostly and supernatural powers. Imagined supernatural terrors are accompanied by
other mysteries that lie closer to home and reality. *A Sicilian
Romance* (1790) describes mysterious hauntings in locked apartments and unravels the family secrets that underlie them. In *The
Romance of the Forest* (1791) the heroine discovers an old manuscript that, to her horror, tells the story of a murdered man. In
The Mysteries of Udolpho a brief glimpse of her father's letters leaves
the heroine to speculate on the horrible secret, a concealed crime,
buried in her family history. Family secrets are resolved and often
rendered innocent, but only after a series of repeated invocations
have encouraged heroine and reader alike to imagine the darkest
possible crimes. Apparently spectral events are similarly explained
after they have excited curiosity and terror over extended sections
of the narrative. This use of suspense characterises Radcliffe's
technique. Involving readers in the narrative, it also encourages
imaginations to indulge in extravagant speculations. The rational
explanations that are subsequently offered, however, undercut the
supernatural and terrible expectations and bring readers and
characters back to eighteenth-century conventions of realism,
reason and morality by highlighting their excessive and ill-judged
credulity. While extremes of imagination and feeling are described in the novels, the object is always to moderate them with a
sense of propriety.

Radcliffe's heroines come from the sentimental genre of fiction
in which fine feelings are signs of virtue and nobility. They have a

tendency, however, to over-indulge their emotions, partaking too heavily of the cult of sensibility which flowered in the eighteenth century. Rarefied abandonments to feeling leave heroes and heroines in tears at the slightest melancholy thought or cause them to faint at the slightest shock. Like the extravagant and superstitious imaginings that are present throughout Radcliffe's works, excessive sensibility is displayed to demonstrate a dangerous evocation of passions that corrupt the heart. Powerful feelings are legitimately expressed in the responses to the magnificence of the scenery through which her heroines pass. Radcliffe draws upon eighteenth-century notions of the picturesque and the sublime as well as the work of travel writers and painters. Elevated by undulating rural landscapes and awed by the craggy grandeur of the Alps and Apennines, the responses of Radcliffe's heroines are thoroughly in tune with prevailing aesthetic taste, and are particularly well versed in Burke's ideas of the sublime and the beautiful. Such taste is reinforced with quotations of poetry from, or in the style of, the works of writers associated with the imaginative genius and natural sublimity of the romantic revival. Invoking poetic power, Radcliffe's texts also set out to contain it within orders of reason, morality and domesticity.

The most famous and most imitated of Radcliffe's six novels was *The Mysteries of Udolpho*. Its four volumes tell the story of Emily St Aubert. Brought up in a rural chateau in southern France by a caring father, Emily is educated in the virtues of simplicity and domestic harmony. She is prone, however, to over-indulge her sensibilities. Her father, before he dies, warns her that all excess is vicious, especially excessive sensibility. Taken in by her aunt, Emily almost marries Valancourt, a similarly sentimental young nobleman. Instead, her aunt marries the Marquis Montoni and takes Emily to Venice and thence to the castle of Udolpho. Montoni is the dark villain of the story who tries by menacing and murderous means to secure Emily's inheritance and estates. She flees from his persecution and the imagined terrors of the castle by way of the mouldering vaults of a ruined gothic chapel. Later, supposedly supernatural terrors are explained, as is the very worldly identity of Montoni: he is leader of a group of banditti, not a demon. Emily returns to France and to the security of an aristocratic family who live in the region in which she was born. Despite the return to the simplicity of country life, fears of ghostly machinations propel the narrative, until an exhaustive series of explanations unravels both the mysteries of the castle and those disturbing secrets closer to home. With the return of Valancourt, absent from most of the narrative as a result of falling prey to the charms of a countess and the corruptions of society, domestic happiness is restored. The novel announces its moral: that the power of vice is as temporary as its punishment is certain and that innocence, supported by patience, always triumphs in the end.

With a clear moral concluding the tale, Radcliffe, like Reeve, gives gothic fiction a more acceptable face. Critics were generally pleased by Radcliffe's novels. *The Mysteries of Udolpho* was praised for its correctness of sentiment, its elegance of style and its bold and proper characterisation in the *Monthly Review* (1794). The author's imaginative and descriptive powers were admired by reviewers in the *European Magazine* (1794) and the *British Critic* (1794). Aspects of her style, however, provoked a degree of critical ambivalence. Her technique of prolonging the mysteries through her use of suspense was considered excessive. In the *Critical Review* (1794), Coleridge argued that 'curiosity is raised oftener than it is gratified; or rather, it is raised so high that no adequate gratification can be given it' (p. 362). A similar air of disappointment is evident in the critic in the *Gentleman's Magazine* (1794) who found the depictions of the picturesque repetitious. Another reviewer, in the *British Critic* (1794), stated that 'the lady's talent for description leads her to excess', before observing that 'too much of the terrific' leads to jaded sensibility and exhausted curiosity (pp. 120–21). These criticisms of the novel's excess point to a contradiction between the style and cautionary project of the novel. Ironically, the criticisms also offer some insight into the ambiguous nature of Radcliffe's technique of heightening mystery, suspense and supernatural speculation by delaying and then deflating expectation with a rational explanation. Like the writer of the satirical essay, 'Terrorist Novel Writing', who hopes that so many tales of ghosts and terror will satiate the most ravenous of reading publics with repetitions,

Udolpho's concern with the dangers of over-indulging sensibility and imagination involves a performative exaggeration of terrifying incidents in order to jade sensibility and exhaust superstitious curiosity. Readers are thus enlisted in the narrative as dupes of the false and terrifying expectations it sets up and then distanced from the credulities and superstitions of heroines and servants by disappointing explanations. By the end, virtue, reason and domestic felicity are restored along with a discriminating readership.

None-the-less, the ambiguity of this technique of inviting and depicting the superstitions that it disavows produces ambivalent effects. The novel as a whole depends on the play of antitheses. It is only in contrast to the dark world of Udolpho that a world of happiness and light can be valued. Only by enduring the effects of her own excessive sensibility and imagination can Emily learn the virtue of moderation. In the passions and selfishness of the unscrupulous Montoni, the terrifying effects of a loss of virtue and self-control are made manifest. Against the rural simplicity and domestic happiness of the family home stands a threatening image of the social world as a place of artifice, corruption and violence. In *Udolpho*'s world of imagination and terror one glimpses the face of evil. This face is as much that of the castle as the villain himself: 'Silent, lonely and sublime, it seemed to stand the sovereign of the scene, and to frown defiance on all, who dared to invade its solitary reign' (p. 227). The castle appears as another figure of power, tyranny and malevolence. Linked to Montoni it is a symbol of egoism, but it is in the imaginative eyes of Emily that it becomes awful and sublime.

Evil, focused in the castle itself, is a result of both the individual passions that are engendered by social corruption and the excessive sensibility that gives it supernatural power. The articulation of these two strands of vicious excess, vicious precisely because they lead away from the simplicity of reason and morality, is made possible by the excesses of the narrative: its artificial stimulation of terrors encourages readers, like heroines, to imagine such power. In this way *Udolpho* is concerned with the effects of representation and the way that it can discriminate between, or blur, the boundaries of good and evil.

Towards the end of the third volume of the novel an exchange takes place that manifests a degree of self-consciousness about gothic novels themselves. Its self-consciousness and satirical edge, indeed, prefigure the exchange about 'horrid' novels between Henry Tilney and Catherine Morland in Jane Austen's satire of the gothic novel in *Northanger Abbey* (1818):

> 'Where have you been so long?' said she, 'I had begun to think some wonderful adventure had befallen you, and that the giant of this enchanted castle, or the ghost, which, no doubt, haunts it, had conveyed you through a trap-door into some subterranean vault, whence you was never to return.' 'No', replied Blanche, laughingly, 'you seem to love adventures so well, that I leave them for you to achieve.'
>
> 'Well, I am willing to achieve them, provided I am allowed to describe them.'
>
> 'My dear Mademoiselle Bearn,' said Henri, as he met her at the door of the parlour, 'no ghost of these days would be so savage as to impose silence on you. Our ghosts are more civilized than to condemn a lady to a purgatory severer even, than their own, be it what it may.'
>
> (p. 473)

The satirical dismissal of ghosts indicates the proper attitude towards the supernatural: it is no more than an effect of a silly, over-indulged imagination associated with women, like Blanche, of a lower class. In the context of the novel, however, the distancing of ghosts from a civilised present is a little more complicated since it is in this family that Emily arrives after escaping the terrors of Udolpho. The two female speakers participating in the discussion of ghosts from the security of their domestic position, as aristocratic daughters or family retainers, constitute doubles of Emily: one is rational and educated, the other over-indulged in imagination and sensibility. These two, indeed, represent the extreme positions allocated to the reader by the novel.

But the secure world of the de Villefort family is not so neatly divided nor so clearly distinguished from Udolpho's world of terrors: the former is also populated by ghosts, suggestively animated by strange noises and spectral figures conveyed along subterranean passages. It is, moreover, the place where the terrors of Udolpho catch up with Emily and are only later explained. Other ghosts, emanating from a source that is closer to home, are raised up. In the rural retreat of the de Villeforts, the horror that Emily felt at seeing her father's letters is revived: ghosts of past family transgressions become the major source of awful emotion. These letters, too, are ultimately furnished with a rational and innocent explanation. It is only Emily's over-sensitive imagination that has turned them into awful crimes, her sensibility and pre-disposition to superstitious fancy turning a few lines from the letters into terrible secrets.

If *Udolpho* restores domesticity, virtue and reason to their proper places in the eighteenth-century order of things, it does so at a price. By presenting vice, corruption and irrationality as evil in the text and as an effect of representations that produce over-sensitive imaginations, it also suggests that the values it espouses and reinforces are effects of representation as well. Like the unnatural or overly imaginative evils the novel tries to cast beyond the pale of good society, the moral and domestic values that it would like to naturalise are glimpsed as part of the fiction. *Udolpho*'s attempt to externalise and expel all forms of vice and evil, including the excessive fancy and superstition encouraged by romances, leaves it, as a work of fiction, in an ambivalent position. Like the ambivalence perceived by critics in its overuse of suspense, there is a degree of uncertainty and instability in the way that the novel returns to conventional eighteenth-century values. This is of particular importance in respect of the roles given to women in the fiction. In many ways the text follows the moralistic pattern of eighteenth-century works like Richardson's *Clarissa* (1748–49) in its depictions of suffering virtue, to affirm values of domesticity and female propriety. In Radcliffe's novels, however, women are never completely confined to the home and family though that is considered to be their proper place. Leaving the security of privileged domestic space, female protagonists, and readers too, are supposed to learn, especially in the encounter with the violence and corruption of the outside world, of the advantages of family life. The escape from confinement, in narra-tive or reading, is no more than a prelude to a welcome return.

Ambivalence remains, not only in the way that the home seems to conceal horrifying secrets but in the possibility that escape, especially for readers, may be more pleasurable than the return to domesticity. Indeed, throughout Radcliffe's novels, it is the heroines who, though subjugated, persecuted and imprisoned, still escape: they and their reactions are the principal focus of the narrative. Apart from the malevolent villains, men play a very small and generally ineffectual part in the narratives. It is for these reasons that, despite the rational explanations and strongly moral conclusions, the distinctions of virtue and vice, good and evil, become rather precarious. While the privileged terms guarantee the sphere of domesticity and society, their antitheses are never fully excluded or completely externalised.

TERROR NARRATIVES

Attempts to define and expunge vice in cautionary tales advocating virtue and family values were regularly repeated in the many novels which followed the model of Radcliffe's sentimentally inflected gothic romances. In stories of orphaned heroines with all the virtues of middle-class domestic values discovering their aristocratic birthright after a series of terrors, persecutions and imprisonments, readers were offered familiar plots, settings and protagonists. Though these became formulaic to the point of ridicule, there was often, as in Radcliffe, some degree of self-consciousness regarding the effects of romance and supernatural narratives. Regina Maria Roche was one of the most successful imitators of Radcliffe. Her novel *The Children of the Abbey* (1794) was almost as popular as *The Mysteries of Udolpho*. Another of Roche's novels, *Clermont* (1798), used a familiarly Radcliffean pattern, but found itself entangled in the ambivalence associated with gothic narratives. Clermont is replete with decaying gothic castles, ruined chapels, underground passages, dark forests and ghostly groans. Its young heroine enjoys the tranquillity of rural life before suffering the terrors of cruelly unprincipled aristocrats and her own imagination. Mysterious events, ineffectual heroes and awful family secrets compose a novel that is made up of partial stories, letters and endless speculation. At the end, when the various stories composing the novel are pieced together, vice is revealed for what it is and virtuous aristocratic identities are finally seen in their true and innocent light. Propriety and familial harmony is restored with a distinctly authorial declaration:

> 'The web of deceit is at length unravelled,' said St Julian, as soon as he concluded it, 'and the ways of Providence are justified to man. We now perceive, that however successful the schemes of wickedness may be at first, they are, in the end completely defeated and over-thrown.'
>
> (p. 366)

The speaker is the heroine's father using his family name and occupying the rightful aristocratic position to which he has only just been returned. For most of the novel he lives in guilty self-imposed exile. While a proper and patriarchal family order is restored and under-written by Providence, its restoration is seen to be an effect of unravelling the stories, the 'webs of deceit', that make up most of the narrative. Demonstrating the dangers of being duped by the deceits of narrative, *Clermont* restores propriety only with difficulty.

Though the innocence of the father is finally explained it is his guilt that constitutes the awful secret of the tale. He is believed to have killed his half brother. This crime is precipitated by his discovery, having grown up an orphan, of his true identity, an identity that he conceals from his daughter for most of the story, along with the fact of his disinheritance. These crimes, alleged or otherwise, result from a tension that the novel tries to resolve between one's duty to one's family and one's own sentimental attachments. The tension is exacerbated by questions of the legitimacy of paternal authority. These questions horrify the heroine, Madeleine, as she begins to uncover her father's guilt. In endeavouring to disentangle the stories of the past the effects of narratives, horrid and otherwise, are brought to the fore. Stories and apparently supernatural events, like ghostly groanings and the mysterious appearance of a dagger, seem to point to the criminal past of Madeleine's father. When she confronts him he employs a conventional eighteenth-century set of terms to deflect the question: "'I trust my love," cried he, "you will not again listen to the idle surmises of the servants: even on the slightest foundation they are apt to raise improbabilities and horrors, which, in spite of reason, make too often a dangerous impression on the mind, and overturn its quiet, by engendering superstition"' (p. 254). The gothic father appeals to distinctly eighteenth-century criteria of judgement which depend on class distinctions. Servants, uneducated and uncultivated, are superstitious; they are the class that believe in horrors, not respectable women. This highlights a class division in readers assumed from Walpole onwards and implied in Radcliffe's manner of enlisting and simultaneously distancing readers from excesses of the imagination. In the 1790s, however, the shifting composition and appetites of the reading public made it a more difficult distinction to draw. In *Clermont*, they are rendered suspect: the rumours that Madeleine's father disavows as superstition are, it later emerges, stories that he believes to be true. Clermont's implied denial is rendered more suspicious when he tells a different story to his own father. Confronted again by his daughter, he offers, not another story, but an appeal to values and character: 'I know your present ideas. But Oh, Madeleine! reflect on the tenor of my conduct, on the precepts I instilled into your mind and then think whether you have done me justice or injustice in harbouring them?' (p. 263). Unconvinced, Madeleine's suspicions might well be a result of the rational precepts she has learned from her father. Character, it seems, is an effect of narrative, not the reverse. Earlier, Madeleine's character has been judged on the basis of her narrative: 'your narrative, my dear, ... convinces me more than ever of the innocence and sensibility of your disposition' (p. 56). Narratives are the vehicles that propel Clermont towards his crime. Letters from his mother, and then a 'horrible narrative' deliberately intended to deceive him, rouse his passions into violent action. Suspicions about character and identity permeate the novel's reversals of apparently good and apparently bad characters. Even at the end the establishment of proper family places and identities depends on the stories and confessions of criminals. The figure, indeed, in whose name the web of deceit is unravelled and Providence invoked has a different name and identity at the beginning.

Clermont finds it increasingly difficult to distinguish good from evil because it acknowledges the importance of narratives in establishing, maintaining and legitimising the difference between the two. The grounds for excluding, punishing and externalising vice become far less secure when implicated in narrative frames. Even as appeals are made to patriarchy and providential authority outside representation, there is a sense in which they are no longer credible in an enlightened and increasingly secular culture. Restoring or securing distinctions requires an effort that, in the works of Radcliffe and her imitators, is offered by the sublime. In Radcliffe's posthumously published essay 'On the Supernatural in Poetry' (1826), a clear critical development of Burke's aesthetic theory, the opposition that is established between terror and horror provides a useful delineation of different gothic strategies: 'Terror and horror are so far opposite, that the first expands the soul, and awakens the faculties to a high degree of life; the other contracts, freezes, and nearly annihilates them' (p. 149). Radcliffe, as in her fiction, privileges terror over horror.

The elevation of terror, moreover, is made possible by a discrimination between the effects of obscurity and confusion, terms which, it is argued, are often used wrongly as synonyms by commentators. The difference is important: 'obscurity leaves something for the imagination to exaggerate; confusion, by blurring one image into another, leaves only a chaos in which the mind can find nothing to nourish its fears and doubts, or to act upon in any way' (p. 150). What is important is that terror activates mind and imagination, enabling an overcoming of fears and doubts, and allowing the subject to move from a state of passivity to activity. This has important consequences: 'if obscurity has so much effect on fiction, what must it have in real life, when to ascertain the object of terror, is frequently to acquire the means of escaping it' (p. 150). Terror enables escape; it allows one to delimit its effects, to distinguish and overcome the threat it manifests. As in much fiction of the 1790s, it is by means of terror that the object of threat is escaped. Indeed, the threatening object can be cast out or away from the domain of rationality and domesticity and, as a result of this expulsion or externalisation, proper order can be reaffirmed as an order that exists outside narratives. By elevating the mind, objects of terror not only give it a sense of its own power but, in the appreciation of awful sublimity, suggest the power of a divine order, an order ('Providence') that is repeatedly invoked at the end of most Radcliffean novels as the way out of vice and the guarantee of social conventions. In many works of Radcliffean gothic, terror enables a return to patterns of sentimental fiction.

HORROR

Horror, however, continually exerts its effects in tales of terror. Horror is most often experienced in underground vaults or burial chambers. It freezes human faculties, rendering the mind passive and immobilising the body. The cause is generally a direct encounter with physical mortality, the touching of a cold corpse, the sight of a decaying body. It arouses the feelings Julia Kristeva associates with 'abjection'. Death is presented as the absolute limit, a finitude which denies any possibility of imaginative transcendence into an awesome and infinite space. It is the moment of the negative sublime, a moment of freezing, contraction and horror which signals a temporality that cannot be recuperated by the mortal subject. Horror marks the response to an excess that cannot be transcended. It is why, despite the repeated attempts to contain gothic machinery and effects within a dialectics of terror, the ambivalences of Radcliffean gothic fiction can neither close satisfactorily nor fully externalise evil.

Horror never leaves the scene. In 1796, it emerged with greatest force in Matthew Lewis' *The Monk* and in the manner it was received. The scandal that greeted the novel's publication placed it among the most notorious works of English fiction. Considered dangerous in its obscenity, the text itself embodied a kind of horror. Its excesses, in part taken from Radcliffe, led to her own subsequent abandonment of much gothic machinery: *The Italian*, published the year after *The Monk*, in 1797, can be seen as, if not exactly a reply to it, a cautious response to the scandal it created. The central figure of *The Italian* is a monk whose villainy and past crimes are never diabolical in a supernatural sense. Indeed, the whole novel moves away from the imagined terrors of Radcliffe's earlier works and towards a more credible and realistic narrative in direct contrast to *The Monk*. The latter goes in the other direction and, turning terror into horror, describes in lurid detail the spectres and shocks that gothic fiction had previously left to the superstitious imagination or explained away.

The Monk eschews and satirises the sentimentality of Radcliffe's work. It draws instead on the *Sturm und Drang* (storm and stress) of German Romantic writers like Goethe and Schiller. During a visit to Germany, Lewis met Goethe, and later showed his interest in German tales by translating several into English. He did the same with drama, capitalising on the vogue for the sensational in the theatre of the time. In the 1790s, German writing was associated with the excessive emotionalism of Goethe's Werther or the shocks and horrors of robber tales by Schiller rather than virtuous sentimentality. The translator's preface to Flammenberg's *The Necromancer* (1794) recommended the text as one with 'wonderful incidents' and 'mysterious events' but without 'tiresome love intrigues' (p. 17). Like Carl Grosse's German horror novel describing the mysterious workings of a powerful and sensually inclined secret society, translated as *Horrid Mysteries* (1797), *The Necromancer* was included in the list of 'Horrid Novels' in *Northanger Abbey*.

While Lewis was influenced by the German tradition, *The Monk* is none-the-less traversed by contradictory, ambivalent impulses. The translator of *The Necromancer* recommends another, similar novel that tells of 'a long series of frauds, perpetrated under the mysterious veil of pretended supernatural aid' (p. 17). In stories like *The Necromancer*, the supernatural is revealed to be no more than hypocrisy or the concealment of very human crimes. In Lewis' novel one of the main targets is a hypocritical monk who conceals his vices beneath a cloak of sanctity. *The Monk*, however, does not refrain from vividly invoking supernatural elements. It often does so in a satirical or brutally mocking manner. The most celebrated incident of this kind occurs in one of the two parallel plots of the novel. Two lovers, Raymond and Agnes, decide to elope against the wishes of their families. To ensure the unimpeded escape of Agnes, they decide to dress her in the habit of a spectral nun believed to haunt the castle. In the course of the elopement their coach crashes and Agnes disappears. The injured Raymond is put to bed and sees, not Agnes, but the actual ghost of the nun. He is petrified with horror. Lewis' marvellous twist to the conventions of the gothic tale is indicative of *The Monk*'s ambivalence as it interweaves horror with a general mockery of the genre. The other ambiguous use of the supernatural in the novel occurs at its end with the appearance of the devil to claim the soul of the villainous monk. As a figure of supernatural justice punishing the sinful monk with eternal damnation, the devil's appearance marks out the Faustian form of the novel with a cautionary note about the dangers of giving in to the forces of desire. Critics, however, were far from convinced by the moral tone of the ending. Indeed, the over-exaggerated style of the punishment works against its supposed avowal of morality and suggests that the cautionary note is merely a weak, even satirical, get-out clause for a novel intent on immorality and excess.

The Monk is about excess, about excesses of passion concealed beneath veils of respectability and propriety. It uses the conventional anti-Catholicism of gothic fiction implied in the monastic setting, but it locates the tyrannical nature of, and barbaric superstitions inculcated by, all institutions, including aristocracy, church and family, as its broader object of criticism. Institutional repression is seen to encourage excess. Family prohibitions produce illicit passions and lead to the imprisonment of recalcitrant members, particularly women, in convents. The spectral nun is the ghost of a female transgressor from the family past of Raymond and Agnes. Justice is harsh and often violently retributive. Religious superstition is similarly rigorous in its policing of social behaviour.

The principal figure of excess is Ambrosio, the monk of the novel's title. He is famed as the most pious and saintly of monks, and crowds flock, adoringly, to attend his sermons. His pride in his own sanctity blinds him to his ambitions and passions. He succumbs sensationally in the gloomy labyrinthine vaults beneath the abbey, his lust initially finding an object in Mathilda, a young woman whose infatuation has led her to disguise herself as a novice monk called Rosario. Strangely attracted to Rosario, Ambrosio finally gives in to very literal temptations of the flesh when Mathilda unveils herself before him. Then Ambrosio directs his desires towards another woman, Antonia. Pure, innocent and belonging to a noble family, she seems an impossible object. Mathilda offers her help, declaring herself to be an agent of the devil. She leads a hesitant Ambrosio through the underground vaults so that he can make the diabolical pact that will ensure the satisfaction of his lusts. The gratification of his carnal appetites involves killing Antonia's mother and spiriting the innocent victim to a secret chamber deep in the underground vaults. There Ambrosio seduces her and then learns that she is his sister. The passion and violence do not finish with this horror. Rumours of Ambrosio's, and other, crimes committed in the monastery provoke outrage among the populace and an angry mob sets about its destruction.

The Monk, similar in terms of its lavish sensual descriptions, its violent images and extravagant scenes to *Vathek*, met with a very different reception. It gave rise to a new and diabolical strand of gothic fiction, evident in the numbers of 'monk' novels that followed it. T.J. Horsley-Curties drew on Radcliffe and Lewis in the title of his romance *The Monk of Udolpho* (1807). Charlotte Dacre, in *Zofloya; or, the Moor* (1806), used the theme of Faustian damnation in a story of a female villain tempted by a black agent of the devil. While *Vathek* was considered a moral tale, *The Monk* was perceived as an outright obscenity. The reviewer for the *Monthly Review* (1797) argued that 'a vein of obscenity' pervaded and deformed the whole novel, making it 'unfit for general circulation' (p. 451). Coleridge, in the *Critical Review* (1796), stated 'that *the Monk* is a romance, which if a parent saw in the hands of a son or a daughter, he might reasonably turn pale'. He went on to describe the 'libidinous minuteness' and the 'voluptuous images' of the novel as 'poison for youth, and a provocative for the debauchee' (p. 197). As an affront to moral, family and Christian values, the novel's potential for corrupting young minds was a particular fear. What exacerbated the potential of its obscene and lewd descriptions was, as a number of critics noted, the elegance of the style. This seems to have contributed to concerns about its poisonous effects on young and undiscriminating minds. Expressing several reservations, the *Analytical Review* (1796) observed that the novel elicited the reader's sympathy for Ambrosio (p. 403). The danger of improper identification and a lack of any clearly stated and convincing moral warranted severe criticism.

There were other reasons that accounted for the savage critical reception. One was that Lewis included, along with his name on the title page, the initials 'MP': he had just been elected to Parliament. Coleridge responded to this detail: 'the author of the Monk signs himself a LEGISLATOR! We stare and tremble' (p. 198). It was not only the position and literary skills of the author that made the novel such an object of anxiety. In the middle of the 1790s there were more serious threats to social and domestic stability with which certain parts of *The Monk* must have had a degree of resonance: its description of the riotous mob destroying the monastery, for example, is likely to have been read alongside accounts of Revolutionary mobs in France.

LABYRINTHS OF LITERATURE AND POLITICS

In T.J. Matthias' *The Pursuits of Literature* (1796) novels and romances are closely linked to fears of revolution spreading across the Channel from France. In encouraging appetites for excitement and sensation and thereby disturbing the balance of domestic harmony and moral propriety, the effects of novels and romances were associated with the passions and violence of Revolutionary mobs in France. One polemical statement among the many that punctuate *The Pursuits of Literature* makes the nature of the connection explicit: 'Our unsexed female writers now instruct, or confuse, us and themselves in the labyrinths of politics, or turn us wild with Gallic frenzy' (p. 244). Departing from the strictures of reason and morality, novels are seen to cause violent frenzy as terrifying as that exhibited in France. By touching on political subjects women writers 'unsex' themselves: they enter with impunity and impropriety a male domain of writing instead of remaining within the domesticated limits of fiction. The metaphor of the labyrinth is also crucial in its articulation of literature, politics and gothic romances. Earlier in the eighteenth century, in writings by Smollett, Pope and Fielding, the labyrinth or maze was used as a figure signifying the complexity and variety of society which remained, none-the-less, unified. It was a positive term. In gothic romances, however, it came to be associated with fear, confusion and alienation: it was a site of darkness, horror and desire. In the labyrinthine vaults of *The Monk* Ambrosio begins his descent into infamy and a pact with the devil. At one point, torn between fear and desire, he almost gives in to conscience and his own horror at what he is about to do. Reflecting on the impossibility of escaping his physical imprisonment in the dark and winding passages, he also understands that he cannot escape or master the desires that have brought him so far. His doubts, fears, dilemmas and helplessness in this labyrinth render him passive like a gothic heroine. Giving in to lust, however, he begins his transformation into a gothic villain. This role is exemplified when, again in the secret depths of the labyrinth, Ambrosio prepares to consummate his desire and violate Antonia. In the labyrinth, hidden and separated from supervision or the laws of the outside world, he is, as he makes clear to Antonia, absolute master. Imprisoned in the labyrinth, she is cut off from all aid and society, dead to the world.

The horror of the labyrinth and its confusion of fear and desire lie in its utter separation from all social rules thus allowing transgression of all conventional limits. In *The Italian* Vivaldi, the hero, is imprisoned by the Inquisition and led to trial in the heart of an underground labyrinth. He describes its horror: 'along the galleries, and other avenues through which they passed, not any person was seen, and, by the profound stillness that reigned, it seemed as if death had already anticipated his work in these regions of horror, and condemned alike the tortured and the torturer' (p. 309). Death, as absolute disconnection from any form of order, signifies the complete alienation of individuals in a finite world. In *Clermont*, moreover, it is narratives that are labyrinthine, spinning their 'web of deceit' and leading protagonists to encounter the insecurity of horrible absence, the death, of any familiar or proper order.

The labyrinth presented in *The Pursuits of Literature* is, ironi-cally, a distinctly gothic locus and works in a manner akin to

Radcliffe's doubled narratives. Its horrors, moreover, are intensified by their association with political terrors. Matthias' text
praises the well-known conservative positions of Burke and the
Abbé Barruel who unmasked the conspirators – the secret societies and radical philosophers – who were believed to have plotted
the whole Revolution. It takes a polemical stance towards revolution, reform and democracy: all forms of change lead to revolution, embodied in France as site of sedition, anarchy, heresy,
deception, confusion, superstitious corruption, wickedness, lust,
cruelty and destruction. France is 'THE MONSTROUS REPUB-
LIC' (p. 164). Modern philosophers, like Rousseau, Paine and
Godwin, are identified as subversive, as are all radicals and free-
thinkers. Novels by Charlotte Smith and Fanny Burney are criticised for over-stepping the 'boundaries of nature and real life'
(p. 58), a transgression which has political implications when
linked to accusations that texts by Elizabeth Inchbald and Mary
Robinson turn girls' heads 'wild with impossible adventures' and
leave them 'now and then tainted with democracy' (p. 56).
Gothic novels, with the exception of Radcliffe's works, receive
short shrift. *The Monk*, however, receives attention as a publication 'too important to be passed over in a general reprehension'
(p. 245). Particular offence is taken at the novel's unashamed
depiction of 'the arts of lewd and systematic seduction' and its
'unqualified blasphemy'; concern is expressed that it has not been
prosecuted for obscenity. Horrified that Lewis is a Member of
Parliament, Matthias finds no excuse in his youth and no relief in
the defence that the novel contains many 'poetical descriptions':

> so much the worse again, the novel is more alluring on that account.
> Is it a time to poison the waters of our land in their springs and
> fountains? Are we to add incitement to incitement, and corruption to
> corruption, till there neither is, nor can be, a return to virtuous action
> and regulated life?
>
> (pp. 248–49)

Style as much as content is, as with many criticisms of the gothic
novel, the main source of anxiety, seducing readers and leading
them astray.

The ambivalence that emerges in respect of questions of style and content has consequences for conceptions of the place and function of literature. Matthias' attacks on unacceptable literary production, and their intensity, are explained by the importance and the ambivalence of literary texts in the preservation or disruption of social values and political order: 'LITERATURE, well or ill-conducted, is THE GREAT ENGINE, by which all civilized states must ultimately be supported or overthrown' (p. 162). Repeated later in *The Pursuits of Literature*, the statement makes plain a bifurcation that Matthias wishes to make absolute in order to sustain literature's properly ideological role. His attempt to distinguish supportive from subversive literature, however, leads him into those strangely gothic labyrinths wherein a Radcliffean strategy is used to find an exit. Labyrinths, as places of radical politics and confusion, are identified as dangerous, subversive sites destroying established boundaries and conventions. Linked to novels that raise the contaminating spectre of democracy and excite readers with a 'Gallic frenzy' that simultaneously upsets proper national and sexual identifications, the labyrinth is also associated with confusion, deception and 'superstitious corruption'. These Protestant constructions of a tyrannical and superstitious Catholicism are combined in the attack on radicals and Revolutionary conspirators, adding force and negative significance to the labyrinth in the process. A place of all forms of excessive, irrational and passionate behaviour, the labyrinth is also the site in which the absence or loss of reason, sobriety, decency and morality is displayed in full horror. *The Pursuits of Literature* sets out to guide its readers through the labyrinth in order to secure 'to this kingdom her political and religious existence, and the rights of society'. It is thus on a mission of life and death that Matthias tenders his services as guide:

> It is designed to conduct them through the labyrinths of literature; to convince them of the manner in which the understanding and affections are either bewildered, darkened, ennervated, or degraded; and to point out the fatal paths which would lead us all to final destruction, or to complicated misery.
>
> (p. 3)

Labyrinths, like novels, seduce, excite, confuse and disturb; they lead readers on 'fatal paths'. Matthias' account describes both narrative form and narrative effects. These have to be endured in order to be escaped, offering a knowledge that will allow their potential destruction to be avoided. The reader, guided through the dark labyrinth, like a Radcliffean heroine, and confronting its dangers – losses of understanding, proper affection, equanimity, virtue and life itself – recognises, by means of a horrified recoil, Matthias' call to preserve the existence of the religious, domestic and political order of the country.

The journey through the labyrinth that is undertaken becomes as difficult and divisive as any in gothic fiction. Matthias' position as both guide and reader duplicates the ambivalent tendencies of the Radcliffean narrative. To provoke a sense of horror Matthias invites superstitious and over-active imaginings on the part of the reader 'in which the understanding and affections are either bewildered, darkened, ennervated, or degraded'. This leads to the emotional recoil that dispels the magical illusions with rational explanation. A frisson of terror leads to the return of reason. This operation, however, inextricably binds literature's supportive function to its subversive potential. This is evident in Matthias' account of reading the work of radical philosophers:

> Philosophy has appeared, not to console but to deject. When I have read and thought deeply on the accumulated horrors, and on all the gradations of wickedness and misery, through which the modern systematic philosophy of Europe has conducted her illuminated votaries to the confines of political death and mental darkness, my mind for a space feels a convulsion, and suffers the nature of an insurrection.
>
> (pp. 17–18)

Rational assurance confronts horror as Matthias is drawn into the corrupting labyrinth of philosophy. This benighted, fatal world is exactly like that described in gothic fiction, only with radicals having taken the place of monks and villains. Similarly, Matthias' response mimics that of a gothic heroine encountering the horrors of the labyrinth, either in the form of a decaying corpse or as her own alienation from the world of conventions and normality.

Acknowledging the power of texts to produce convulsion or insurrection in the rational mind, Matthias depends on an excess of feeling to restore reason to its privileged place. The horror depicted in his account, like Radcliffe's, is designed to produce similar effects. As a warning about the dangers of texts, *The Pursuits of Literature* presents a world of death as the consequence of any social, political or literary deviation. The duplication of gothic patterns remains ambivalent. In the labyrinth Matthias reaches the bewildered and enervated limits of his own understanding, losing his reason in a convulsion of horror, a sublime encounter with his own limits and those of social value. Duplicating the divided position offered by gothic texts, as rational and imaginative, knowing and superstitiously emotional, the convulsion of horror borders on the 'Gallic frenzy' he fears will be produced by the texts of 'unsexed female writers'. Distinctions that hold rational, sexual and moral identities in place are threatened by the labyrinth's confusions. Representation and its ambivalent powers to stabilise, seduce and subvert come to the fore. The force of representation in maintaining order, moreover, involves a reinscription of gothic patterns and strategies. In Matthias' text France and the French are constructed along the lines of gothic narratives. Not only subjects of Catholicism's 'superstitious corruption', Frenchmen are thoroughly gothic in their villainy: 'always brutal', 'neighing after the constitution of their neighbours, in their lawless lustihood', 'they first deflower the purity of the struggling or half-consenting victims, and then with their ruffian daggers they stifle at once the voice, and the remembrance of the pollution. Such are their abominations; such are their orgies of blood and lust' (p. 4). Magnifications of gothic bandits and villains in every respect, French men are represented as the outcome of any deviance from order.

The gothic figures that are invoked not only testify to the power of narratives and representation in sustaining political and social order, but also display the conservative function of sublimity and history in the process. The tone and intensity of Matthias' text is drawn from its main influence, Burke's *Reflections on the Revolution in France* (1790). Burke's reaction to the threat he sees emanating from France and from radicals in England itself invokes a gothic form of narrative. Given the influence of Burke's theories of the sublime and the beautiful on many gothic writers, especially Radcliffe, it is hardly surprising that his writings on the French Revolution are painted in powerfully monochromatic hues. He construes events in France as a darkly sublime threat in contrast to the gently enlightened tones of English social and political stability. In the darkest colours of confusion, obscurity and selfish passion, the new social formation ushered in by the Revolution is seen as a chaotic assemblage of vice, depravity, self-interest and commercial opportunism: France's 'monster of a constitution' gives free reign to 'attornies, agents, money-jobbers, speculators, and adventurers, composing an ignoble oligarchy founded upon the destruction of the crown, the church, the nobility, and the people. Here end all the deceitful dreams and visions of the equality and rights of men' (p. 313). All ideas and writings advocating revolution or reform, in England as well as France, are associated with the 'monstrous fiction' that Burke sees enacted in France. Wanting to countermand the 'deceitful dreams and visions' of radicals, Burke's text acknowledges the forces of social and political change and anxiously produces his own representation, his own fiction, in opposition.

Burke's defence of constitutional monarchy, aristocracy, landed property and the Church as the bases for an ordered society takes the form of a nostalgic romance imbued with chivalric values. Vividly presenting an account of the capture of the French Queen by a riotous mob, Burke bemoans the absence of gallantry that left her undefended and waxes lyrical about the time he viewed the splendours of the French court: 'I thought ten thousand swords must have leaped from their scabbards to avenge even a look that threatened her with insult – But the age of chivalry is gone –. That of sophisters, oeconomists, and calculators, has succeeded; and the glory of Europe is extinguished for ever' (p. 170). The French Revolution turns into a gothic romance. The role of the heroine clearly delineated, that of the villain falls to the French Assembly: 'they have power given to them, like that of an evil principle, to subvert and destroy; but none to construct, except such machines as may be fitted for further subversion and further destruction' (p. 161). The romantic polarisation of good and evil enables the renunciation of all things French and therefore evil. The polarisation, however, involves the reinvigoration of romance fictions in order to combat those of English and French radicals: as with gothic novels, it is representation that is both at stake and the crucial weapon in the contest. Burke's appeal to a romance tradition attempts to establish a sense of continuous history and awake a series of associations that wrest words like freedom, nation and order from the grasp of radical texts. It also imagines the dissolution of English society in order that readers' terror, like his own, at the events in France, will completely purge their minds of any radical ideas. The evil in France and in radical writings is expelled from the shores of England.

The language Burke uses and the meanings of gothic he draws upon have particular political associations with a Whig tradition that emerged in the later seventeenth century. In this context gothic signified the northern European tribes, admired for their love of freedom and democratic institutions. In using this gothic significance to support English institutions of monarchy, family and government, Burke pre-empts radical calls for democracy and political equality by suggesting that the continuity of English tradition has already established them. A very different sense of the word gothic is employed by many of the English writers who spring to the defence of radicalism in response to Burke's *Reflections*: for Thomas Paine and Mary Wollstonecraft, two radicals who replied to Burke's revolutionary polemics with accusations directed at his gothic ideas, the term signified, quite conventionally, everything that was old-fashioned, barbaric, feudal and irrationally ungrounded. In *The Rights of Man* (1791–92), Paine uses Burke's lament at the passing of the age of chivalry to criticise the *Reflections* as a piece of imaginative and evocative fiction in the manner of a drama or quixotic romance. Paine's main political targets are the institutions and customs Burke defends: despotic government and its arbitrary power, religious authority, hypocrisy and property, aristocracy, its insistence on primogeniture and its hereditary privileges. Wollstonecraft, also, is critical of Burke's 'gothic' ideas and the way they reinforce an uncivilised and dehumanising set of values and socio-economic practices. In her *A Vindication of the Rights of Men* (1790), Wollstonecraft criticises the lack of humanity and liberality implied in Burke's position: 'Man preys on man; and you mourn for the idle tapestry that decorated a gothic pile, and the dronish bell that summoned the fat priest to prayer' (p. 58). Linked to the religious superstitions and hypocrisies of Catholicism common in gothic works, Burke's irrationality is seen as a defence of a barbaric aristocracy, savage property laws and feudal injustice. For radicals, all that is gothic is signified by the *Ancien Régime* in France. Defending the French National Assembly against Burke's attacks Wollstonecraft again uses gothic associations as a form of insult: 'Why was it a duty to repair an ancient castle, built in barbarous ages, of gothic materials? Why were the legislators obliged to rake among heterogeneous ruins ... ?' (p. 41). In Wollstonecraft's rational humanism, the mention of Burke's gothic nostalgia can only be an insult. These invocations of the word gothic in defences of revolution were written before the Terror in France gave new weight to those conservative writers of tales of terror in England.

The continuing ambivalence and polarisation of the word 'gothic' until the end of the eighteenth century were significant not only in the changes of meaning that it underwent but in its function in a network of associations whose positive or negative value depended on the political positions and representations with which gothic figures were associated. Indeed, the gothic figures that appeared in so many novels, as well as critical, aesthetic and political discussions, became signs of a pervasive cultural anxiety concerning the relation of present and past, and the relationship between classes, sexes and individuals within society. Gothic figures were also indicative of changing notions of culture and nature. Markers of a lost order or of a feudal practice that continued to oppress people, the castles, counts and monks of gothic fiction remained politically ambivalent, seen as figures of nostalgia or criticism. The term itself was a site of struggle and an effect of contests to represent an authoritative, singular and legitimate version of identity, sexuality, culture and its history. As such, invocations of the word 'gothic' could not fail to be ambivalent, could not fail to disclose as much as they tried to discard, bringing questions of evil and vice to the fore as political constructs, themselves dependent on partial and politically interested representations. The problem of locating, defining and policing the effects of representations bound gothic writing and history to a political arena in which singularity and order vanished into mythical pasts. Threats to society and convention that were depicted in gothic terms altered notions of representation and literature beyond repair. From being a way of containing and warning against vices, evils and anti-social behaviour, gothic romances became advocates of subversion. Irreparably divided, tortuously ambivalent, these narratives could only attempt to maintain conventions and identities by repeating, identifying and externalising examples of evil in a movement that embraced their own narrative form. Under pressure from contradictory demands, those narrative forms, moreover, began to change in the 1790s. From identifying villains and practices to be excluded as vicious or evil, narratives ceded to the ambivalence that shaped them and became increasingly uncertain of the location of evil and vice. In the 1790s, as fears of gothic fiction are bound up more and more with processes of representation, the locus of evil vacillates between outcast individuals and the social conventions that produced or constricted them.

5

ROMANTIC TRANSFORMATIONS

She was an elfin Pinnace; lustily
I dipped my oars into the silent lake;
And, as I rose upon the stroke, my boat
Went heaving through the Water like a swan:
When, from behind that craggy Steep, till then
The horizon's bound, a huge peak, black and huge,
As if with voluntary power instinct,
Upreared its head.– I struck, and struck again,
And, growing still in stature, the grim Shape
Towered up between me and the stars, and still,
For so it seemed, with purpose of its own
And measured motion, like a living Thing
Strode after me.

(Wordsworth, *The Prelude* [1850], Bk I, ll. 373–85)

In the period dominated by Romanticism, gothic writing began to move inside, disturbing conventional social limits and notions of interiority and individuality. The internalisation of gothic forms represents the most significant shift in the genre, the gloom and darkness of sublime landscapes becoming external markers of inner mental and emotional states. Many gothic elements found their way into the work of writers from Wordsworth to Keats, though the significance and resonance of gothic devices and themes were undergoing notable transformations. While standard plots and narrative machinery of the sort established by Walpole, Radcliffe and Lewis continued to be imitated in many novels and stories well into the nineteenth century, major innovations, or renovations, of the genre drew it closer to aspects of Romanticism. It is at the level of the individual that Romantic-Gothic writing takes its bearings. The individual in question – rebellious hero, alienated outcast, creative quester – stands at the edges of society and rarely finds a path back into the social fold. The critical distance taken with regard to social values derives from radical attacks on oppressive systems of monarchical government. Instead, consciousness, freedom and imagination are valued.

Usually male, the individual is outcast, part victim, part villain. Older gothic figures and devices, over-used to the point of cliché, are transformed into signs of aristocratic tyranny, leftovers from an unenlightened world. The disturbing and demonic villain, however, retains a darkly attractive, if ambivalent, allure as a defiant rebel against the constraints of social mores. The sympathies for suffering, doomed individuals find expression in Romantic identifications with Prometheus and Milton's Satan, regarded as heroes because of their resistance to over-powering tyranny. The villain or outcast, unlike in much Radcliffean writing, is not the cause of evil and terror, an object to be execrated so that order can be restored. It is a position which calls for respect and understanding. Real evil is tyranny, corruption and prejudice, identified with certain, often aristocratic, figures and, more frequently, with institutions of power manifested in government hierarchies, social norms and religious superstition.

The prevailing narrative forms accord with the focus on Romantic individuals. First-person tales highlight the psychological interest in the dilemmas and suffering that attend social alienation. Subject as they are to imaginations, passions and fears they can neither control nor overcome, the heroes' imaginative transgressions of conventional values encounter the limits, laws, rules and forces that are not their own. Seekers after knowledge of themselves and metaphysical powers beyond and in deified nature, these individuals can be associated with the way that notions of human identity, mental and natural powers were being transformed and secularised, not only in political theory but also in the scientific discoveries of the time. In political terms, the failure of the French Revolution to realise hopes for human progress and equality contributed to the inward and darkening turn of Romantic speculations. Alienated from society and themselves, Romantic-Gothic heroes undergo the effects of this disillusion, doubting the nature of the powers that consume them, uncertain whether they originate internally or from external forces. Without an adequate social framework to sustain a sense of identity, the wanderer encounters the new form of the gothic ghost, the double or shadow of himself. An uncanny figure of horror, the double presents a limit that cannot be overcome, the representation of an internal and irreparable division in the individual psyche.

PERSECUTORY ROMANCE

In his *Enquiry Concerning Political Justice* (1793), William Godwin describes the feudal system as a 'Voracious monster', the remnant of which in the eighteenth century continues to bolster aristocratic power and privilege in the form of a stuffed monster that terrifies humankind into 'patience and pusillanimity' (p. 476). A small but important part of the book's radical and rationalist attack on forms of government riddled with relics of a feudal past in the shape of monarchy, courts and inherited wealth, the metaphor of the stuffed monster highlights the barbarity and tyranny of feudal power. Moreover, it stresses both the extinction of feudal economic power and its strange persistence at a superstructural level. As a stuffed monster, aristocratic power is an illusion, a phantom of a barbaric and superstitious past that lingers, forcefully, in the present. The terrors seem at once real and imaginary, strangely effective yet ungrounded and insubstantial. In the reaction to the Revolution in France, the monster had very real effects: laws were passed enabling the suppression of radical texts and the arrest, imprisonment and persecution of radicals.

In *Caleb Williams* (1794), written immediately after *Political Justice* and originally entitled *Things as They Are*, Godwin detailed the oppressions that existed in the society of the time. Injustice and persecution, very real issues in the novel, are also imaginary in the wider sense implied by the stuffed monster: they describe the terrifying and superstitious beliefs that irrationally persist and govern ideas about and actions in the world. In the trial scene of *Caleb Williams*, where Caleb is falsely accused of stealing from his master, he is called a monster when he rejects the findings of the mock court which condemns and frames him, his disrespect for the law and the title of 'gentleman' earning him the appellation and the identity of outcast. The greater monstrosity, the real horror, however, is that presented in the first-person narrative detailing the injustices and crimes that can be committed in the name of the law. The metaphor of the stuffed monster links politics and fiction by associating feudalism and tales of terror with the persistence of superstitious, barbaric and irrational values. In this respect *Caleb Williams* criticises the gothic romance as an oppressive and conservative form. The novel none-the-less uses gothic strategies, not satirically, but politically to display social and psychological oppression.

The novel assembles various stories in its account of what *Political Justice* describes as 'the gothic and unintelligible burden' borne by readers of romance and inheritors of feudalism (p. 477). While the first-person narrator, Caleb, an orphan taken in as secretary to Squire Falkland, is the central figure later in the novel, his master provides the principal interest at the start. Caleb collects stories of Falkland's past which testify to his talents, generosity, grace and benevolence, qualities that make him popular in local society, much to the chagrin of another squire, Tyrell, whose brutish, tyrannical, selfish and uncultured demeanour is Falkland's aristocratic antithesis. Their rivalry culminates in the murder of Tyrell. Tried for the crime, Falkland is acquitted, while other victims of Tyrell's cruelty are blamed and subsequently hanged.

Caleb, suspicious of his master's moody behaviour, eventually draws a confession from him. The truth has a price: Caleb has sold himself 'to gratify a foolishly inquisitive humour' (p. 142).

Charged to remain forever in the service of a master who hates him, Caleb is subjected to external forms of discipline and sur- veillance in the shape of Falkland and the legal and aristocratic code that protects him. This surveillance is also internalised. Tormented by the secret, 'a source of perpetual melancholy', Caleb says he has made himself a prisoner of guilt as well as the caprices of his master: 'the vigilance even of a public and sys- tematical despotism is poor, compared with a vigilance which is thus goaded by the most anxious passions of the soul' (p. 144). Daring neither to flee Falkland's power nor able to stay under its subjugation, the novel describes Caleb's sufferings under both forms of vigilance as he tries to escape an unbearable double bind.

The dilemma and self-divisions are intensified by the manner in which external and internal persecutory vigilance is shown to be an effect of Caleb's identification with Falkland. His crime of spying against Falkland is a crime against his own self, whose values have been modelled on an idealised version of his master: his guilt is defined in terms of the values he has internalised. Attempting to escape unbearable physical and psychical impri- sonment, Caleb enlists the help of Falkland's brother-in-law, Forrester. Trusting in the latter, Caleb is again disbelieved, framed for theft and imprisoned. The prison conditions suffered by Caleb before his trial, echoing the darkness and coldness of gothic dungeons, foreground the horrors of judicial systems. In distinct contrast is the band of thieves joined by Caleb after his escape. They are modelled on Schiller's Romantic robbers, 'thieves without a licence' who are 'at open war with another set of men who are thieves according to law' (p. 224). Rational, democratic and humanitarian principles among thieves reflect critically on wider society's false pretensions to justice.

In one of the reversals that dominate the novel, a member of the band, Gines, becomes the agent of Falkland's persecution of Caleb, hounding him wherever he goes, no matter what identity he assumes. A decisive turn by Caleb, however, brings the novel to its climax: he decides to challenge Falkland in court and, tor- tured by guilt and self-loathing, to shatter the codes of secrecy and honour fatally binding his master and himself together. By now the dual relationship of master and servant has a bleaker aspect: Falkland is a broken man, a ghostly remnant of his former self worn down by guilt and publicly admitting his villainy. Ideals are sacrificed, reputations obviously false. In their self-loathing and betrayal, Caleb and his master are again doubles of each other, not ideal images, but inverted mirrors, shadows of suffering and persecution. Previously the antithesis of brutal Squire Tyrell, Falkland, now that his murderous secret is out, becomes the same, an agent of irrationality and oppression. Caleb, the initiator and victim of the vigilance in his spying on Falkland, casts himself as both victim and villain who, in destroying his previously idealised master, destroys himself: 'I began these memoirs with the idea of vindicating my character. I have now no character that I wish to vindicate' (p. 337).

In the original ending of the novel Caleb is again imprisoned and injustice continues. The revised version sees Falkland die and Caleb become the living gravestone of a human being. In both versions, however, there appears no way out of the imprisonment marked by the first-person narrative, indeed, to escape or resolve matters happily would be to return to those conventional and gothic narrative patterns that are challenged throughout the novel. Falkland is a figure from a gothic romance, marked by his ideals of chivalry, honour and personal reputation. He speaks 'the language of romance' (p. 182), becomes a 'fool of fame' (p. 141) and, having imbibed the 'poison of chivalry', is driven to passion and violence like a gothic villain: 'Begone, devil! ... or I will trample you into atoms', he cries in a characteristically demonic manner (p. 10). The assumption of terrifying, gothic, power is reiterated later in threats against Caleb (p. 150). In the novel, these internal states and individual statements indicating psychical delusions, paranoia and persecution are coloured in more distinct gothic terms than accounts of external persecution. Imprisonment and injustice is a real horror that needs little gothic colouring, whereas the turmoil induced by alienation and mental suffering appear in more menacing shades. *Caleb Williams'* use of gothic extremes also reflects, like much of the novel, on the poisonous, alienating and imprisoning effects of narrative: much of Caleb's persecution is enacted through the circulation of false stories, leading to his expulsion from secure communities and to his assumption of various false identities. His torment is in part to live a life without unified or authentic identity: he must don a 'counterfeit character' that reduces him to bestial degradation (p. 265). External forms are deceptive, inhuman and evil: they lead to alienation, guilt and self-destruction and eclipse values of humanity, justice and identity. With social forms as corrupt, unjust and persecutory as they are in *Caleb Williams*, the horror seems to be that there is no alternative or resolution in either political or psychological terms to the unbearable conflicts that are produced.

Internal conflicts and external contradictions, the play of ideals, deception and duplicity recur in Godwin's other novels. Depicted in historical, romantic and fantastic modes, the outcasts and wanderers are, like Caleb, both agents and victims of their conditions, drawn by pride and passion, by social prejudice and accidents of circumstance to transgress convention. In Godwin's fifth novel, *St Leon* (1799), the promise of the elixir of life and the philosopher's stone turns out to be a curse that leaves the immortal wanderer isolated from all comforts of family and society. Bringing Faustian elements of gothic fiction to the fore and alchemists from a feudal past into the present, the novel highlights the way human aspirations to knowledge, wealth, certainty and power become impossible, exclusive ideals that lead only to the despair and alienation depicted in *Caleb Williams*.

ROMANTIC HEROES

The hopeless and doomed quest of a cursed wanderer in *St Leon* discloses a darker current within the Romantic imagination's visions of unity and transcendence, a gothic strain that inhabits much of the period's poetry. The darker, agonised aspect of Romantic writing has heroes in the gothic mould: gloomy, isolated and sovereign, they are wanderers, outcasts and rebels condemned to roam the borders of social worlds, bearers of a dark truth or horrible knowledge, like Coleridge's Ancient Mariner. Milton's Satan or Prometheus are transgressors who represent the extremes of individual passion and consciousness. Blake's mythical creations, the tyrant Urizen and the suffering Los, inhabit a violent world of fire and struggle. Drawing on the anti-rational and mystical powers associated with a bardic romance tradition, Blake's poetic mythology values liberty, especially of the imagination, above any restraint, particularly of religious and political institutions. Byron's heroes, and his own impersonation of the Byronic hero, possess the defiant energy of a gothic villain. In 'Manfred' (1817) the disenchanted solitary hero defies the powers of natural and spirit worlds. He is alienated from humankind:

> From my youth upwards
> My spirit walked not with the souls of men,
> Nor look'd upon the earth with human eyes ...
>
> (II, II 50–52)

Seeking something more than quotidian existence, like Faustus, he pursues the secrets of alchemical thought:

> And then I dived,
> In my lone wanderings, to the caves of death,
> Searching its cause in its effect; and drew
> From wither'd bones, and skulls, and heap'd up dust,
> Conclusions most forbidden.
>
> (II, II 78–82)

He quests in vain: existence remains unbearable to 'fools of time and terror' (II, 164) for the ideal form of his lost love is irrecoverable, even when conjured up by mysterious and magical powers. The setting of the verse drama, too, is important: the awe and terror inspired by the sublimity of wild, mountainous realms not only signifies a grandeur beyond human powers, but also mirrors the internal world of the heroic sufferer, the magnificence of his suffering. In the throes of excessive feeling and tormented consciousness Romantic subjectivity is mystified, becoming the shadowy image of the grander forces of natural creation and destruction or the mysterious power of the imagination.

Percy Shelley's 'Alastor' (1816), the story of a Romantic solitary in search of his ideal, uses wild, mountainous and stormy settings to present an external image of the alienated wanderer. His youthful literary efforts included two gothic novels, *Zastrozzi* (1810) and *St Irvyne* (1811), and he returned to gothic themes in 'The Cenci' (1820). This poem, recounting the story of a debauched and vicious father whose cruelty and incestuous passions drive his victim, his daughter, to murder, has a recognisably gothic framework in its themes of parental wickedness and filial suffering. Shelley, moreover, is quick to make the link between domestic and political tyranny. Following the Godwinian model, in which individual crime is set in the context of wider social forces, Shelley contrasts the daughter's suffering at the hands of the state with the protection the father received throughout his life while pursuing his nefarious activities. The daughter's punishment compounds the injustice embedded in domestic and political institutions.

In other poems of the Romantic period the use of romance forms, language and settings connects the writing more directly with the medieval poetic tradition used by gothic writers to give Romantic themes of individualism and naturalism an atmosphere of strangeness and mystical distance. Byron's *Childe Harold's Pilgrimage* (1812–16) is subtitled 'A Romaunt', an archaic rendering of romance. The use of medieval language and Spenserian stanzas adds to the archaic atmosphere in the account of the wanderings of the 'shameless wight/Sore given to revel and ungodly glee' (I, 2, 14–15). While the roving adventures of a lonely hero can be located in the romance tradition, the focus on inner states of turmoil and passion testify to the Romantic nature of this hero:

> I have thought
> Too long and darkly, till my brain became,
> In its own eddy boiling and o'erwrought,
> A whirling gulf of fantasy and flame ...
> (III, 7, 55–58)

The wild natural images, internalised as the sign of a tormented consciousness, give force to the sense of individual dislocation. In other uses of medieval settings, historical and poetic distance provides the mysterious atmosphere for the discussion of love and passion. Coleridge's 'Christabel' (1816), following the patterns of eighteenth-century imitations of feudal romances, is set in a world of knights, ladies, honour and portentous dreams. In a similar vein, in Keats' 'Eve of St Agnes' (1820), the superstitions associated with the chivalric world give an air of mystery to the tale of illicit love.

In contrast, the popular Romanticism of Sir Walter Scott domesticates or assimilates romance forms, settings and adventures within the bounds of his historical context. He employs less extravagant or dramatic features from the gothic romance. Influenced by eighteenth-century antiquarianism and the romance tradition, Scott's novels use familiarly gothic environments, highly appropriate to the Scottish settings and imbued with Scottish folklore and history. In *The Bride of Lammermoor* (1819), the spectral return of a past family horror is implicated in fierce clan rivalries. The romance tradition is used with a degree of ironic detachment: the past and its gothic trappings provide the background for romanticised adventures of warriors, pirates and lovers, adventures that are often used self-consciously as signs of youthful enchantment and folly. The hero of Scott's *Waverley* (1814) is in this mould: steeped in romances, his love of adventure is presented in a lightly quixotic manner as the amusing naïveté of a young dreamer. Romances thus provide a way of modifying the eighteenth-century novel of manners and morals by flavouring it with the charms of adventure and superstition that are kept at a distance from the bourgeois values of professionalism, industry and legality in the present. Scott tames the excesses of gothic romance by assimilating it within acceptable literary bounds.

Scott, more enamoured of the antiquarian aspect of the romance revival, nonetheless enjoyed gothic fiction, and was one of the few reviewers who approved of Mary Shelley's *Frankenstein* (1818). For him, writing in *Blackwood's Edinburgh Magazine* (1818), the novel used marvellous incident to enquire into the conditions and implications of human knowledge and imagination. Other critics, like the reviewer for the *Edinburgh (Scot's) Magazine* (1818), deprecated the evident Godwinian influence in its lack of piety, its 'monstrous conceptions' marking the consequences of 'the wild and irregular theories of the age' (p. 253). He also noted, in its 'dark and gloomy views of nature and man' (p. 249), a distinctly unwelcome version of gothic writing. *Frankenstein*, though one of the texts now synonymous with gothic, deploys standard gothic conventions sparingly to bring the genre thoroughly and critically within the orbit of Romanticism. Its villain is also the hero and victim, while diabolical agency has been replaced by human, natural and scientific powers. Pervaded by the political, philosophical, aesthetic and scientific issues of its time and set in the eighteenth rather than the fifteenth century, the novel has few, though important, traces of older gothic elements: ruined castles only appear, significantly, in the distance, perched on rocky outcrops and lost in the striking romantic scenery of mountains. Graveyards and charnel houses appear briefly to signal the horror of Frankenstein's enterprise and associate it with the work of necromancers. It is later, in the 1831 introduction to the novel, that Mary Shelley offers another gothic frame in her account of readings from *Fantasmagoriana*, a French translation of a German collection of tales published in Paris in 1812 and, with a new title, *Tales of the Dead* (1813), in England a year later. These stories stimulated the ghost story competition held between Byron, Shelley, Polidori and herself and, in the Introduction, are identified as the origin of the novel. Written after a number of popular stage productions had added sensational aspects to the first edition of the novel, the Introduction not only provides an origin, but also, retrospectively, a moral for the novel as the tale of man 'mocking' the work of the divine creator. In the brief sketch it offers of the scientific machines of creation, moreover, it provides a hint for the sets that, a century later, would provide film versions with their striking, and gothic, visualisations of the story.

The belated Introduction inscribes another frame around a novel composed of frames. Using different first-person narrators and collecting various stories and letters, the novel alludes to the complexity and mystery of gothic narratives. With the silent reader presented on the margins of the text as the addressee of the letters that compose the novel, the figure of the eighteenth-century reader is invoked. These features do not close the novel in a conventionally moral manner, but produce a distance from the different figures in the tale to leave a sense of uncertainty and irresolution. Fragmented, assembled from bits and pieces, the novel is like the monster itself, and like the unnatural, disproportionate monsters of gothic romances. The monster is also a political figure, an allusion to the monsters that proliferated in the debates concerning the French Revolution, debates in which Mary Shelley's parents, William Godwin and Mary Wollstonecraft, took an active part. A metaphor of the violent mob loosed in times of political upheaval, the monster, in the powerful critique he enunciates of human social and political institutions, also represents a form of radicalism too disturbing to be countenanced by the existing order and which, in the manner of *Caleb Williams*, highlights the monstrosity of systems of law, religion and family.

The most striking scene of the novel, replayed and rewritten in many films, is its moment of creation, a moment that has become the most enduring aspect of the tale's mythological dimensions. Signalling the effects of human aspirations for natural and physical powers beyond the limits of humanity, the monster has come to represent the fears about the existence of both natural and artificial mechanisms that not only exceed the boundaries of a humanised world but also emerge, transgressively and destructively, from uncontrollable desires and imaginings in the individual mind. The scientific replacement of nature and humanity, the various means of producing and reproducing the material world and the creation of entities that threaten human existence, is a recurrent horror, undermining the naturalness and stability of any order of identity or society.

Victor Frankenstein is not just a scientist in the modern empirical sense. His project is imbued with the grander speculations of alchemical power, speculations which, in the context of natural philosophy, promise, not supernatural knowledge, but the awesome secrets of nature, the mind and the body in the manner laid out by chemical and electrical experiments of the time. In the attempt to deliver life in full and forever, Frankenstein delivers a humanist dream, associated as much with poetic as with scientific imagination. As a dream it is an aesthetic as much as scientific enterprise that is horribly realised in monstrous form, natural and unnatural, living and dead, human and inhuman.

Though Frankenstein descends into a world dominated by the monster, violently raving in his destructive pursuit of his abortive creation, the novel does not present this as a simple case of delusion or madness. The monster is not simply an alter ego of Frankenstein, not simply the passionate returning of the repressed energies of a deranged individual mind. For, attending to psychological details, the novel presents the monster as both a private and public horror: he has an autonomous existence manifested by his eloquence and critical intelligence and in responses he elicits from others.

This is underlined by the patterns of doubling and reversal in the novel. The first narrator, Walton, is an explorer, possessed of dreams to discover the North Pole and its secrets of magnetism, dreams that are akin to Frankenstein's in that they envisage a world of eternal light. His sympathy, on meeting Frankenstein, also signals their proximity. The process of doubling is extended in the figure of Clerval, who dreams of learning Eastern languages in order to participate in the colonial commercial exploitation of the East, an enterprise analogous to Walton's hopes of entering a new northern land and Frankenstein's wresting of the secret of life from a feminised Nature. The exclusive and totalising ambition of these masculine projects is encapsulated by Frankenstein's statement that he intends to transcend the bounds of life and death, flood the world with light and create a 'new species' that will adore him like a father. Assembling a creature designed to be beautiful he is repulsed at its ugliness when animated by the spark of life. His vivid nightmare signals the total reversal of his project: images of death, decay, sexuality and woman return, like the monster, to haunt him with the antitheses and consequences of his idealist fantasy. The total and absolutely unified vision that animated his project, a vision in which self predominates, is reversed and shown to be dependent on the figures of difference it tried to negate. Frankenstein's subjectivity disintegrates, its imagined and vain sovereignty turning into the passions and violence of a gothic villain: creation cedes to destruction, mastery to slavery, unity to monstrosity.

While the doublings and reversals suggest a critique of the gothic implications of the distinctly masculine Romantic imagination, of a humanism grown monstrous as a result of excessive and exclusive aspirations to power and ideal unity, the novel, while presenting the destructive effects on family, gender and social relations, does not end with either an affirmation of domestic values or a moral reprimand. Monstrosity has left the novel open, its frames broken: all boundaries are left in question, divided between the positions of Frankenstein and the monster. The creator dies, the monster disappears in darkness and distance, while Walton, having agreed to return home, still gazes towards the Pole. Home and domestic values, after the early descriptions of Frankenstein's ideal upbringing in a republican and bourgeois Genevan family, are rendered suspect. Moral and legal systems, too, are tainted by monstrosity in the trial and execution of an innocent woman. As a result another woman, Frankenstein's fiancée Elizabeth, comments on a horror that pervades the novel: that all distinctions have irrevocably collapsed, that nothing is certain or grounded but teeters on the brink of an abyss. It is on a similar brink that the novel ends, divided by a monstrous transgression that is doubled, both internal and external, embedded in psychological and social forms, leaving all boundaries uncertain, delivered to a horrified glimpse of movements and powers shaping identity but beyond any human control.

Exceeding any authorial control, *Frankenstein* crossed generic boundaries to be disseminated in popular culture and modern mythology as a byword for scientific over-reaching and horror. First staged in 1823, in Richard Brinsley Peake's *Presumption; or the Fate of Frankenstein*, the novel was dramatised, in burlesque and melodramatic forms, some fifteen times by 1826. The theatre was important in the process of popularising gothic terrors and horrors and often framed texts with new and more acceptable meanings as the title of Peake's production of *Frankenstein* indicates. The melodramatic and sensational aspects of gothic fiction were also suited to the stage, and many novelists, Lewis and Walpole included, wrote plays. Another writer of novels and dramas was the Irish clergyman Charles Robert Maturin, whose *Bertram* (1816) was a popular success. In gothic terms, however, Maturin's most significant work is the perplexing and tortuous *Melmoth the Wanderer* (1820), often considered the last directly gothic text.

WANDERERS AND DOUBLES

In the dedication to *The Milesian Chief* (1812), Maturin describes his literary talent as the gothic capacity 'of darkening and gloomy, and of deepening the sad; of painting life in extremes, and representing those struggles of passion when the soul trembles on the verge of the unlawful and unhallowed'. He goes on to describe an earlier novel, *Fatal Revenge* (1807), as an exploration of the 'ground forbidden to man; the sources of visionary terror; the "formless and the void"'. In *The Milesian Chief* he says he has tried 'the equally obscure recesses of the human heart' (pp. iv–vi). The examination of similar gothic extremes, with particular emphasis on psychological horror and human evil, is continued in *Melmoth*. Appearing, as a contributor to the *Monthly Review* (XCIV, 1821) observed, at a time when, 'overwhelmed by their own extravagance', gothic novels were in decline, the novel revives 'the predilection for impossibility', and 'the passion for the violent, ferocious, and dreadful in poetry' (pp. 81–90).

The novel is also compared to the works of Radcliffe and Godwin, a combination that describes its generic strangeness, its belated use of characteristically eighteenth-century gothic machinery alongside agonised outcasts and psychological horrors. *Melmoth*'s extensive and intertwined narratives describe terrible and fantastic adventures that traverse Ireland, England, Spain and Indian islands. Horrors are encountered among ruined churches, in stormy and desolate landscapes and in the subterranean passages, burial vaults and prisons of Catholic monasteries. Mob violence, domestic tyranny, seduction and various forms of oppression are documented in gothic terms. The narrative frame, a manuscript of an obscure family history, its mystery emphasised by a portrait that seems strangely alive, recalls standard gothic devices. Catholicism and its Holy Inquisition, associated by gothic convention with tyranny, injustice and superstition, are strongly attacked by Maturin, a Protestant cleric in Catholic Ireland. Other religious doctrines, even the Calvinism to which Maturin adhered, are implicated in general criticisms which blur doctrinal distinctions in the ambiguous malevolence of the Wanderer. Ambiguous, like the novel, Melmoth is drawn from the models of Radcliffean villain and Godwinian Romantic outcast. His malevolence, violent rages, despotic power and blazing eyes are similar to the characteristics of Radcliffe's Montoni but in contrast do not depict a mortal made supernaturally diabolical by superstitious imagination: he actually possesses unnatural longevity and magical powers of movement, literalising the ghostly and diabolical capacities that are only imagined by Radcliffe's heroines.

Though described in religious terms as satanic throughout the course of the novel, Melmoth appears as a spectral double of the human, his image and story emerging gradually from the stories of his many victims. He disavows his satanic role, appearing more like a tempter who preys upon human desperation and desire. The evil he discloses is distinctly, intrinsically, human rather than externally diabolical: 'Enemy of mankind!', Melmoth exclaims, 'how absurdly is that title bestowed on the great angelic chief ... what enemy has man so deadly as himself?' (p. 436). Evil has a banal, human existence, produced from accidents and circumstance to escalate beyond human control. Melmoth's criticisms of religious tyranny also encompass the mundane absurdities, perversities and corruptions of human passions, vanities and social habits.

Much of the drama in *Melmoth* is internalised in details of horror, suffering and anguish. Melmoth is also a victim, like Caleb or Falkland. A Faustian figure, like St Leon, he sells his soul for knowledge and power, to become a Cain figure, a Wandering Jew, an outcast and a rebel. A cursed wanderer, he will only be free to die if another takes his place, exchanging his powers and cursed condition for their sufferings of which he is not the cause: everyday life and the corruption of social and religious institutions take care of that. The persecution and torment caused by these institutions is detailed in the novel's many accounts of alienation, desperation and mental deterioration. One sufferer, Moncada, describes the psychological effects of monastic imprisonment as 'something like the conspiracies so often occurring in the convent' which are 'an attempt to involve me in some plot against myself, something in which I might be led to be active in my own condemnation' (pp. 231–32). Such paranoia, and the delusional loss of any sense of self and reality that it entails, is not, however, enough for him to be seduced by Melmoth's offers of freedom.

Melmoth is a particularly unsuccessful tempter, a victory perhaps for the personal faith engendered by the Reformation. That faith remains a bleak hope in a novel in which physical and psychological torment constitutes the only basis for human reality and dignity: 'while people think it worth their while to torment us, we are never without some dignity' (p. 251). Humanity, communication and feeling tenuously emerge as effects of suffering, betrayal, disillusion and guilt, an inevitable condition emphasised by the form of the novel. The complexity and density of the narrative frames, do not, like conventional gothic texts, restore a moral order or explain a mystery, but suggest that the human condition is as inescapable as the narrative labyrinth itself, a relentless chain of cruel events without purpose, unity or meaning. In this respect the novel performs an ironic reversal of romance ideals and their homogenising effects.

'Reality' is repeatedly contrasted with gothic fictions. During the relation of one characteristically gothic adventure romances are described as habituating readers to 'tales of subterranean passages, and supernatural horrors' but failing to represent the real 'breathless horror felt by a being engaged in an enterprise beyond his powers, experience, or calculation, driven to trust his life and liberation to hands that reeked with a father's blood' (p. 191). Reality and fiction are not clearly separated, but are tortuously entwined in this self-conscious twisting of distinctions that appears at once serious and silly. Romance distinctions are undercut by challenges to readers' expectations, like the comments on Isidora's display of anxiety and terror in a situation all too common to a romance heroine. The grandeur of gothic terrors is steadily and comically undercut by the absorption of gothic horrors into the banal and everyday world:

> Romances have been written and read, whose interest arose from the noble and impossible defiance of the heroine to all powers human and superhuman alike. But neither the writers nor readers seem ever

to have taken into account the thousand petty external causes that operate on human agency with a force, if not more powerful, far more effective than the grand internal motive which makes so grand a figure in romance, and so rare and trivial a one in common life.

(p. 372)

The internalisation of grand gothic devices is ambivalently externalised, diffused throughout an everyday world itself composed of fictions. Maturin's disturbing reflections render reality in part an effect of fictions, and yet worse, not better, than gothic terrors. Grand romantic aspirations, internalised and reproduced in social and generic codes and fictions, are inverted as superstitious misconceptions: horror is banal in origin, an inescapable reality, internal to the workings and subjects of everyday circumstances. *Melmoth* becomes an anti-romance in contesting the purgative functions of terror that externalise and aggrandise quotidian evils. Art, life and horror are tortuously intertwined in a vicious play that refuses distinctions of fiction and reality:

there was no luxury of inventive art to flatter the senses, or ennervate the attention, – to enable the hearer to break the spell that binds him to the world of horrors, and recover the soothing realities and comforts of ordinary life ...

(p. 398)

Maturin's fiction offers no conventional novelistic escape and recuperation of reality, only the pervasively literal horrors of a world painted in gothic colours. The inter-relation of fiction and reality, internal and external worlds of horror, of irreconcilable conflicts and warring extremes, for Maturin, is characterised by Ireland:

the only country on earth, where, from the strange existing opposition of religion, politics, and manners, the extremes of refinement and barbarism are united, and the most wild and incredible situations of romantic story are hourly passing before modern eyes.

(dedication to *The Milesian Chief*, p. v)

Gothic romance again transcribes and displaces anxieties and horrors in the everyday.

The gothic nature of Maturin's Ireland is not unique. Scott's novels present his native Scotland as wild and romantic and thus appropriately gothic settings. James Hogg's *The Private Memoirs and Confessions of a Justified Sinner* (1824) also uses the Scottish context to gothic effect. While Maturin coloured the world in the dark hues of gothic fiction, Hogg's novel focuses on a similar collision of extremes in an individual psyche. In the *Memoirs*, too, the religious ideas of Calvinism, Presbyterianism and anti-nomianism predominate among scenes of Scottish political conflicts between prelatic and covenanter mobs. From the social context and descriptions of the political and familial conflict and the strict religious environment in which the protagonist is brought up, an increasingly disarming world of delusion and uncertainty emerges. An 'editor's' narrative explains events as the fratricidal and cunning crimes of a man determined to inherit the family wealth that has been denied him from birth. There are, however, some mysterious events, especially the appearance of a dark stranger, that allude to supernatural machinations. In the subsequent confessional account by the criminally Cain-like brother, Robert Wringhim, the boundaries of social and sub-jective reality are shattered. Wringhim, raised by a local Rever-end instead of his aristocratic family, is taught that as one of the Elect his place in Heaven is secure no matter what he does on earth. Meeting a stranger capable of transforming his physical appearance, Robert is encouraged in crime, initially haunting his brother, George Colwan, before luring him into a duel in which the latter is stabbed in the back. Taking possession of the Colwan estates, Robert discovers he has indulged in bouts of drinking, love affairs and business deals of which he has no recollection. He speculates that a 'second self', his own likeness, or some spirit possessing his body, is responsible: it is never clear whether these are excuses for evil, figures of unconscious forces, temporary lapses of sanity or effects of diabolical agency. The strange double, exe-crated in gothic terms as a 'monster of nature' and a 'devil incar-nate' (p. 189), persecutes Wringhim to the extent that, psychologically and physically wretched, he is tortured by terrible voices and hideous, nightmarish fiends: no longer possessed of any sense of self, nor daring to look in a mirror 'for I shuddered at my own image and likeness' (p. 205). The image, like his double, only exacerbates his alienation, misery and self-loathing. In a world of fantastic images and distorting doubles, he can only be divided from himself, drawn in by their lure, an image, a semblance, 'liker to a vision than a human being' (p. 216).

Framed by an editorial account of events using eye-witness reports, journal evidence and even an article by a writer named Hogg, the confessions are held at a distance as the auto-biographical ravings of a madman. The editorial frame ironically plays with gothic devices aimed at verisimilitude and, after trying to assess the authenticity of the confessions and their significance as allegory or parable, the 'editor' offers other possibilities:

> In short we must either conceive him not only the greatest fool, but the greatest wretch, on whom was ever stamped the form of humanity; or, that he was a religious maniac, who wrote and wrote about a deluded creature, till he arrived at that height of madness that he believed himself the very object whom he had been all along describing.
>
> (pp. 229–30)

An ironic comment on the identifications and doublings of Romantic and gothic writing, this suspicious recognition of writing's uncanny powers and reading's strange effects is made after the events comprising the story have been written twice. The *Memoirs*, it seems, is similarly doubled, ambivalently negotiating between two forms of narrative in a process that repeats gothic dynamics of internalisation and externalisation.

The *Memoirs*' ironic distance manages to sustain a distinction between internal and external worlds even as it acknowledges the curious, ambivalent effects of writing's duplicity. Its fascination with delusion and psychological disturbance maintains an individual case as its object. The fascination with deranged states and uncanny experiences, uncertainly imagined or horribly real, recurs throughout later gothic fiction in attempts to represent these conditions subjectively or objectively. The different narratives of

Hogg's novel perform both strategies, one looking at mental deterioration from the inside, the other from the outside. Both these angles are explored in nineteenth-century renderings of the uncanny where they are internally presented with the attention on doubles and mirrors, and externally objectified as cases of criminal or psychological degeneration. Between the two, the status of human identity, social forms and gothic styles underwent significant changes in location and significance.

6

HOMELY GOTHIC

In general we are reminded that the word 'heimlich' is not unambiguous, but belongs to two sets of ideas, which, without being contradictory, are yet very different: on the one hand it means what is familiar and agreeable, and on the other, what is concealed and kept out of sight ... everything is unheimlich that ought to have remained secret and hidden but has come to light.

(Freud, 'The Uncanny', pp. 224–25)

In the mid-nineteenth century there is a significant diffusion of gothic traces throughout literary and popular fiction, within the forms of realism, sensation novels and ghost stories especially. Eighteenth-century gothic machinery and the wild landscapes of Romantic individualism give way to terrors and horrors that are much closer to home, uncanny disruptions of the boundaries between inside and outside, reality and delusion, propriety and corruption, materialism and spirituality. These are signified by the play of ghosts, doubles and mirrors. In both American and British writing the influence of Radcliffe, Godwin and Scott is still evident, though their gothic styles are significantly transformed. The bourgeois family is the scene of ghostly returns, where guilty secrets of past transgression and uncertain class origins are the sources of anxiety. The modern city – industrial, gloomy and labyrinthine – is the locus of horror, violence and corruption. Scientific discoveries provide the instruments of terror, and crime and the criminal mind present new threatening figures of social and individual disintegration. The traces of gothic and Romantic forms, however, appear as signs of loss and nostalgia, projections of a culture possessed of an increasingly disturbing sense of deteriorating identity, order and spirit. The development of the American novel owes much to the reception and transformation of European romantic literature. Significant differences appear in the use of gothic images in writing that was predominantly realist. Hackneyed gothic machinery was abandoned, but contrasts of light and dark, good and evil, were inflected in texts in which the mysteries of the mind or of family pasts were the central interest, the human and social world completely replaced the grand gothic terrors of a supernatural kind. In the North American context a different geography and history were available to writers: romantic adventures could take place in the wilds of an uncharted continent, or horrors could be found in the Puritan witch trials of Salem in the seventeenth century. Psychological and narrative disturbances raise questions about how strange incidents are framed by a reality subject to different historical pressures: of rationalism, democracy and religious organisation, and their relationship to individual freedom, slavery and social control.

The malevolent aristocrats, ruined castles and abbeys and chivalric codes dominating a gloomy and gothic European tradition were highly inappropriate to the new world of North America. They were too far removed to have the same significance or effects of terror. As Nathaniel Hawthorne, in the preface to *The Marble Faun* (1860), rather optimistically observed:

> No author, without a trial, can conceive of the difficulty of writing a romance about a country where there is no shadow, no mystery, no picturesque and gloomy wrong, nor anything but commonplace prosperity, in broad and simple daylight, as is happily the case with my dear native land.
>
> (pp. x–xi)

In Hawthorne's earlier novels there were many peculiarly American shadows that fell upon the 'broad and simple daylight' of American life. Though the grand architectural gloom of European gothic was inappropriate, the commonplace of American culture was full of little mysteries and guilty secrets from communal and family pasts. In 1865 Henry James, who wrote many ghost stories later in the century, criticised, in an essay on the sensation novelists Mary Braddon and Wilkie Collins, Radcliffe's external and extravagant sources of excitement, when there were more interesting, terrible and strange events closer to home. James states that a good ghost story 'must be connected at a hundred points with the common objects of life' (p. 742). The newness of the American world, however, retained some shadows of superstitious fancy which appeared in concerns with the relation of the individual, mentally and politically, to social and religious forms of order. The negotiation with fictions of the past, as both a perpetuation and disavowal of superstitious fears and habits, attempts to banish certain shadows haunting the American daylight and, in the process, discovers new dark shapes.

NEW WORLD, NEW TERRORS

Charles Brockden Brown, the first native-born American professional writer, occupies an important position in regard to transformations in gothic writing. Negotiating European and American gothic traditions, he was one of the Shelleys' favourite writers. Brown's novels drew on Godwin's fiction and philosophy, but he adapted themes of persecution, criminality and social tyranny as well as Enlightenment notions of freedom and democracy. Mystery underwent a similar transformation: psychological motivations and delusions were examined in relation to their social and aesthetic implications. Between 1798 and 1800 Brown published four novels concerned with persecution, murder and the powers and terrors of the human mind. *Wieland*, his first, describes the life of two orphans, Clara and Theodore Wieland, growing up in the context of religious evangelism and enlightened rationality. A balance between these two discourses appears to be sustained until the sound of strange voices disrupts the community. Wieland interprets these voices as emanations from God. It is, however, his devout faith that leads to the horrors that destroy the community: believing it to be God's will, Wieland kills his wife, children and himself.

The strange occurrences are subsequently explained in the memoirs appended to the novel as the effects of a human *diabolus ex machina*. The memoirs tell the story of Carwin, a 'biloquist' or ventriloquist able to throw his voice and perfectly imitate the voices of others. His talent makes him an outcast and, after years of wandering and persecution, he settles near the Wieland's community to haunt its members with his biloquistic skills. What is never explained or confessed is Carwin's involvement in Wieland's crimes, whether he urged their commission or whether they really were the result of a deluded religious imagination. The interweaving of distinct tales that links *Wieland* to the gothic romance also underlines its different perspective, questioning how mysteries are located in the empirical world, in the natural powers of Carwin and in the chain of events that lead to crime. The implication of the two tales, and the way key issues are left uncertain, disclose a greater realm of mystery in the complexity of motivations and fantasies that determine and delude individual behaviour. Rational explanation of natural powers and its mechanistic image of a universe beyond human control shift the realm of mystery from supernatural agency to a physical and empirical world. But the force of delusion inspired by religious devotion still remains mysterious and inexplicable, and presents, not the victory of enlightenment, but a new and different type of darkness.

The uncertain relation between religion and rationalism is, in *Wieland*, located at the level of political and aesthetic representation. The ambivalence, like that of gothic concerns with the dangerous effects of imagination and novel-reading, is not resolved. In the American context the ambivalence reflects an anxiety about the constitution of American society itself, its culture shaped by a movement from colonial struggles to independence. In part demystifying European gothic traditions of superstitious and aristocratic terror, and in part relocating their mystery from the supernatural to a human and natural sphere,

Wieland refuses the dichotomy of religious mysticism and enlightened rationalism: it casts suspicion on the authority and effects of their representations and identifies the shadows that fall as a result of the lights of either reason or revelation to be manifest as individual pathology, an effect of the repressions and desires produced by authoritative representations.

Nathaniel Hawthorne's engagement with romance, in contrast to Brown's, departs in the direction of realism. Less concerned with criminality and individual psychopathology, Hawthorne demystifies gothic representations of a haunting past and associated superstitions lingering in the present to look at the play of sunshine and shadow in family and society. In *The Scarlet Letter* (1850) the spectre of Puritan intolerance and witchcraft trials hangs over the community that condemns a young woman, Hester, to wear a large red 'A' as a mark of her adultery. Demonised, Hester and her child live defiantly as outcasts on the fringes of the community. The child's father lives a guilty and anxious life in the community, wearing a veneer of respectability that becomes increasingly thin. The boundaries and conventions distinguishing good from bad are, in the exclusions they legitimate and the repressions they demand, as much a site of darkness and uncertainty as Hester's 'immorality'.

While *The Scarlet Letter* focuses on the limits of social propriety, other Hawthorne stories imbue the past with more psychological interest. In 'Young Goodman Brown' (1835), a young man's nocturnal journey into a forest at night leads to an encounter with respected churchgoers and elders. His mysterious companion suggests that they are not the shining examples of propriety that they appear to be. Arriving at a witches' sabbath Goodman Brown discovers a social spectrum of supposedly respectable as well as disreputable figures. The short story ends on an uncertain note, unable to decide whether the events were dreamt or real, whether they were the deluded visions of a superstitious young man or the dark side of the community as a whole. One thing is sure: the diabolical effects of the account itself. Brown returns a changed man to an apparently unchanged community, deeply suspicious of all outward appearances and all forms of faith, distrustful and gloomy until his dying day.

The play of appearances, of past and present, superstition and reality, remains in the lighter tones of Hawthorne's second novel, *The House of the Seven Gables* (1851). As in conventional gothic texts, it centres on a building. Not an old castle or mansion, Hawthorne's edifice is a family house. Like a gothic castle, however, it is a gloomy and grotesquely ornamented repository of ghosts. Harking back to the early days of American colonisation, the story centres on the theft of the land on which the house was built (a theft, of course, that occludes prior colonial expropriations of land). The victim, Maule, curses Pyncheon, the new owner, who dies shortly afterwards, establishing the basis for local superstition. Two generations later, the family is in decline and, like ghosts, haunting rather than inhabiting the house and its memories of transgression. The arrival of a stranger, a young daguerrotypist, and the death of the senior member of the family in the same manner as the grandfather, precipitate a very gothic conclusion. The stranger, the heir of old Maule, reclaims the property by marrying the youngest member of the Pyncheon family. Because he knows past secrets about the house, he also finds the deeds entitling him to great estates. These have been hidden in the house for years. The ghosts are thus purged, replaced by the values of property and domesticity. Mysteries are explained, the deaths resulting, not from the curse, but from apoplexy. Superstitions linger in the reaction to more modern features. Old gothic portraits are superseded by daguerrotype photography, demonic possession by the science of mesmerism. While the present excises the superstitions of the past and domesticates gothic terrors, daguerrotype representations have uncanny effects in bringing the dead to life, until, that is, the picture is revealed to be of a living rather than dead relative.

The uncanny effects of representation are addressed elsewhere by Hawthorne in stories dealing with artistic creation. In 'The Artist of the Beautiful' (1844) a clockmaker labours for years to replicate perfectly a flying butterfly only to have his successful mechanical wonder destroyed by the clumsy grasp of a child. The production of beauty is not an idealised enterprise in Hawthorne for it involves obsessive and wearying labour that undermines a sense of reality. The lures of beauty are presented in the

Hoffmanesque fantasy 'Rappacini's Daughter' (1844). E.T.A. Hoffman, the German Romantic writer of marvellous and ghostly tales, was a strong influence on Hawthorne and Poe. Stories like 'The Golden Pot' (1814) describe fantastic, dream-like worlds full of magical events and exotic imagery, while others, like 'The Sand-Man' (1815), describe an individual's descent into states of delusion and insanity. In 'Rappacini's Daughter' both the daughter of the reclusive professor, Rappacini, and his marvellous garden of exotic plants are extremely attractive and lethally poisonous, their allure drawing a young man to the brink of death. The world of artifice and representation is seen to possess mysterious powers in the stimulation of fantasy and hallucination.

The distortions of the imagination are best presented in the macabre, hallucinatory stories of Edgar Allan Poe. In Poe's tales and stories the outward trappings of eighteenth-century gothic, the gloom, decay and extravagance, are, in chilling and terrific evocations, turned inward to present psychodramas of diseased imaginings and deluded visions that take grotesque fantasies to spectral extremes. The horror in Poe's tales exhibits a morbid fascination with darkly exotic settings mirroring extreme states of disturbed consciousness and imaginative excess, presenting fatal beauties, bloody hauntings, premature entombment and ghastly metempsychosis. Human desires and neuroses are dressed in the lurid hues of the supernatural to the extent that nightmare and reality become entwined. Poe's extensive reading in the works of British and German gothic writers shapes his ambivalent attitude to the genre. Aware of the humorous possibilities of the formulaic gothic tales popularised in periodicals like *Blackwood's Magazine*, and the ironies inherent in Romanticism and outlined by August Schlegel, one of his favourite authors along with the novelist and dramatist Ludwig Tieck, Poe's tales sustain a distance from Romantic investments in unified imaginative vision. Indeed, his characters manifest a predilection for mental states that are disturbed, drugged or diseased, delusional or pathological states from which neither they nor the tales recover.

Poe's use of gothic images and effects draws out the darker moods of setting and psyche and, moreover, draws them to the surface. Landscapes are wild, misty and desolate; buildings, like the house of the Usher family or the Abbey in 'Ligeia' (1838) are gloomy and grey. They are designed to produce effects on narrators and readers alike. The interior decorations in Poe's stories, such as arched gothic frames, armorial carvings, arabesque wall-hangings, enhance their disturbed, feverish and nightmarish effects. The description of a tapestry in 'Ligeia' powerfully demonstrates the gothic effects aimed at in the tales, not only depicting ghastly forms but made even more disturbing by the draft that causes it move (p. 120). Attention to external and internal scenes extends further, mental space becomes a site of gothic disturbances, the genre's outward forms providing images of deranged, unhinged states in which distinctions of fantasy and reality become blurred. In 'Berenice' (1835), where the hero grows up in an inverted world in which fantasy appears real and reality seems fantastic, memory is registered in architectural form as 'ruin', while in 'The Fall of the House of Usher' (1834) the palpable but immaterial effects of fear immediately assume gothic shape as a 'grim phantasm' (p. 146). Physical space and material things seem thoroughly inter-penetrated with fragmented, pathological and feverish forms of consciousness. Women, especially, figure the fatal and sexual intensities of emotional disturbances made almost solid and then returned to a phantasmal state. Their lack of substance – pale, evanescent, ghostly, dead – like the uncertain animation of décor and storytelling, mirrors the lack of consistency and assurance assumed by male protagonists, narrators and tales themselves.

Stressing the darker trajectories of the imagination, Poe's fiction leaves boundaries between reality, illusion and madness unresolved rather than, in the manner of his contemporaries, domesticating gothic motifs or rationalising mysteries. In 'William Wilson', first published in 1839, Poe's schooldays in England are recalled in a story that has all the architectural and atmospheric trappings of earlier gothic forms. The tale of a boy encountering another of the same name who infuriates him by means of vocal and sartorial imitation, 'William Wilson' exploits the theme of doubling, but without the distancing effects of the editorial frame used by Hogg in his *Memoirs*. The hero of the tale leads a dissolute life, but finds that, wherever he travels, his illegitimate schemes are thwarted by the figure who haunted him at school. He finally locks his double in a duel, to find, on running his opponent through, that he is alone and bleeding before a great mirror. His mortal foe has been his inverted image, an alter ego that, unlike the doppelgänger, is a better self, an external image of good conscience described as having a spectral 'officiousness' in spoiling egotistical indulgences (p. 175). The climax turns the tale around so that what appeared to be an account of some external haunting is seen as individual hallucination. Self, in Poe's model, is never made whole, the mirror encounter not only shows one to be two, but does so in a language of double negativity: 'not a thread in all his raiment – not a line in all the marked and singular lineaments of his face what was not, even in the most absolute identity, mine own!' Neither dress nor visage shows any signs of deviating from exact likeness. At the same time an absolute difference is suggested in the accumulation of negatives: self is singular yet utterly divided and, moreover, unable to regain identity. As the other yields in death, Wilson notes a further blow to identity. He will also be dead 'to World, to Heaven and to Hope', an irrevocable separation from material, ideal and spiritual supports of self (p. 178).

In 'The Fall of the House of Usher' consciousness and reality are as extensively disturbed. The house is both an architectural ruin set in a desolate and gloomy landscape and a family suffering physical and psychological decay, dying from an unknown and incurable illness and subjected to all sorts of diseased imaginings. A friend arrives to witness the family's disintegration, seeing brother, sister and house disappear in an atmosphere of attenuated gloomy sensibility. The luxurious and languid decline is punctuated by a shocking gothic climax. At the point of death the brother announces that his sister has been buried alive. Suddenly her enshrouded form reappears, falling upon her brother. Both die. Rather than ponder the erotic implications of this macabre moment the narrator flees as storms gather and the house itself crashes in utter ruin. The imagination, suspended and tortured in this gloomy and unreal world, reaches its own collapse, caught up in the otherworldly, claustrophobic environment of mists, darkness, feverish fancy and delusion.

The morbid and macabre images of premature burial and the return of the dead are given a more human and more realistic twist in 'The Cask of Amontillado' (1846). Premature burial constitutes the climactic horror of a tale of chillingly executed vengeance. Preying upon the weakness of an old enemy – his pride in his knowledge of wine – the narrator relates how he is enticed into vaults to taste an uncertain vintage. The narrator then relates how he chained and walled his victim within a recess deep in the vaults. More horrible still are the self-satisfied tones of the narrator. The vaults lend a gothic atmosphere to what is a horror story about a callously inhuman intelligence. Crime, in 'The Tell-Tale Heart' (1843), is treated with a similar ambivalence concerning subjective and objective phenomena: a murderer is driven to confess his crime by what is assumed to be the pounding heart of his victim's corpse concealed beneath the floorboards. In 'The Facts in the Strange Case of Mr Valdemar' (1845) contemporary scientific themes provide the basis for a more metaphysical exploration of the horror attendant on disturbances of the boundaries between life and death. In the tale the mesmerising of a dying man leaves him in a state of suspended animation. The body does not decay but it, or something, can speak, uttering the impossible words 'I am dead'. This statement confounds distinctions between life and death as they are maintained by realistic and linguistic conventions, indicating the fragility of the boundaries of nature that are manipulated by the scientific imagination's attempt to gain knowledge of death. The horror surrounding the question of who or what is speaking is followed by the release of the body from a mesmeric limbo and its speedy decomposition into a liquid mass.

Throughout the tales the lurid settings and extravagant scenes raise, often playfully, questions about the nature and effects of representation. 'The Oval Portrait' (1845), a very short story self-consciously using conventional gothic devices like the old castle, the life-like portrait and discovered manuscript, discusses the capacity of representation to reverse the relationship of life and death: the life-like portrait is a perfect representation of the beautiful love of the artist, completed precisely at the moment the original died. Art, it seems, sucks the life out of things, doubling nature with a disturbing imaginative power, a macabre power of death that recurs throughout all Poe's tales. It is not only the morbid fascination and macabre auras that make them interesting as gothic works. The various devices, styles and subjects that Poe uses, and transforms, influence all of subsequent gothic writing: the doubles, mirrors and the concern with modes of representation; the scientific transgressions of accepted limits; the play of internal and external narrations, of uncertain psychological states and uncanny events; and the location of mysteries in a criminal world to be penetrated by the incisive reason of a new hero, the detective. All have become staples of the gothic.

Poe's tales take gothic devices in new directions, opening up disturbing recesses within mental and realistic spaces and, in a claustrophobic paring down and darkening of imaginative potential, closing down avenues of certainty or escape. Other tales, like 'The Narrative of Arthur Gordon Pym' (1838), enjoy the romantic and adventurous aspects of fiction produced in the context of the open and threatening spaces of a new world in which exploration, discovery and trade were as much about the frontiers of individual identity as about affirming the virility of a new country. The fiction of Herman Melville plots the entanglement of romance and psychology with new commercial and social motifs where sublimity and terror are associated with savage, vast and threatening new spaces, frontiers and attitudes. Melville, departing in different directions in his use of romance and gothic forms, returned from a trip to England in the 1840s, with a selection of gothic novels. *Moby Dick* (1851), in which the whaling ship has decorations reminiscent of European gothic structures, plots a different journey in which the sublime is associated with the power of a marine nature (the sea and the great whale that inhabits it) lying beyond the mastery of humans. The mirror of this sublime and unconquerable vastness, the novel suggests, is found in the darkness of the human mind, in the way Ahab's obsession and desire exceed all constraints.

Melville's 'Benito Cereno' (1855) offers another pairing of conventional gothic motifs with new concerns in a short tale in which reading and misreading have powerful social implications. Told initially from the perspective of the Captain of a sealer, with events recapitulated and corrected in legal documents and records, the text begins with the encounter with a distressed vessel near a deserted Pacific island off the coast of Chile. Assuming the ship, a Spanish slaver called *The Tryal*, has been badly damaged by storms, the sealer's Captain goes aboard to offer his help and finds himself increasingly disturbed by small events and observations he cannot explain: the odd demeanour, actions and comments of the Spanish Captain and his black servant, the mixed condition and behaviour of crew (ill-kempt Spanish sailors) and cargo (unchained slaves) induce an unease that, despite the 'phantoms' – the suspicions – that haunt him, he cannot pinpoint (p. 280). At one point he fears that they are pirates keen to commandeer his own ship. That fear, however, is shown to be another romantic misperception among the many that litter the Captain's account. For example, at first sight the Spanish vessel appears to be full of monks in 'dark cowls'; 'battered and mouldy', it seems like a floating gothic ruin with 'castellated forecastle' and 'ancient turret' (p. 220). The references to romance equate the Captain with a heroine who misperceives the world in gothic and archaic terms rather than in a rational and empirical manner. Only on departing the ship, in a chaos of leaping sailors, does he glimpse the actual situation: the slaves had taken control of vessel and crew.

The American Captain's romantic naïvety and simplicity is linked to his blindness towards the reality of slavery. It is not the fact of the mutiny – the tale was based on actual events – but the focus on its representation that generates critical strangeness. Hidden yet in plain view is an unthinkable situation: the idea that African slaves rather than Europeans should be in control is so ungraspable it shows just how embedded and naturalised racism can be. In drawing attention to his misapprehensions, in highlighting its link to romantic, and significantly superstitious, tales, Melville's suggests that the Captain's perspective is itself a fantasy – a romance – that shapes and occludes reality and, through its critical strangeness, also how fragile and false it is, confounding ideas of reality and fantasy. The actual situation is misunderstood due a perspective that is simultaneously real (slavery was an actual, widespread and accepted practice) and fantastic (slavery was so naturalised that imagining Africans or African-Americans in control was unthinkable). The tale's allusions to romance have further critical implications: the associations of romance with irrational, superstitious, tyrannical and barbaric practices are turned from a feudal past to present conditions. The story draws attention to an enduring and powerful context for the production of fiction in North America: slavery. New terrors of frontiers and open spaces also mean confronting and killing indigenous populations, new horrors shadow the free and rational outlook, the 'commonplace prosperity' and 'broad and simple daylight' of homes and estates built in the process. Here freedom is haunted by slavery, homes cleaned and lands worked by people that are treated as nothing more than items of property.

CITIES, HOMES AND GHOSTS

In Britain in the mid-nineteenth century distinct forms of gothic writing were less discernible, having been dispersed among a number of other genres. Ghost stories and sensation novels, shaped by earlier gothic texts, were popular sources of terror and horror. Though the influence of Scott, Radcliffe and Godwin was evident, significant transformations were made, reflecting the different concerns of the time. A major shift was evident in the domestication of gothic styles and devices within realistic settings and modes of writing. Domestic, industrial and urban contexts and aberrant individuals now provided the loci for mystery and terror. Haunting pasts were the ghosts of family transgression and guilty concealment; the dark alleyways of cities were the gloomy forests and subterranean labyrinths; criminals were the new villains, cunning, corrupt but thoroughly human. Prisons, social injustice and rebellious individuals were not Romantic sites or heroes of gloomy suffering, but strange figures threatening the home and society. Traditional gothic traces were strongest in representations of scientific innovation, being associated with alchemy and mystic powers. The lingering dark Romanticism that surrounded accounts of scientific or individual excess was both a threat to social mores and a sign that, in the increasingly normalised and rationalised worlds of family and commerce, there was something missing: a spiritual passion which, in opposition to the more real horrors of everyday corruption, was nostalgically represented in gothic terms or in the ghost story as a contrast between narrow reality and lost, metaphysical dimensions.

In the popular fiction of the 1830s and 1840s plenty of gothic and Romantic elements were still used. Edward Bulwer-Lytton's fiction embraced the old romantic forms that he had enjoyed in his youth. A fascination with aristocracy and past ruin is counterbalanced by Godwinian accounts of criminal underworlds, incarceration and individual corruption. The alchemy associated with Godwin's *St Leon* provides the basis of another important strand in Bulwer-Lytton's work, though the latter departs in more arcane directions. A visionary and Romantic mixture of alchemical, Faustian and scientific themes is framed with a mystical idealism that aspires to a supra-rational humanism. *Zanoni* (1842) describes the search for metaphysical unity and new dimensions in terms of a hero schooled in occult reading, experimenting in ancient black arts in a search for the elixir vitae of the alchemists. In a later, shorter, novel, 'The Haunters and the Haunted' (1859), arcane instruments and occult lore are combined with a quasi-scientific discussion of energies and fields in a story framed by a sceptical and rational investigator's narrative. The examination of the vulgar superstitions surrounding a supposedly haunted London town house, in order to debunk them, leads the empiricist narrator into an encounter with extremely powerful supernatural forces. Though these are associated with the haunting energies that result from past criminal horrors, they also disclose awful and superhuman secrets, for example, in a secret room the narrator discovers clues to a being possessed of extraordinary mental powers that combine occult and scientific knowledge. These, a later encounter with this being reveals, involve skills in mesmerism as well as inexplicable paranormal abilities and the possession of eternal life. A supermind, the figure that appears in various guises in the story, represents the desirable peak of Gothic-Romantic imaginings, the total fusion of matter and spirit and the terrible and threatening implications of such power. While this current of visionary horror lingers throughout the nineteenth century, to resurface strongly at its end, fiction in the middle of the century tended to realise terror and horror, fascinated by their irruption in the shadows of the everyday world.

In the popular romances by William Harrison Ainsworth there is a less visionary blend of gothic forms that looks at the darkness of crime and the city. His productions were varied, however. In *The Lancashire Witches* (1849), a historical novel beginning with witch trials in the seventeenth century, secret covens and witchcraft rituals are the subject matter. Other novels, involved in the Newgate controversy over fiction that was considered to encourage crime, focus on the villains and their propensity for corrupt and criminal action. In a later novel, *Auriol* (1885), it is the city that is described as a distinctly gothic scene. Earlier work by G. W.M. Reynolds also examines this new gothic scene. Though he wrote supernatural tales with standard gothic themes – *Faust* (1845–46), *Wagner, the Wehr-Wolf* (1846–47) and *The Necromancer* (1852) – Reynolds' darkly realistic work *Mysteries of London* (1845–48) provides a good example of the city viewed through a gothic lens. Tyranny and horror are both nightmarish and real in its gloomy descriptions of aristocratic corruption and depravity which, in the city's labyrinth of immorality, also enmeshes the behaviour of the working classes. The apparent reality of the city's horrors evokes emotions that ask questions of the social order, emotions relating to fears in the immediate present rather than displaced on to a distant past.

These horrors also influence the gothic elements of more literary works. Charles Dickens' *Bleak House* (1853), for example, presents a grimly blackened city, while *Oliver Twist* (1838) shows the violence and cruelty lurking just below the surface of acceptable Victorian reality. A great reader of gothic romances, Dickens deploys their devices in diverse ways and for various effects throughout his fiction, a good example of the dispersal of gothic elements. In *Dombey and Son* (1848), the transformations of industrial and technological progress seem apocalyptic and demonic. Here the novelty of train journeys is accompanied by anxiety and, in climactic scenes where the villain is run over, their destructive aspect is described in terms of a monster. In *Great Expectations* (1860–61) aspects of gothic fantasy, in the shape of Magwitch and Miss Havisham, satirically undercut the aspirations of Pip, who, like superstitious readers of romances, is duped by his own expectations. As creations of distorted imaginings both Pip and Estella are fabricated like Frankenstein's monster. Coketown, in *Hard Times* (1854), is a grimly inhuman industrial labyrinth, a realisation of a distorted and reductive rationalism that has its ideological equivalent represented by the tyranny of numbers and facts which, in Gradgrind's school, are ground into young heads without the spiritually ameliorating influence of any imagination. Traces of gothic fear and power shadow the bourgeois family and its house in *Little Dorrit* (1855). Having the melancholic and gloomy appearance of the castle, the house and the family within it are haunted by secrets of disreputable class origins and the ghostly presence of the father signified by his foreboding portrait.

Dickens was also influential in the growing popularity of another related but distinct genre, the ghost story. Like much gothic writing in the early part of the nineteenth century, the ghost story was circulated and popularised in literary magazines and periodicals. While the gothic crossed various historical and natural boundaries in an extravagant fashion, the ghost story's limited encounters with the spectral world focused on the vacillation between real and supernatural dimensions. Generically more contained, the ghost story presents a more definite idea of reality in order to evoke a specifically uncanny effect by the appearance of supernatural figures. As realism's uncanny shadow, the ghost story produces gentle tremors along the line separating the supernatural world from that of Victorian empirical and domestic order. The supernatural is not rationalised, however, but is affirmed as a distinct and unknown presence occupying a narrative that, though incompatible, runs parallel to realist representations. Though very popular throughout the century, the ghost story seemed more a diversion from serious writing. With the exception of the most productive of ghost story writers, Sheridan Le Fanu, who none-the-less engaged with realism and gothic forms in his novel, *Uncle Silas* (1864), many of the writers of ghost stories spent more time writing novels along conventional realist lines. In 'The Signalman' (1866), Dickens produced a ghost story of place describing the uncanny recurrence of a tragic event in the same location years later. Mrs Gaskell's 'The Old Nurse's Story' (1852) uses the presence of a child's ghost to disclose a guilty secret in a family's past. In other tales, like Mary Braddon's 'At Chrighton Abbey' (1871), the ghost is not only a figure representing the past, but also returns in spectral anticipation of disaster in the immediate future. The more distant future, too, makes phantom appearances in the present in George Eliot's 'The Lifted Veil' (1859), a tale describing the disarming effects of an individual's extraordinary ability to catch glimpses of the future.

By the end of the century stories of haunting extended the realm of uncertainty to include the reading mind. Henry James, practising his ideas about the importance of suggestion over explicit and hackneyed conventions, opened ghost tales to an undecidable form of haunting. 'The Turn of the Screw' (1898), while acknowledging Radcliffe's work in a story of a young governess arriving in an isolated country house, developed techniques of narrative framing to leave issues of haunting unresolved. Whether the children in the story are actually possessed by a demonic spirit or whether everything stems from projections of her own disturbed state of mind are never explained, thereby extending the realm of haunting from text to reader. Given ghosts' associations with home and family, the question of female consciousness remains a significant issue in other tales written in the same decade. Charlotte Perkins Gilman, in 'The Yellow Wallpaper' (1892), details a dramatic mental unravelling which may – a cause is never made explicit – arise from post-natal depression, conjugal constraint or self-doubt. Beginning like a gothic romance with a visit to an old US colonial mansion that has been untenanted for a long period, and may be haunted, the story draws outs ghosts of the mind rather than the past represented by the building. Suffering from an unidentified 'nervous depression', the heroine's 'hysterical tendency' is treated by her rational and practical doctor-husband with a prolonged rest cure (Baldick, *Gothic Tales*, p. 249). Not even allowed to write, though she secretly does, she is little more than a domestic prisoner whose condition emerges in her account of, and obsession with, the wallpaper of her bedroom. From appearing ugly and ill-kept, the pattern changes, with her growing absorption in its surfaces, into shapes, lines and suggestive forms. It mirrors her isolation: its 'bloated curves' suggest a Romanesque 'delirium tremens', diagonal lines exaggerating 'optic horror' and nervous distraction (p. 254). Shapes seem to move behind the paper, a woman creeping behind bars. Rendered passive, thoroughly constrained by the domestic environment, she, like the wallpaper, seems no more than surface and decoration, her identification and absorption performing a commentary on the role she internalises to the point of delirium.

Though affirming, often self-consciously, the reality of ghostly events, tales frequently address the question posed in the title of a Mrs Wood story, 'Reality or Delusion?' (1868): poised between scepticism and supernaturalism, it leaves readers uncertain about the story's reality. The uncertainty about individual perception and interest in other, supernatural dimensions stimulated by the ghost story, like the more material horrors of social depravity and criminal corruption displayed in gothic representations of the city, indicate some disaffection with the present. Excursions beyond the everyday world, the disturbance of boundaries between present, past and future indicate both fear and nostalgia in relation to Victorian attitudes and society. What is missing, in a thoroughly secular, rationalised and scientifically ordered material world, the ghost story suggests, is a sense of unity, value and spirit. Ghosts return from a greater darkness surrounding the culture, from a sense of spiritual loss of which criminality and social degeneration were symptoms.

Gothic and Romantic images were ways of engaging with the alienation from the past as both a repository of the fears of disintegration and the hopes of regaining a sense of unity and value. In Robert Browning's nineteenth-century poetic version of the quest romance, 'Childe Roland to the Dark Tower Came' (1855), the bleak landscape and uncertain destination of the wandering hero give form to a sense of cultural and spiritual desolation and general aimlessness. In Alfred Tennyson's reworking of Arthurian legend, the romantic figures, particularly female as in 'The Lady of Shalott' (1833), are identifiable as figures of mourning and separation, their loss mirroring the sense of cultural emptiness that demands a unifying national myth. Romance forms, for some cultural critics, provided a way out of social alienation. John Ruskin's accounts of gothic architecture uncover a fierceness and strength that, like the freedom and imagination associated with gothic and romance forms in eighteenth-century antiquarianism, has a vigour and spirit lacking in the soul-destroying and monotonous conditions of Victorian England. An antiquarian angle is pursued by William Morris' use of romances as a utopian and precapitalist alternative to the oppressive forms of industrial capitalism.

SINS OF THE FATHER

The extravagant effects of gothic and Romantic elements tended, in nineteenth-century fiction, to be refracted through the domestic world central to realism. As the privileged site of Victorian culture, home and family were seen as the last refuge from the sense of loss and the forces threatening social relations. The home, however, could be a prison as well as a refuge. In two novels of the period, novels that engage very differently with gothic themes, the home is the site of both internal and external pressures, uncanny and terrifying at the same time. In Emily Brontë's *Wuthering Heights* (1847) gothic and Romantic forces of individual passion are fearful and invested with a sense of loss. In Wilkie Collins' adaptation of Radcliffean themes in his sensation novel, *The Woman in White* (1860), gothic terrors are purged from the social and familial world through the determined exercise of rational, legal and investigative powers.

The desolate, stormy and wild landscape and decaying family house of *Wuthering Heights* embody gothic and Romantic elements that, as in Charlotte Brontë's *Jane Eyre* (1847) and *Villette* (1853), signify darker forces of individual passion, natural energy and social restriction. The novel's hero/villain, Heathcliff, combines the roles of gothic villain and Romantic outcast in his anti-social demeanour, fierce temper, mercenary and unlawful plotting, and his quest for vengeance. With Cathy's rebellious passions, there is a similar refusal of the niceties of domestic passivity, propriety and duty. The narrative structure of reported stories and its uncanny movement between past and present are gothic elements signalling an untamed and wild invasion of the home rather than comfortable domestication. The gothic theme that the sins of the father are visited on the offspring is manifested in the representations of the illegitimacy and brutality of paternal authority, the repetition of events, and the doublings of figures and names in successive generations. Earnshaw's domestic tyranny, Hareton's wildness, Linton Heathcliff's unmanliness and Catherine's energy are all displaced duplications of the roles and characteristics of the previous generation. The duplication that signals the dependence of past structures on those of the present is also evident in the dependence of individual identities on those of others. The relationship between Heathcliff and Cathy is the most powerful example of doubling: one constituting the other's narcissistic image of his or her own unified self. The powerful desire for unity, however, disturbs all social and familial relations. Heathcliff's desire demands the transgression of all rules, and casts him in the figure of a fiend, a devil and a vampire. He is also associated with natural wildness, and his temperament mirrors the hostile and stormy environment he occupies.

The distinctions between nature and culture, between individual passions and social rules do not simply distinguish the artificial repressiveness of social forms from the eruption of primitive desires. They are as artificial as the constructions of an originary and natural gothic world to which they allude, a legacy of eighteenth-century and Romantic distinctions between civilisation and wildness. Heathcliff's passions are produced: he is found in the city and then miserably domesticated by a hostile middle-class family whose criticisms, exclusions and prohibitions of his progress towards the properly bourgeois ends of marriage make him wild and vengeful. Heathcliff represents the outer limit of Romantic individualism, possessed by the desire of an impossible unity invested in the figure of Cathy. If Miss Linton can elope with Heathcliff under the illusion, as the latter scornfully observes, of his romantic heroism, then antithetical characterisations of his wild, untamed nature are similarly illusory constructions signalling the spectral return of gothic and Romantic forms.

The ghosts of the novel are an effect of the internalisation of a Romantic tradition on a social rather than individual level.

Ghosts are not only seen by the narrator Lockwood on his first visit to the Heights, they reappear throughout the text: Heathcliff is seen with a strange lady by members of the local community. These uncanny effects in the story are, like the effects of the story on Lockwood, signs of the return of a lost world whose contours he does not fully understand. At the end of the novel the perspective moves from the happy domestic scene at the Heights to Heathcliff's grave. Like a Graveyard poet of the eighteenth century, Lockwood imagines tranquillity after death, a return to proper unity in the earth. It is a peace that remains imaginary, part of the projections of the beholder-narrator's sense of loss and his nostalgic dwelling upon the scene, indeed, it is as a reader of the story's romantic passions that he has identified with its subject. The text, framed by Lockwood's longing gaze, has constructed a lost natural passion and spirit that is at once strange and desirable as a site of unity.

In *The Woman in White* the transgressions of individual desire threaten family and society from within. Wilkie Collins was pre-eminent among the sensation novelists of the 1860s. Sensational effects, however, owe much to gothic, particularly Radcliffean, styles of evoking terror, mystery and superstitious expectation. The plot, figures and narrative form of *The Woman in White* also resemble structurally Radcliffe's gothic, although they have been transposed into shapes more appropriate to the nineteenth century. Henry James, in his essay 'Mary Elizabeth Braddon', in the *Nation* (1865), credits Collins with 'having introduced into fiction those most mysterious of mysteries, the mysteries which are at our own door'. 'Instead of the terrors of "Udolpho"', James goes on, 'we were treated to the terrors of the cheerful country-house and the busy London lodgings. And there is no doubt that these were infinitely the more terrible' (p. 742). None-the-less, gothic patterns pervade Collins' novel. The gothic heroine, passive and persecuted, is presented as an image of loss and suffering, especially when seen through the eyes of that new Victorian hero, the amateur detective. Anne Catherick, the woman of the title, is scarcely present in the novel, her spectral appearances in dark city streets, deserted graveyards and garden retreats gesturing towards the mysteries and terrors the narrative resolves. As a ghostly figure pointing to the past crimes of an illegitimate aristocrat and the sufferings and persecutions which he inflicts on her, Anne Catherick's appearances also anticipate the trials of the novel's gothic heroine who, as a half sister, is both literally and narratively her double. As a reminder of older gothic family romance patterns, the double is also used to present a more terrible possibility as a figure that threatens the loss of identity.

The novel, indeed, is framed quite self-consciously as a gothic romance. Towards the end, the hero, Hartright, reviews the story:

'The sins of the father shall be visited on the children.' But for the fatal resemblance between the two daughters of one father, the conspiracy of which Anne had been the innocent instrument and Laura the innocent victim, could never have been planned. With what unerring and terrible directness the long chain of circumstances led down from the thoughtless wrong committed by the father to the heartless injury inflicted on the child!

(p. 514)

Echoing Walpole's partial justification for *The Castle of Otranto* the oldest gothic plot of all is re-enacted in the story of the consequences of secret paternal crime. The self-consciousness and the duplicity of the gothic is presented in the text's doubles: Anne and Laura, mirror images of female oppression, fortitude, passivity and sacrifice, within and in the name of the family, are not the only gothic pairing. The role of villain is also doubled. One is Sir Percival Glyde, who persecutes Anne to keep his own dark family secret, and marries Laura in the hope of dispossessing her of her inheritance. He is the selfish, brutish example of economic and oppressive villainy. The other, Count Fosco, is a figure of aesthetic and imaginative villainy. His diabolical cunning and creative intelligence are combined with a vain, self-indulgent and cruel character that, in a corpulent body, signal him to be the real and ambivalent object of horror. He devises the most callous schemes with the same delight that he exhibits while playing games. His intellectual vanity and aesthetic self-consciousness are displayed with a flourish when, in the confession he is forced to write at the end, he recommends his idea of abducting and substituting Laura for Anne as a model plot for English romance writers (p. 568).

As in the Radcliffean romance, the mysteries surrounding the spectral appearance of Anne Catherick are finally furnished with a rational explanation. Through the investigative efforts of Walter Hartright and Marian Halcombe, Laura's relation, the aura of mystery and terror is disclosed as an intricate but material plot. Unlike earlier gothic narratives, the interwoven narratives composing the novel, such as lawyers' reports, domestics' statements and villains' confessions, are all presented as extended legal documents. The legalistic form is central to re-establishing a proper narrative against the webs of deceit woven by the villains, with the consequence that law, reason and identity are linked as narrative forms. The careful comparison of narrative clues and temporal consistency regarding events, in the analysis of dates, times and timetables, provide the means to rescue the abducted Laura. The secret of Glyde's illegitimacy is found in a text. Moreover, it is the manipulation of stories that enables the substitution of Laura for Anne, while a properly legal account of events proves her identity and establishes her rights to her inheritance and property.

A rational explanation of criminal mysteries by means of detection and law rather than the hand of Providence situates gothic patterns in a thoroughly Victorian context. It is an amateur detective who comes to the rescue of a persecuted wife. Female persecution and imprisonment are of a more modern cast with the asylum replacing the convent and the country house the castle. The dark labyrinth of terror is located in the city, a 'house-forest' populated by spies and conspirators (p. 379). Fosco, an adept chemist, especially when it comes to drugs, embodies the villainous potential of scientific intelligence. As a refugee from a Europe that, in 1848, was wracked by revolutionary upheavals and subversive conspiracies, he is also associated with dangerous, and imported, political ideas. The superiority of English values of law, liberty and domesticity is reaffirmed only after the terrors of losing one's identity, freedom and life have been encountered. Happy domesticity is restored in the marriage of Hartright and Laura, but only at the price of the sacrifice of her double. It is, moreover, a displaced sense of closure since, at the beginning of the novel, it was the spectral, mysterious and helpless appearance of Anne that excited Hartright's interest and became his object of desire. Sacrificed, she became a sacred and impossible object, her ghostly distance and her death a sign of the fragility of a social order caught between the duplicitous power or impotence of fathers and husbands.

Closure is partial, a sense of loss remains. Threats to law, domestic relations and cultural and sexual identity are only temporarily rebuffed. In Victorian culture, too, a loss, increasingly irreparable by reason or law alone and articulated in terms of spiritualism and horror, governs perceptions of science, nature, crime and social degeneration. Later in the century the threats to cultural identity reappear, to be presented, in a different combination of scientific rationality and sacred horror, as distinctly sexual in nature.

7

GOTHIC RETURNS IN THE 1890s

> Human beings whose nature was still natural, barbarians in every
> terrible sense of the word, men of prey who were still in possession
> of unbroken strength of will and lust for power, hurled themselves on
> weaker, more civilized, more peaceful races, perhaps traders or cattle
> raisers, or upon mellow old cultures whose last vitality was even then
> flaring up in splendid fireworks of spirit and corruption. In the
> beginning the noble caste was always the barbarian caste: their pre-
> dominance did not lie mainly in physical strength but in strength of
> the soul – they were more whole human beings (which also means, at
> every level, 'more whole beasts').
>
> (Friedrich Nietzsche, *Beyond Good and Evil*, pp. 391–92)

At the end of the nineteenth century familiar gothic figures, the
double and the vampire notably, re-emerged in new shapes, with
a different intensity and anxious investment as objects of terror
and horror. Recurrent since the late eighteenth century, doubles
and vampires made an impressive reappearance in the two major
gothic texts produced in the period, *The Strange Case of Dr Jekyll
and Mr Hyde* (1886) and *Dracula* (1897). Though harking back to
Romanticism, it was in the context of Victorian science, society

and culture that their fictional power was possible, associated with anxieties about the stability of the social and domestic order and the effects of economic and scientific rationality. Earlier nineteenth-century concerns about degeneration were intensified, not in relation to cities and families, but in the different threats that emerged from them, threats that were criminal and distinctly sexual in form. In scientific analyses the origin of these threats was identified in human nature itself, an internalisation that had disturbing implications for ideas about culture, civilisation and identity, as well as a socially useful potential in the process of identifying and excluding deviant and degenerate individuals. The ambivalence towards scientific issues led, in the fiction of the period, to strange realignments of the relationship between science and religion, a relationship shaped by spiritualism and the continuing popularity of the ghost story.

The ghostly returns of the past in the 1890s are both fearful and exciting incursions of barbarity and, more significantly, the irruptions of primitive and archaic forces deeply rooted in the human mind. Supernatural occurrences, also, are more than manifestations of a metaphysical power: they are associated, in scientific and quasi-religious terms, with the forces and energies of a mysterious natural dimension beyond the crude limits of rationality and empiricism, exceeding the reductive and deterministic gaze of materialistic science. These forces, seen as non-human, are also in-human, embedded in the natural world and the human mind. While these powers were threatening, they were also spiritually elevating in their provision of a framework to articulate disaffections with the reductive and normalising limits of bourgeois morality and modes of production, limits whose repressions produced the divided lifestyles of the middle classes, respectable by day and pleasure-seeking by night. Individual moral degeneration was also considered to be a problem of class and social structure: capitalist modes of organisation produced a society in which individuals were parasitic upon each other. In *Civilisation* (1889) Edward Carpenter argued that primitive cultures were stronger and healthier because their members were not separated along class lines or restricted to single occupations and because they were more self-reliant, they did not need to prey upon each other. In the city and the factory, where divisions of class and labour were most extreme, alienation and cultural corruption were most acute. It is no wonder that Dracula selects London as his new hunting ground.

The ambivalence of scientific theories, manifested in the indifference of Jekyll's drug, had to be contained by the cultural and moral values it threatened. Darwin's theories, brought humanity closer to the animal kingdom, thereby undermining the superiority and privilege that humankind had bestowed on itself. Along similar lines, the work of criminologists like Cesare Lombroso and Max Nordau attempted to discriminate between humans: some were more primitive and bestial in their nature than others. Anatomical, physiological and psychological theories were brought to bear on identifications of criminal types, those who, it was claimed, were genetically determined to be degenerate and deviant. Atavism and recidivism marking regression to archaic or primitive characteristics, dominated constructions of deviance and abnormality. Physiognomy, too, was important in the process of making atavistic tendencies visible. The fiction of the period is dominated by marked descriptions of facial features as telling signs of character. In studies of the brain, theories of dual or split human nature were given a physiological basis. Paul Broca's work, for example, on the division of the brain into left and right hemispheres, observed that one side governed intellectual faculties and the other emotions, thus apparently grounding dichotomies in human nature.

In disclosing threatening natural forces scientific theories gave shape to the anxieties about cultural degeneration and provided ways of disciplining and containing deviance. Combining science with religion, however, provided a new way of envisaging a sacred or metaphysical sphere. Spiritualism was one meeting place, with groups like the Society for Psychical Research, founded in 1882, legitimating investigations into paranormal powers. Science, as in Frankenstein's distinction between the reductive perspective of Krempe and the visionary outlook of Waldman, disclosed new natural miracles and powers. From theories of magnetic, chemical and electrical forces the divination of greater powers was imaginable: from experiments in hypnotism, mesmerism and theories of unconscious cerebration, as Van Helsing suggests in *Dracula*, the telepathic transference of thoughts becomes a distinct possibility.

While science disclosed grand unifying powers, horror was another mode of cultural reunification, a response to the sexual figures that threatened society. One of the main objects of anxiety was the 'New Woman' who, in her demand for economic, sexual and political independence, was seen as a threat to conventionally sexualised divisions between domestic and social roles. The loosening moral, aesthetic and sexual codes associated with *fin-de-siècle* decadence, the spectre of homosexuality, as narcissistic, sensually indulgent and unnaturally perverse, constituted a form of deviance that signalled the eruption of regressive patterns of behaviour. A more pervasive, biological manifestation of the sexual threat was perceived in the form of venereal disease: syphilis was estimated to have reached epidemic proportions in the 1890s. Though linked to the immorality of certain identifiable groups and deviant behaviour, the threat of venereal disease was particularly intense as a result of its capacity to cross the boundaries that separated the healthy and respectable domestic life of the Victorian middle classes from the nocturnal worlds of moral corruption and sexual depravity.

SCIENCE, CRIME AND DESIRE

In *Jekyll and Hyde* the austere, rational and respectable world of the lawyer, Mr Utterson, is gradually eclipsed by a dark and obscure arena of mystery, violence and vice. The stark division of good and evil, in part an effect of Stevenson's Calvinism, echoes the disturbing dualities of Hogg's *Memoirs* in their uncanny relation of everyday realities and fantastic irruptions of hidden wishes. The horror emanates from the revelation of the extent and power of these buried energies. Strangely natural, the emergence of Hyde as a figure of evil is only partially explained in gothic terms as the return of Jekyll's dark past: the 'ghost of some old sin', 'black secrets', haunts Jekyll as some suspected transgression. Jekyll's scientific practice is also implicated in that his are 'transcendental' ideas, opposed to the prevailing 'narrow and material views' of his one-time colleague, Dr Lanyon (p. 80). Like Frankenstein, these visionary and metaphysical ideas have monstrous results. Enfield's first encounter with Hyde, for instance, describes him as a 'Juggernaut' callously trampling over a young girl and speculates on his preying upon the sleeping rich, drawing back their bed curtains and forcing them to succumb to his awful power (p. 37).

The story's setting suggests a gothic image of the city in a 'dingy neighbourhood' of which Jekyll's windowless laboratory is a ruined reminder of gothic decay, a 'sinister block' bearing 'marks of prolonged and sordid negligence'. Its 'blind forehead of discoloured wall' personifies the building with the physiognomic signs of a regressive nature. The city also recalls a primitive past: a forest, its darkness, only intensified by the glow of streetlamps, resounds with a 'low growl' (p. 38). The narrative, unlike the omniscient and singular perspective of realism, is composed of fragments, partial accounts that are gradually articulated in the disclosure of the mystery surrounding Dr Jekyll. Unlike the gothic romance's collage of manuscripts and stories, the journals, letters and first-person narratives in *Jekyll and Hyde* are combined with legal documents, distinguishing a world dominated by professional men who are lawyers, doctors and scientists. Indeed, the 'strange case' that is related is a matter of legal, medical and criminal investigation, a challenge to the mechanisms of reason, law and order. Jekyll's experiments, while endowed with diabolical, Faustian or alchemical suggestiveness, are performed with scientific instruments and chemical compounds; their results, moreover, are described in contemporary secular and scientific terms: Hyde is 'troglodytic', 'ape-like', a manifestation of human regression to primitive and animal states (pp. 40–42). Good and evil are similarly articulated as the line separating culture, progress and civilisation from barbarity, primitivism and regression. The line, however, is easily crossed in that the elaborate performance that culminates in the empirical demonstration of the reversibility of human identity for Dr Lanyon makes manifest the inextricable relation of antitheses (p. 80).

Scientific theories disclose the instability of the dualities that frame cultural identity. The proximity and reversibility of good and evil cannot be restricted to a case of individual pathology, having 'no discriminating action', 'neither diabolical nor divine', the ambivalence, the moral indifference, of Jekyll's drug undermines classifications that separate normal individuals from deviant ones. Its ambivalence discloses a doubled human condition that is not symmetrical: 'although I had now two characters as well as two appearances, one was wholly evil, and the other was the same old Henry Jekyll, that incongruous compound of whose reformation and improvement I had already learned to despair' (p. 85). The drug distils evil while leaving the same old human compound of good and evil. It is no longer a question simply of good and evil, of human nature divided between a higher or better self and a lower or instinctual self, but of an ambivalence that is more disturbing to the constitution and classification of human nature. The indifference of the drug is linked to a realm of chance, a result of accidents and circumstances beyond rational understanding or control. Indeed, the success of Jekyll's experiment is due not to technical expertise, but, it is deduced, to an impurity in a particular batch of chemicals (p. 96).

The ambivalent and disturbing effects of a realm beyond human control or understanding disclose an imbalance in notions of identity that draws the 'better side' inexorably towards evil. In the guise of Hyde, Jekyll enjoys 'vicarious depravity', selfishly 'drinking pleasure with bestial avidity' (p. 86). For Hyde, Jekyll is no more than a respectable mask, a cavern in which a bandit hides from pursuit (p. 89). The unevenness of the splitting displays an inherent instability in notions of human identity. The drug, manufactured and not natural, controls and shatters 'the fortress of identity', 'rattling the doors of the prison-house of my disposition' (pp. 83–85). It is the better self, Jekyll suggests, that is both castle and prison, an external image that is shaken by the drug taken internally. Identity, moreover, seems to be an effect of images, shaping and crossing the boundaries of inside and outside. Seeing the 'ugly idol in the glass' does not evoke revulsion on the part of Jekyll but is a welcome image: 'this, too, was myself. It seemed natural and human'. The image of Hyde, moreover, is also more unified, seeming 'more express and single, than the imperfect and divided countenance, I had hitherto been accustomed to call mine' (pp. 4–5). While the repetition of 'seem' implies a distinction between deceptive appearance and true reality, conventions associated with images of personal identity are, in the rather disinterested tones of the word 'accustomed', presented as strangely arbitrary. At this point, also, the conventional dualities invoked by Jekyll in terms of a difference between his 'original and better self' (p. 89) and a lower or secondary self are undermined. The secondary self seems primary, growing in power in inverse proportion to the sickliness of the better self. The doubling in the novel, then, does not establish or fix the boundaries of good and evil, self and other, but discloses the ambivalence of identity and the instability of the social, moral and scientific codes that manufacture distinctions. These external structures are seen to be crucial as well as disturbing and contradictory. Hyde uses Jekyll to escape reprimand and punishment, while the latter preserves his respectable reputation and enjoys vicarious pleasures in the guise of the former. Jekyll owes his existence to the law since, without it, he would be of no use to Hyde. These external pressures sustain his better self: 'I think I was glad to have my better impulses thus buttressed and guarded by the terrors of the scaffold' (p. 91). His hesitation regarding the external legal supports for his inner being is elaborated in the ambivalence the story uncovers in the law itself. While the law buttresses the fortress of identity called Jekyll, it also produces the radical evil called Hyde, and the ambivalent doubling they both employ as a masquerade against punishment. Law, establishing particular limits between good and evil as taboos and prohibitions, also produces the desires that can only be manifested secretly, in the guise of an other being.

The production of illegitimate desires, and their construction as unnatural by a system that is itself seen to be arbitrary, has a significant bearing on the cultural context of the novel. The supposedly natural power of law, presented in Jekyll's paternal interest in Hyde (p. 89), is strangely unbalanced so that the exclusively male world of the novel itself seems unnatural. It is reflected in the speculations concerning the relationship between Jekyll and Hyde, with the mirror in Jekyll's cabinet offered as evidence of a horrible kind of narcissism. In Oscar Wilde's *The*

Picture of Dorian Gray (1891) the portrait as an inverted image is, like the mirror, bound up with the reversibility of individualised good and evil as well as homosexuality. Moreover, the idea that Hyde is blackmailing Jekyll, and the luxurious, indulgent but tasteful decoration of Hyde's rooms, imply a past relation of some intimacy and the unnaturalness of homosexual pleasures. The associations of unnaturalness with homosexuality, however, seem to be undercut rather than reinforced in a text in which notions of human nature are neither stable nor dual, but bound up with an ambivalence and uncertainty that leaves boundaries between nature, culture, law and identity both in doubt and strangely interconnected.

While the doubling of *Jekyll and Hyde* discloses horrors and questions concerning human nature and sexuality in terms of law and science, other versions of atavism employ different fictional and discursive arrangements, involving mythological figures from the past and the occult and contemporary scientific practice. In Arthur Machen's *The Great God Pan* (1894) a scientist specialising in cerebral physiology and also, like Jekyll, a doctor of 'transcendental medicine' rearranges a few cells in the brain of a woman patient and produces startling and occult results: she encounters 'the great god Pan', becomes a gibbering wreck and dies nine months later after giving birth to a daughter. The narrative gradually pieces together the ghastly incidents that surround the daughter's life, though she takes on many disguises. Her power seems to be of a terrifyingly sexual nature, seducing her male victims who are often from the respectable echelons of society, before revealing to them something so unspeakably horrible that they commit suicide. As a daughter of Pan, the woman reveals secret forces at the heart of things, forces that should, the narrator moralises, remain buried, no doubt because their sexual nature is linked to female desire. The mythological and occult frame, moreover, presents science as a kind of alchemy, dabbling with powerful forces it cannot understand and producing effects it cannot control. In 'The Novel of the White Powder', from *The Three Imposters* (1895), science opens on to a similarly occult dimension. A serious law student, after taking a drug prescribed by his doctor, becomes a decadent pleasure-seeker before regressing totally into a horrible mass of black primordial slime. Theories of atavism are rendered occult: scientific analysis explains that the drug obtained from a perfectly respectable chemist's shop had been affected by a long process of temperature variations that turned it into the *vinum sabbati*, the potion for a witches' sabbath. Reformulating regression in terms of the occult, the conclusion also places science within a greater, sacred and mystical universe of force and energy, matter and spirit.

Science, at the time, was also arming itself with a more horrifying, and realisable, potential for destruction. One of the four narrators of Richard Marsh's *The Beetle* (1897) is a gentleman scientist working for the British government, developing a gas capable, in the tiniest doses, of killing any form of life. The main horrors of the novel, rivalling *Dracula* in popularity at the time, are not scientific but sexual, Oriental and occult, and are linked to corruption, imperialism and cultural decline. Set in a foggy, nocturnal London of fashionable neighbourhoods and seedy suburbs, it is told in different narrative sections, from the perspectives of a destitute clerk, a rich heiress and New Woman, a scientist and a private investigator. The plot takes its bearings as a tale of vengeance in that having participated against his will in orgies and sacrificial rituals conducted by the secret cult of Isis, the politician's past catches up with him in the shape of the eponymous beetle. Able to assume male and alluring female shapes, this mysterious scarab is also capable of controlling minds. With scenes of striking body horror, sexual and moral corruption is conjured up and associated with occult and Oriental powers and a lack of imperialist self-control.

VAMPIRES

The play between mythological and modern significance, between mystical and scientific visions of horror and unity, sexuality and sacred violence, is focused in the figure of the vampire. In Mary Braddon's 'Good Lady Ducayne' (1896) the vampire theme signals the barbarities that result from human vanity and scientific illusions. Centring on a naïve young companion growing weaker and weaker from a mysterious 'mosquito bite', the mystery is explained as a series of blood transfusions designed to extend her old and withered mistress's life beyond its natural limits. A scientific version of the quest for eternal life, the story highlights the horrible illusions of alchemical powers that surround contemporary science. In contrast, Sheridan Le Fanu's 'Carmilla' (1874) makes no attempt to rationalise superstition within the bounds of everyday realism or nineteenth-century science. The gothic features of the narrative temporally and geographically distance the story from the present. The events are framed as a case from the files of Le Fanu's psychic doctor, Martin Hesselius. Castles, ruins, chapels and tombs signal the gothic tradition and its atmosphere of mystery and superstition. At the centre of the mystery is Carmilla, a beautiful young woman who arrives at the castle of an aristocratic family. Uncannily, Carmilla is the very image of a figure appearing years before in a childhood dream of the family's daughter, Laura. The latter, attracted to and repulsed by Carmilla, establishes an intimate acquaintance. Deaths occur in the locality, accompanied by superstitious rumblings. Oblivious, Laura soon becomes the prey of Carmilla. Laura is saved, however, by the intervention of the guardian of one of Carmilla's other victims. As vampire lore is expounded, and her tomb discovered, Carmilla is subjected to the traditional measures of decapitation and a stake through the heart, a perfectly natural end in a story in which superstition, legend and folklore are part of the everyday reality.

The story's sexual images, none-the-less, have a resonance in the context of the late nineteenth century. Female sexuality, embodied in Carmilla's languor and fluidity, is linked, in her ability to turn into a large black cat, with witchcraft and contemporary visions of sexual, primitive regression and independent femininity. Feline, darkly sensual and threatening in its underlying, cruel violence, Carmilla's unnatural desire is signalled in her choice of females as her victims and the alluring as well as disturbing effects she has on them. Exciting amorous emotions in Laura that are far from innocent, the attraction is shadowed by an incomprehensible fear and anxiety when Carmilla's romantic passions are articulated in terms of blood, sacrifice and fatal possession. Laura's susceptibility to Carmilla's disturbing charms is finally interrupted by the reassertion of a male order of meaning and sexual differentiation. The secrets of Carmilla's behaviour and her resemblance to an old portrait are explained as vampiric immortality. Her changing yet singular identity is disclosed as a play on words: she has masqueraded under names that are anagrams of Carmilla. The curiously ambivalent power, the superstitious allure of the vampire herself, lingers in the memory of Laura, haunted by the dual images of 'beautiful girl' and 'writhing fiend' (p. 314), images that only partially described the polymorphous representations of female sexuality.

As a haunting figure from past narratives like legends and folklore, and as an eruption of unavowable energies from the primitive past of human sexuality, the vampire remains disturbingly ambivalent. The female vampires in *Dracula* display the effects of desire and horror attendant on the dangerous doubleness of sexuality. In Stoker's use of the legend, however, the principal vampire is male, a feature in line with the legacy of gothic villainy and Dr Polidori's Romantic and Byronic hero, Lord Ruthven, in 'The Vampyre' (1818). Wresting diabolical ambivalence and agency from its association, in 'Carmilla' and a whole host of other tales of female demon lovers, Stoker's novel subordinates feminine sexuality to a masculine perspective in which women serve as objects of exchange and competition between men. *Dracula* recuperates the gothic romance in making men the primary subjects of terror and horror, thereby addressing and attempting to redress, in its movement between figures of the past and present, the uncanny mobility of normal, natural and sexual boundaries in the 1890s. Akin to Radcliffe's Montoni, Polidori's Ruthven and Maturin's Melmoth, the malevolence of the Count, his pale, gaunt features, demonic eyes and callous libertinism are bolstered by supernatural attributes of metamorphosis, flight and immortality. Dracula's heritage extends deeper into the gothic past with the account of his family history full of tribal migrations and conquests, a militaristic, warrior past characterised by values of blood and honour (pp. 42–43). This history is, in part, that of the romance as traced by eighteenth-century antiquarians; stories of uncertain origin, romances, according to different versions, began among the nomadic warlike tribes of northern

Europe or peoples migrating from the East. The Carpathians formed the crossroads where these traditions met. The vampire is not only associated with the dissemination of the romance. In travellers' accounts from the eighteenth century onwards the significance of the vampire in the folklore, superstitions and customs of Eastern peoples was recorded and assessed. The origins of the vampire were explained as fears of the Plague, thought, since the Middle Ages, to have emanated from the East. Dracula's principal companions and alternative forms – rats, wolves and bats – were associated with disease.

In the setting of *Dracula* stock features of the gothic novel make a magnificent reappearance: the castle is mysterious and forbidding, its secret terrors and splendid isolation in a wild and mountainous region form as sublime a prison as any building in which a gothic heroine was incarcerated. The place of a heroine, however, is taken by the naïve young lawyer Harker. Throughout the novel ruins, graveyards and vaults, all the macabre and gloomy objects of morbid fascination and melancholy, signal the awful presence of the gothic past. Dracula is more than a gothic villain, however, more than the mercenary and mundane bandit that they too often turn out to be. As the sublime synthesis of the human and supernatural terrors of gothic writing, he is both villain and ghostly diabolical agent whose magic and power cannot be reduced to mere tricks or effects of over-indulgent, superstitious imagination. More than rational, he serves to elicit rather than dispel superstitious beliefs, demanding, not a return to reason and morality, but a reawakening of spiritual energies and sacred awe. The form of the novel testifies to the excessive, unpresentable nature of this demand. The letters and journal entries telling different but connected parts of the same story compose a whole whose immensity, like the unrepresentable horror of Dracula's unreflecting image, remains obscure.

Dracula's narrative fragments are of a distinctly modern cast. Though alluding to the gothic devices of lost manuscripts and letters, it is recorded in the most modern manner: by typewriter, in shorthand and on phonograph. There are other indicators of modern systems of communication. Telegrams, newspaper cuttings, train timetables are all signs of contemporaneity as are the medical and psychiatric classifications, the legal documents and the letters of commercial transaction. Not only useful in recording the story, these systems provide the information necessary to follow Dracula's trail and investigate his plot. The modernity of the novel's setting is also signalled by the professional status of the men who combine against the vampire. Apart from the aristocratic leftover, Arthur Holmwood, they are lawyers and doctors at the centre of late Victorian commercial life. Even Mina, by no means a 'New Woman', acknowledges in her secretarial abilities shifts in the nature of work within and outside the family. Van Helsing is a combination of professor, doctor, lawyer, philosopher and scientist. Like his former student, Dr Seward, and his systems for classifying psychiatric disorders in his asylum, Van Helsing is well versed in contemporary theories like the criminology of Lombroso and Nordau, Charcot's ideas concerning hypnotism and Carpenter's notion of unconscious cerebration. Dracula's archaic, primal energy is reformulated in scientific terms: his 'child-brain' a sign of criminal regression which is also characterised by his egocentricity (p. 389). Renfield, the inmate of Seward's asylum and 'index' of the Count's proximity, also displays the characteristic criminal traits of secrecy and selfishness. In his strange eating habits, progressing from flies to spiders, sparrows and, he hopes, kittens, Renfield selects a bizarre food chain which links animal to human life in a caricature of Darwinian theory. Reconstructing natural events with its scientific explanations, modernity also supplants the myths, the explanations of the past, with its own version of things. The occult powers of Dracula's castle, Van Helsing suggests, might well be natural, mysterious forces of geological and chemical origin (p. 411).

The progress of modernity, threatened by Dracula throughout the novel, is not as secure as its explanations suggest. Harker observes: 'unless my senses deceive me, the old centuries had, and have, powers of their own which mere modernity cannot kill' (p. 51). Irrepressible forces from the past continue to threaten the present. In response to the deficiencies of contemporary culture and society, in part embodied in its scientific values, the science in *Dracula* does not simply replace superstition with deterministic knowledge, the latter bound up with cultural degeneration and the parasitic nature of capitalist social organisation. A want of culturally unifying and elevating values underlies the repeated invocation of sacred forms in the novel. The threat of wanton and corrupt sexuality is horrifically displayed in vampiric shape. Their decadence, nocturnal existence and indiscriminate desires distinguish vampires as a particularly modern sexual threat to cultural mores and taboos. They are modern visions of epidemic contagions from the past, visited on the present in a form that, like venereal disease, enters the home only after (sexual) invitation. Against the threats of contagion and disintegration a sacred order is reconstituted. Dispensing with its inadequate materialism, science offers grander visions of a mysterious and sacred universe. Significantly, Van Helsing is more than a scientist, he is also a metaphysician who deals with 'spiritual pathology' as well as physical disease, a psychic investigator or transcendental doctor like Le Fanu's Hesselius or Stevenson's Jekyll. Van Helsing does not discount superstition and is the first to use sacred objects like the crucifix and the Host. Science involves mysteries and opens on to a more than rational plane in line with Victorian attitudes towards spiritualism and psychic investigation. The fusion of scientific knowledge and religious values is made possible by the demonic threat of Dracula. His diabolical powers and primitive energy lead to a 'baptism of blood' for his victims (p. 414), and mark the utter profanity that demands a more than rational response.

Under the unifying and priestly command of Van Helsing, the men of middle-class Victorian England reinvigorate their cultural identity and primal masculinity in the sacred values that are reinvoked against the sublimity of the vampiric threat. In the face of the voluptuous and violent sexuality loosed by the decadently licentious vampire, a vigorous sense of patriarchal, bourgeois and family values is restored. Out of the collective fragments of the text a new masculine image is assembled in opposition to the dark, inverted figure of pure evil and negativity. Dracula is the dark double of the brave and unselfish men whose identity is forged in their struggle; he is the regressive in-human otherness lifted from the realm of individual psychopathology into a cultural field as its absolute antithesis. Without mirror image or shadow, Dracula is a pure inversion. On a symbolic level he is the mirror and shadow of Victorian masculinity, a monstrous figure of male desire that distinguishes what men *are* becoming from what they *should* become. He forms a mirror that must be destroyed since its already fragmented textual composition signals regressive narcissism, perverse egoism and a terrible duplicity of appearance, unreality and un/naturalness that threatens all cultural values and distinctions. Dracula's duplicity is multiple, doubling Harker by donning his clothes in order that his disappearance is not linked to the castle. Dracula is also a foreigner trying to pass as English. On a symbolic level he passes for Christ, Beast and various identities within the family. This has the effect, as in the case of his interception of Harker's letters and ordering him to write brief notes, of a dissimulative disruption of proper systems of communication.

Dracula's crossing of boundaries is relentless. Returning from the past he tyrannises the present, uncannily straddling the borders between life and death and thereby undoing a fundamental human fact. In crossing the borders between East and West he undoes cultural distinctions between civilisation and barbarity, reason and irrationality, home and abroad. Dracula's threat is his polymorphousness, both literally, in the shapes he assumes, and symbolically in terms of the distinctions he upsets. His significance is dangerously over-determined. In the scene where he is interrupted in the act of pressing Mina's mouth to his bleeding breast he appears as an inversion of Christ as Pelican, nourishing his subjects with his blood in an unholy communion, and as a mother suckling Mina with the milk of his blood. 'The blood is the life', as Renfield reiterates throughout the novel. The exchange of bodily fluids renders the scene shockingly sexual, its violence as masculine as any act of rape. Blood, indeed, is linked to semen. Arthur, after giving blood to his fiancée, Lucy, states that he feels as if they are married. The fluid exchange present a perverse sexuality, unnatural in the way it exceeds fixed gender roles and heterosexual distinctions. Dracula's fluid, shifting and amorphous shape is, like Carmilla's, threatening because it has no singular or stable nature or identity. Meanings, identities and proper family boundaries are utterly transgressed in the movements of vampiric desire and energy. For all his sovereignty and violence, Dracula is, in respect of his polymorphousness, strangely feminised and, like Lucy, condensed into an objectification of total excess, 'a Thing' (p. 277, p. 293), as inhuman, 'hellish' and 'inorganic' as Hyde (*Jekyll and Hyde*, pp. 94–95). Lucy is presented as a 'Thing' just before the band of men symbolically subject her to phallic law by driving a stake through her heart and decapitating her. Restoring the boundaries between life and death, body and soul, earth and heaven, the ritualised killing of vampires reconstitutes properly patriarchal order and fixes cultural and symbolic meanings. The vampire is constructed as absolute object, the complete antithesis of subjectivity, agency and authority. The ritual killing also restores systems of communication in which women remain objects for male exchange. By way of women Dracula attacks men; through women he will contaminate and colonise the teeming metropolis of London. In the name of women the good men respond to the threat. Through and over women, male bonds, relations and identities are established, hence the significance of Lucy being courted by Arthur, Quincey and Seward.

Women constitute the objects and supports for male exchanges and identities, supports that are narcissistic in their reflections on and between men. Dracula's mirror thus returns the novel to its specific cultural and sexual context even as it serves to project sacred identities into a universal, metaphysical dimension. Dracula's effects, imaginarily in the way individuals perceive his threat, and symbolically in the cultural significance assigned to him, are infectious, producing doubles and reversals in images that contaminate all limits. As the males of the novel consolidate themselves against Dracula they begin to duplicate as well as reverse his effects. The mirror that Dracula composes for them becomes a mirror of male desire, of what men, in the 1890s, have to become in order to survive. The hunter becomes the hunted, and vice versa, as Dracula is driven out of western Europe. In the process Western civilisation and rationality grow increasingly barbaric and irrational. Superstition, both religious and folkloric, takes precedence over reason. Male emotions become more visible as Van Helsing lapses into hysteria after Lucy's funeral (p. 225);

Arthur sobs hysterically on the paternal and maternal shoulder of the professor after impaling her and later bursts into tears in Mina's arms (p. 279, p. 295). Having found its maternal place by arriving on Mina's shoulder, male hysteria is a sign of the breakdown and longing for proper social bonds. These are nostalgically invoked by Quincey in his recalling of 'yarns by the campfire', dressing 'one another's wounds' and drinking 'on the shore of Titicaca' (p. 83). The bonding produced by exclusively male adventures forms an idyllic boy-scout past that is reconstituted and sanctified in the pursuit of the vampire. In the final stages of the chase Seward observes how 'those adventurous days of ours are turning up useful' (p. 461). Van Helsing appeals to this spirit when he describes how the vampire may be beaten by the 'power of combination' and the unselfish devotion to a cause (p. 306). It is a cause that requires the letting of blood. In an earlier context, Van Helsing says to Quincey 'a brave man's blood is the best thing on this earth when a woman is in trouble. You're a man, and no mistake. Well, the devil may work against us for all he's worth, but God sends us men when we want them' (p. 194). The jolly fortitude of this statement is tested later when Quincey loses more than the amount of blood required in a transfusion.

Manhood, blood and bravery form the cornerstones of Van Helsing's fatherly notion of cultural and spiritual renewal. The appeal to male strength, blood and bravery culminates in the violence of the hunt that marks the return of a buried warrior tradition represented and mourned at the beginning of the novel by Dracula's description of his heritage: 'the warlike days are over. Blood is too precious a thing in these days of dishonourable peace; and the glories of the great races are as a tale that is told' (p. 43). Engaging in battle with Dracula, Van Helsing's vampire-killers reawaken racial memories and myths of blood and honour: Quincey is described as a 'moral viking' and Arthur is compared to Thor as he impales Lucy (p. 225, p. 277). To combat the racial myths associated with the creature originating in the East, myths of northern tribes, myths linked to gothic notions of freedom and strength, are invoked. A warlike paganism is combined with Christianity, a sacralisation of racial myths whose function within an embattled and aggressive cultural and imperialist imagination is starkly emphasised when Van Helsing invokes divine sanction for their project: in God's name they 'go out as the old knights of the Cross' (p. 412). The appeal to past history and romance is not merely invocative of a fictional tradition, but also alludes to the belligerent pursuit of a religious cause, in the Crusades, against the non-Christian peoples of the East. In the context of gothic fiction this seems like a nostalgic appeal to a long-dead world, a disappeared past imagined as noble, strong and purposeful. It is also a return to myths and fictions that try to reinvent a sacred unity for the degenerate 1890s. The return to myth, the invocation of romantic fictions within a gothic fiction, has an uncanny effect on the values of domesticity and patriarchy whose superiority, stability and naturalness are finally affirmed at the close of the novel. These start to seem like myths themselves. Indeed, throughout the novel there are no examples of model families. The only biological parents, Lucy's mother and Arthur's father, die, while other paternal and maternal figures are only surrogates: Hawkins bequeathes his property to Harker and Mina in a fatherly gesture, Van Helsing is a good father to everyone, as Mina is their mother. Dracula is allotted the role of bad father. The absence of family underlines the nostalgia for the family that is literalised by the birth of a child at the end. Structurally inscribed throughout the novel in the paternal and maternal duplicates, the myth is only realised in the closure of the fiction.

The making real of this mythical model of the family demands, for a culture disintegrating without it, blood, expulsion and sacrifice. Family values are restored by the ritual destruction of Dracula and the sacrifice of female sexuality embodied by Lucy, and are vitally monumentalised in the self-sacrificing death of Quincey and his subsequent and nominal immortalisation in the Christian name of the Harkers' son. The romance quest provides the structure of a male fantasy of sacred, immortal power, its values restored in the present by violent, sacrificial energy. The horror embodied by Dracula reawakens the primitive and powerful emotions of his opponents, emotions of attraction and repulsion in which his intimate doubleness is expelled and repeated in another terrible expenditure of energy. Civilisation and domesticity need to retain and channel their buried natural, even barbaric energies, signified in hunter and warrior myths, their spirit, unity, strength and immortality are nourished by myths of their own duplicitous self-image.

Turning the gothic romance into a male quest romance, *Dracula* feeds off prevailing cultural anxieties concerning corruption, sexuality and spirit. For Van Helsing, the penetration of evil mysteries and the redemption of proper identities by means of sacred horror involve clerical and ideological powers. As a scientist and psychic doctor his powers are rational and more than rational, like the world investigated by Hesselius and another popular, secular and yet strangely magical figure, the detective, as exemplified by Arthur Conan Doyle's Sherlock Holmes. The mysteries, terrors and horrors explained by his penetrating mind, endowed with a rationality that seems more than rational, are, though ultimately mundane and deviously criminal, imbued with an aura of the fantastic, spectral and diabolical. *Dracula's* adventurous romance also alludes to the tales of adventure that, from Scott's romances onwards, provide a more popular and exciting alternative to domestic realism. The associations of Dracula with the East are important in this respect. For the East, at the high point of Victorian imperialism, provided many wonderful adventures and strange tales, which, in Kipling's stories about India and, similarly, in Rider Haggard's narratives of Africa, projected the darkness of gothic fears and desires on to other cultures, peoples and places.

8

PHANTOMODERNISMS

The world dominated by its phantasmagorias ... is 'modernity'.
(Walter Benjamin, *The Arcades Project*, p. 26)

Dracula looks back. In conjuring up images of atavism and degeneration as threats to a patriarchal, bourgeois and imperial morality it enacts a sacrificial gesture aimed at the restoration of a very English order of social and family values. This occurs in a modern context of commercial, scientific, social and technological change and innovation, in a novel full of the machines and media of urban modernity: typewriters, phonographs, photographs, telegraphy, an infrastructure of newspapers, guidebooks, commercial and legal records, railway timetables. Fragmentary and with multiple, mediated perspectives, the novel's form seems modern but is itself a sign of a need for a single and unified vision to counteract the cultural threat embodied by the vampire. It engages with the present and looks back. Other versions of fears about changing culture, science, empire and technology look forward. In *The Island of Dr Moreau* (1896), horror is associated with the in-human potential of scientific research and articulated with a perversely Darwinian creation of hybrid creatures. In *The War of the Worlds* (1898), with powerful alien invaders threatening imperialist England, inhumanity comes from outside. Unlike the vampire, who feeds lasciviously on human blood, the aliens inject it. Science fiction marks one important divergence among the many generic shifts and relocations of gothic motifs that occur through the twentieth century, divergences that see gothic shapes redefined in many literary, medial and popular forms.

Technological innovation, scientific, economic and social change shape the progressive but ambivalent forward movement of modernism as an apparently relentless and mechanical force. The pressure to make artistic technique new, to devise adequate ways of presenting an increasingly fluid sense of the world and the self, never fully overcomes the weight of history or tradition, never excises other cultural forms in a flight of high aesthetic vision. Moreover, it never returns, it seems, to a sense of material solidity or secure selfhood in the frequently violent entanglements of humanity and its machines. Like the Vorticists who found artistic and social energy in the forceful conjunction of human and mechanical forms, F.T. Marinetti's Futurist manifesto (1909) appeals to a world of speed, engines and energy, of cars and crashes, accelerating beyond safe and stolid institutions of culture and tradition like museums and galleries. He writes excitedly of 'electric hearts' and 'snorting machines', yet acknowledges a sense of darkness, danger and horror at the heart of cities and industry, referring to the 'infernal stokeholes of great ships' or the 'black spirits which rage in the belly of rogue locomotives' (pp. 3–4). Spirit, violent emotion, body and machine co-exist bringing antitheses into close proximity and moving from the patterns of exclusion and suppression enacted by a Victorian order to a manifestation of disturbing conjunction and incomplete incorporation. Civilisation does not exclude barbaric and savage energies, it reinvents them. The changing configurations of cities, crowds, commodities and consciousness compose a new 'phantasmagoria', the metaphor of the magic lantern from the eighteenth century reactivated by Walter Benjamin to signal the uncertain extent to which the modern world involves a blurring of perception and hallucination, a flux of impressions, realities, machines and media forms, in which both a sense of the solidity of things and security of selves is supplanted by multiple and sometimes monstrous movements that engender apprehension but cannot be easily apprehended. It is as if the uncanny disturbances, spectres and ghosts that once were limited as effects of gothic fictions extend, via other media, into the fabric and shadowy formation of modern life, a kind of 'phantomodernity'.

The diffusion of a sense of ghostliness indicates why there is no new or distinctive generic manifestation of gothic writing at the time of modernism. Though older popular forms of romance and ghost story continued to be produced in the period and newer forms of fantastic and science fiction emerged, separate innovations in fiction are less evident. In part this is because the aesthetic experiments and aspirations of modernism aimed higher and appealed to a cultural elite that had little time for popular and formulaic fiction (though many writers, like D.H. Lawrence, wrote ghost stories). Also, modernist identifications of a very different sense of life, one in which reality, time and consciousness were perceived to be fragmented, transient and in flux, used metaphors of phantom, ghost or spectre as appropriate registers for the everyday instabilities of subjectivity and materiality.

ALL THAT IS SOLID MELTS ON THE SCREEN

Gothic modes and figures assume a distinctive role in one new medium of the time. Many early films took themes, characters, titles and plots from well-known novels and tales. For example, the Selig Polyscope presented a version of *Dr Jekyll and Mr Hyde* in 1908; Edison Studios made a single-reel version of *Frankenstein* in 1910. *The Student of Prague* (1914) brought the double to the screen. Scientists with mesmeric and hypnotic powers, doubles and vampires were the focus of German expressionist films: Robert Wiene's *The Cabinet of Dr Caligari* (1920) and Friedrich Murnau's versions of *Jekyll and Hyde* and *Dracula*, *Der Januskopf* (1920) and *Nosferatu* (1922), which, with their grotesque villains and stylised sets, played on the gloomy artificiality of gothic scenes of terror. The use of strong lighting in Expressionism created stark and looming shadows on screen, presenting a distorted and sometimes grotesque world where spatial dimensions, such as shots from odd angles, produced disorientating effects in which characters and action were subordinated to visual effect. *Caligari* and its sparse geometric sets dislocate reality and perception, a hallucinatory and nightmarish quality appropriate to a film about mesmerism and murder. Film made a gothic literary aesthetic visible as a shadowplay in which light and darkness were its principal motors. It was a medium in which unreal things could happen and unreal beings could exist, where the dead came back to life as moving images. Double exposures and over-exposure enhanced the hallucinatory qualities of cinematic vision; stop-frame editing in which objects could appear and disappear, or split screens in which one figure could appear twice, enabled apparitional effects. These new moving images composed of light and shadow could mesmerise or hypnotise audiences, suggesting a technical magic that not only disturbed perceptions of the external world but also made inner life visible. Shocking or terrifying audiences in realising the unreal, cinema was also seen to present the workings of the desires, demons and suppressed energies of the human psyche on screen. One film from this period offers a particularly striking blend of modern concerns and gothic images. Fritz Lang's *Metropolis* (1926) blends old and new forms and topics together to compose a powerful example of modern gothic. Angelic heroines, tyrannical fathers and sequences of pursuit through underground tunnels and caverns are combined with a mad scientist who creates a robotic heroine; the gloomy city is divided between a class of industrially enslaved workers forced to live a dark impoverished subterranean existence maintaining the machinery powering the city, and the rich who enjoy the luxuriously decadent pleasures of the light and clean world above. The monstrous and inhuman oppression of one class by another is starkly presented in the voracious machines that feed on the labour and life of workers. The film operates against the backdrop of the city's gothic cathedral and the cavernous spaces of a subterranean existence. The manufacture of an automated anti-heroine who is demonically seductive as a sign of the artificiality and deceptiveness of ideological manipulation and the bright modernity of the city above provides templates for future science fiction cinema. Produced in a period when the economic and political systems of Europe were undergoing revolutionary challenges, the dark vision of capitalist modes of production and social reproduction is striking. In contrast, the film's romantic ending, in which love wins out over class, is thin. Combining and reimagining various genres, *Metropolis* is located at a juncture where all sorts of divergences become possible. The film itself, its director and the Expressionist style all offer different trajectories for presenting terror and horror, trajectories which assume generic shapes of their own, from crime and detection ('film noir') to romance, science fiction and the 'horror' genre itself (the name with which cinema moves beyond gothic modes).

In 'The Cinema' (1926), Virginia Woolf notes how film develops a new relationship between eye and brain, image and writing. Cinema presents something that is magical and primitive and monstrous and 'wordless', linking perception and instinct in 'hubble-bubble, swarm, and chaos': it feels like looking 'over the edge of a cauldron in which fragments of all shapes and savours seem to simmer' (p. 268). Though rich in potential, cinematic forms present 'life as it is when we have no part in it' and deliver a beauty that is inhuman, that 'will flourish whether we behold it or not' (p. 269). Woolf notes how, during a technical error in a performance of *Dr Caligari*, a 'shadow shaped like a tadpole' moved across the screen: 'for a moment it seemed to embody some monstrous, diseased imagination of the lunatic's brain' (p. 270). This inhuman tendency of media to depart from recognisably human dimensions was also a concern for Franz Kafka. His writings vacillate between horrors of individual alienation and grotesquely distorted images of everyday family and social life. In 'Metamorphosis' (1916) a young man awakes to find he has become an insect. An image of self-loathing, it also serves, in the domestic context in which it is situated, as a projection of the anxieties regarding family structure and feeling. In *The Trial* (1925) individual guilt is inscribed throughout social and legal systems as a mysterious, arbitrary and impenetrable condition as the hero, Josef K., is lost in a bewildering labyrinth of bureaucracy and indifference. The unapproachable and unfathomable nature of law and authority is presented, in *The Castle* (1926), as a looming impenetrable edifice of terror. For Kafka, the modern world and its system of communications seem to threaten a sense of humanity, his letters maintaining that ghosts inhabit all technical forms and media, from writing to telegraphs, telephones and radios, feeding on human emotions and natural communication: 'the ghosts won't starve, but we will perish' (*Letters*, p. 229). The 'gothic' element of technology and media that Woolf and Kafka notice at the start of the twentieth century involves an extension of the alienation, separation and distortion of the human world.

GHOSTWRITING

A sense of spectrality, associated with a loss of substance and stability, ranges across modern modes of communication, perception, consciousness and life to disturb the imagined security of ideas of human culture and civilisation. Gothic reflections are evident in some of the major writing of the period. Joseph Conrad's *Heart of Darkness* (1902) questions the uncomplicated imperialism of adventure stories, like those popularised by H. Rider Haggard, that reinforce constructions of the savagery and otherness of Africa's 'dark continent'. In Conrad's frame narrative of a journey in search of a colonial trader, Kurtz, who has become immersed in the environment he was supposed to be exploiting, the encounter between white Western powers and black Africa blurs distinctions between morality and corruption, civilisation and savagery, right and wrong to offer a horrified glimpse of darkness within late Victorian society and values. Told aboard a boat floating in the Thames estuary, the story of a journey upriver in the Congo never rests on solid ground or moves in a progressive direction. Its language moves through self-referential frames and misty images to encounter a primordial and impenetrable landscape that dwarfs human attempts to master it. The 'dark faced and pensive forest' reduces all humans to ghostly figures, from the 'black shadows of disease and starvation' on the land to 'phantoms' gliding past on a riverboat (p. 24, p. 51). Even the object of the quest, Kurtz, is reduced to a phantom, only his crazed eyes, voice and mind possessing the intensity his exhausted body lacks. The overriding sense of uncertainty and futility is underlined by the failure to grasp the meaning of

Kurtz's now famous words: 'the horror, the horror'. More than a horror of African otherness or colonial cruelty, the darkness into which the story journeys locates the darkness where it begins and ends: on the edge of that 'monstrous town', London, and on the river that 'seemed to lead into the heart of an immense darkness' (p. 7, p. 111).

The horror, in *Heart of Darkness*, becomes political terror in *The Secret Agent* (1907), the locus of fear having shifted from colonial outposts to the centre of the British empire. The London of *The Secret Agent* is dark and labyrinthine, its areas of industrial production and working-class housing are populated by anarchists and political activists, émigrés from European states engaged in plots and conspiracies. Political, economic and technological transformation was not always seen as progress. A concern with the decline of cultural and aesthetic values haunted much of the poetry that strove to create innovations in literary form adequate to maintaining a relationship with great writing of the past and appreciating the movement of life and consciousness in the urban present. Ezra Pound's long reflection on art and the artist, 'Hugh Selwyn Mauberley' (1920), considers a degraded civilisation and uses the metaphor of the phantasmagoria to suggest how his poetic double's work delivers optical and perceptual illusion rather than new artistic vision. In the interplay of voices, media and urban environments of T.S. Eliot's poetry, phantasmagoria offer an image of a fragmented, transient, alienating and unreal world. The speaker of 'Love Song of J. Alfred Prufrock' (1920), caught up in novels, banal consumption and empty socialising, finds his attempt to discern meaning replaced by a 'magic lantern' throwing nerve patterns on a screen (l. 105); London in 'The Wasteland' (1922) is often dark, foggy and decayed, pictured as a modern hell of desolate spaces, material desires and degradation punctuated by multiple voices in different locations, songs from public houses, accents of fallen women and aging men, platitudes of salons. Darkness is physical and phantasmatic, haunting minds as much as actual spaces. James Joyce's Dublin, too, is traversed by many fragments of a changing culture, its living rooms, schoolrooms, chapels and brothels resonating with the diverse discourses of patriarchy, nationalism, Catholicism

and aestheticism, which impinge on a developing artistic consciousness. Among the different modes composing *The Portrait of
the Artist as a Young Man* (1916) there are moments, at school,
in the city and at university, when phantoms and darkness come
to the fore.

Modernism's sense of consciousness is considered fleeting; its
sense of time and life is accelerated. Scientific ideas of relativity
transform appreciations of materiality and substance; thought and
perception become flux, a 'stream of consciousness'; 'civilised' self
is pressured by returns of sexual energies from the unconscious.
Atomistic and transient relationships between language, life,
perception, consciousness and memory, the ghostly sense of
modernity, are suggested throughout Virginia Woolf's writing.
In 'The Mark on the Wall' (1921), a stream of consciousness
experiment, stable frameworks for understanding life through a
stable patriarchal knowledge become suspect and ghostly, 'the
masculine point of view' becoming 'half a phantom' (p. 80). In
'Street Haunting' (1930), a routine trip to buy a pencil turns into
an exciting threshold experience of modern urban spaces and
commodities, the half-light of streetlamps and storefronts illuminating the half-life of evanescent existence. If modern life is
haunted, its phantoms are not only figures of memory, guilt or
indebtedness that return from the past, they are figures, fragmentary, insubstantial, fleeting, for the present's dislocation in
time, space and consciousness from itself. Haunted houses, in this
context, are not only the settings of traditional ghost narratives,
but designate the newly phantasmatic locations of modern life,
consciousness and the city. Woolf's short story, 'A Haunted
House' (1921), both acknowledges an entire tradition of haunting
and, highly poetically, sketches its contemporary significance.
The form is pared down to the minimum; it leaves almost everything to the reader in the manner that Woolf found most effective in Henry James' ghost stories (1921), observing how his
ghosts 'have nothing in common with the violent old ghosts –
the blood-stained sea captains, the white horses, the headless
ladies of dark lanes and windy commons. They have their origin
within us. They are present whenever the significant overflows
our powers of expressing it; whenever the ordinary appears tinged

by the strange' (p. 323). In Woolf's story, there is a house, a 'ghostly couple', heard but unseen, wandering through it as if searching for something; a figure reading, pencil in hand; movement through rooms, sounds within and without, curtains drawing, doors shutting, wind blowing, birds and trees; an outside reflected on windows, apples, roses; gardens and sunlight; and the voices of ghosts (pp. 116–18). Nothing is specified of the where, when and who of the story, there is no geographical or historical location of the house nor are the identities of past and present tenants announced. What is imagined and what is real are confounded: are actual ghost voices heard or are they misperceived noises in the house? Is there some romantic tale sketched in the ghostly couple's movements or is it a projection by the current occupants? What are the treasures, losses and joys mentioned in their search? Setting and mystery, while acknowledging traditional romantic formulas, are extended; the vagueness and ambiguity of the telling suggests multiple interpretations and links haunting to the narrating consciousness of the story and to the process of reading in which sense and meaning remain elusive.

With modernism, the minimum of form, rather than an excess of formula, constitutes the basis for a powerful re-enactment and expansion of the uncanny. When the figures and tropes traditionally located in specific genres and relegated to subordinate dimensions (the unconscious; subterranean spaces; wildernesses) move into general and normal usage or when everyday reality seems to be suffused with the strangeness previously located outside mundane existence, then the question of the uncanny as a return of the repressed has to be rethought. How does one make the uncanny uncanny again? This is addressed in the *Uncanny Stories* (1923) of May Sinclair, a prolific novelist, critic and philosopher interested in theories of spiritualism and psychoanalysis. Her stories acknowledge the shift in the location and significance of ghosts, and make attempts to recover the uncanny. If the uncanny has been absorbed into everyday life and consciousness or if its generic patterns have become too familiar, how does one recapture the disturbing effects it once provoked? While Sinclair's tales affirm uncertain boundaries between material and ghostly planes of existence, her tales do not rest on separations between matter and spirit, hallucination, disturbed consciousness or supernatural power but, with some (pseudo) scientific under-pinning, they move beyond the extant frames of contemporary reality onto more palpable but immaterial dimensions in which distinctions are confounded. 'The Flaw in the Crystal' hovers between spiritual powers of an empath and medium, sustaining late nineteenth-century interests in psychical research, and sug-gestions of desire and sexual impropriety. Able to influence emo-tional states of others, she finds herself caught between two men, one married, one engaged. Her ability to help their nervous con-ditions has contrary effects on her own state of mind. With one of the men she feels benevolent and positive, open to the flux and energy of vibrant intensities; with the other, her experience is of malignancy and danger, being consumed by darkness. In 'Nature of the Evidence' an unnamed narrator berates the main character, a lawyer with an utterly rational and moral Victorian outlook, as a 'bigoted materialist' who is unable to credit that consciousness extends beyond corporeal existence (p. 114). When his wife dies, he remarries but is unable to consummate the relationship because his first wife, in disembodied form, interrupts every attempt at coupling. He is 'shocked', not by the 'phantasm' of his first wife, but by the 'uncanny and unnatural thing' that his second wife appears to be: wearing a diaphanous white night-gown it seems the latter is both too spectral and too fleshly (p. 120). They divorce, with the lawyer advocating the benefits – and pleasures – of 'discarnate passion', a passion that touches 'all points of being' (p. 122). Sexuality and the world of spirits are not, in this strange twist, opposed or contradictory. With 'The Victim' Sinclair tackles another traditional theme of murder and its spectral consequences. A servant kills his master, having pre-pared his act with the obsessive precision of one of Poe's villains. Such is the perfection of his execution that he remains free of suspicion. His master, of course, returns as a ghost, setting off a chain of appropriate thoughts and feelings in the murderer. When he returns again, curiously 'clear and solid' in form, he asserts that he is 'more natural and real' than ever before (p. 156). He does not, as one might expect, demand vengeance but forgives his killer and even thanks him! Death was the best thing that could have happened to him, a release from the limitations of a frail and sick body and into an exquisite realm of meta-physical continuity in a universe of energies and powers beyond imagination. Here Sinclair's new sense of the uncanny affirms not a disturbance of existing borders of a Victorian idea of reality, but imagines their transformation into something even weirder.

SOUTHERN GOTHIC

Modernism and ghosts conjoined in the innovative fictions composed in the USA in the first half of the twentieth century. Fragmented narratives and consciousness, shifting perspectives and a sense of strangeness emerge in Southern gothic's encounters with modernisation and cultural change. Decaying traditions are manifested in old buildings; the contours of familiar environments appear increasingly strange; and ghosts abound. Often located in houses – buildings that embody family lines in the manner established by Poe and Hawthorne – ghosts draw out a pervasive sense of distortion and mystery and, oddly amid the brightness and heat of the landscape, emphasise desolation and occasionally menacing and unresolved violence. The disjointed perspectives of William Faulkner's, Flannery O'Connor's and Carson McCullers' fictions disclose a grotesque and absurd world seen through the eyes of misfits, freaks and malcontents, a world of quiet yet desperate haunting. Southern gothic is barely gothic in any European sense. Even Poe's terrors and horrors seem extreme in respect of the gently haunted reality of class, racial and familial tensions, of spectres marking displacements of cultural status and memory, of consciousness dispersed in the haze of heat and dust. Changes in American modernity, its speed and urbanisation shadowing a world whose social fabric unravels in the shade of porches and long-gone family dramas, tilt and topple the axis of a way of life that seems to have forgotten how to die.

Southern gothic evinces strange sensitivities to generic and cultural history. Attentive to the romance and gothic modes at the heart of American culture, it acknowledges how romance is also social and political. Encapsulated in the manners, customs and character of the Southern gentleman that provided the ornate façade of a, now fading, economic prosperity based on agricultural property and slavery, Southern gothic ghosts recall values of family honour and shame, duty, corruption and violence in a modern present of factories, automobiles, commodities and civil freedoms. In contrast to the pattern of US fiction, however, history (including identification with European aristocratic culture) remains more visible in the South; the darkness projected onto frontier spaces or onto slaves is closer to the surface of everyday life and thus fear, guilt, transgression remain close at hand, to possess the mind, turning inwards. Where the North might have more readily embraced reason, modernity and democracy, the heritage of the South, tied to agriculture and a slave economy that it fought to preserve, follows a different trajectory.

Recollecting the mid-nineteenth century, Mark Twain's critical comments on Southern life and character focus on customs and manners drawn from a European heritage (French and Spanish as much as English) that persist in romantic ideas, festivals and architecture. Infected by 'Sir Walter Scott disease', Southern character clings on to ideas of gallantry, gentlemanly conduct, patriarchal patronage of women, family honour and history, good manners, inflated eloquence and 'reverence for rank and caste' in which every man furnished himself with the title of Judge, Major, Colonel or General (pp. 218–19). Acknowledging the pretensions of romance at a time when the Confederacy was more than a memory pressing upon defeated descendants, Twain's version of the South does not pursue the way that martial affiliations were more than affectation. Its other side is a world of battle, violence and slavery. Writing years later (1935) and coining the phrase 'Southern gothic school', the popular southern novelist Ellen Glasgow is similarly attentive to the double-edged nature of romance. Her criticism of the new style of fiction produced by Faulkner attacks 'aimless violence' and professional rebelliousness and is not ashamed to recall the Confederate dead or appeal to gentility and character. 'We remain incurably romantic', she asserts, going on to note that only 'a puff of smoke' separates the 'fabulous Southern hero' and 'tender dreams' from the 'fabulous Southern monster' and 'fantastic nightmares'. Acknowledging the importance of gothic – 'as gothic' – in Southern fiction and recognising the importance of romance's doubled aspect, Glasgow objects to Faulkner's 'pseudo-realism', to its promotion of decay, and to its single 'vast, disordered sensibility'. There is a wider, and ironic, complaint about the state of fiction: 'is the whole tedious mass production of degeneracy in our fiction – the current literary gospel of futility and despair – merely a single symptom of the neuroses inflicted on its slaves by the conquering dynamo?' (pp. 3–4). Modern fiction is associated with the domination of Northern industry and mass culture, 'slavery' meaning the aping of its fallen sensibility, aesthetic mores, existential attitudes and psychological disorders. The description of literary subservience as 'slavery' is ill-considered. Yet it does acknowledge that a very real and violent spectre accompanies the battlefields, gentility, heroes, dreams, nightmares and monsters of Southern romance: the economic, social and political subordination of a whole group of people.

The proximity of hero and monster, dream and nightmare is very much part of the indissociable relation between opposites that characterises Southern fiction. 'Good and evil appear joined in every culture at the spine', notes Flannery O'Connor, indicating the extent to which antitheses inter-relate in Southern fiction (p. 856). Re-examining romance and realism, and objecting to terms like 'the School of Southern Degeneracy', Flannery O'Connor observes that the 'tradition of the dark and divisive romance-novel has combined with the comic grotesque tradition'. 'Grotesque' articulates a technical and topical link between fiction and reality in which unusual experience is brought to ordinary attention: 'strange skips and gaps' allow mystery, and wildly combine discrepant elements like violence and comedy. Southern fiction introduces 'distortion' and a new vision altering normal perspective: 'seeing near things with their extensions of meaning and thus seeing far things close up'. Through this approach characters are 'forced out', beyond themselves to 'carry an invisible burden' and 'fix us with eyes that remind us that we all bear some heavy responsibility whose nature we have forgotten' and, shedding comic aspect, manifest a 'reproach' that is 'not merely eccentricity' (p. 860). In times of displacement (of loss of values and traditions), grotesque fiction demands grotesque characters. The penchant of Southern writing for ghosts, monsters and freaks is related to its sense of distortion, and the recognition of freakishness involves a 'conception of the whole man' and becomes 'a figure for our essential displacement'. Though related to the isolated and alienated outsider, the freak is, ironically, more human. The former, who also populates Southern fiction, is 'rootless' and 'can go anywhere' while belonging 'nowhere': 'being alien to nothing, he ends up being alienated from any kind of community based on common tastes and interests. The borders of his country are the sides of his skull' (p. 856). Bearing the weight of belonging to a community and a heritage that has gone or suffering the isolation and psychological consequences of having no place to go, the freak and the outsider reflect the very distortion of which they are composed.

Carson McCullers' *The Heart is a Lonely Hunter* (1940) offers a poignant view of freaks and outsiders living in a southern mill city. Her characters – two mutes (one sent early in the novel to an asylum), a tomboy, a bartender, a mechanic and an African-American doctor – all lead isolated lives punctuated by infrequent social gatherings. When the mute, who serves as an unacknowledged hub of humane and social bonds, dies, the gently grotesque account of alienation opens up briefly to the distortion that haunts all their lives. After the funeral the bartender reflects on the elevation and terror of the occasion. He glimpses his face askew and asymmetrical in the bar-room mirror, reflecting bifurcated emotions: one eye looks to the past while the other, larger and wider, stares 'into a future of blackness, error and ruin'. Between 'radiance and darkness', 'bitter irony and faith', his position is grotesque and true (p. 312). *The Ballad of the Sad Café* (1943), a novella about the curious communal spirit fostered in a run-down town by a tall, strong and masculine woman and a sickly hunchbacked dwarf, begins with a similarly telling image of distortion. The building once housing the café, though large, is boarded up and leans as though it is about to collapse; it appears cracked, an optical effect caused by only half of the front having been painted. Its deserted appearance is another illusion. At times a hand will open the shutter on the one clear window and a face will look down, 'like the terrible dim faces known in dreams –

sexless and white, with two gray crossed eyes which are turned inward so sharply that they seem to be exchanging with each other one long and secret gaze of grief (p. 3). Yoking various aspects of the grotesque, both face and building draw out the effects of distortion to include the café's geometry, its inhabitant's ghostly, nightmarish face and the manner in which it turns on itself in sorrow. That face also looks out on the town.

Flannery O'Connor's characters, too, engender effects of distortion. The first encounter with the outsider-hero of *Wise Blood* (1952) occurs on a train, returning from four years of active service as an infantryman abroad. He wears a new shiny bright blue suit and carries a broad-brimmed black hat. He is repeatedly mistaken for a preacher, like his grandfather. But, belonging nowhere since his family are dead and their rural home is a 'skeleton', he is heading for a fictional modern city with its electric lights and advertisements, museums, cinemas, boarding houses and whores in order to start afresh. He remains haunted by a strong evangelical upbringing: the figure of Jesus – his preacher-grandfather's Christ – moves 'from tree to tree in the back of his mind, a wild ragged figure motioning him to turn around and come off into the dark where he was not sure of his footing, where he might be walking on the water and not know it and then suddenly, know it and drown' (p. 13). Disturbing and comic, almost a trickster, Jesus is a figure that leads him astray. Setting out to purge his past and its grand-paternal shadows, he begins, perversely, to preach his own gospel: the 'Church without Christ' proclaims the non-existence of Jesus and denounces belief based on blasphemy, sin, miracles, redemption and hypocrisy. His evacuation of religion, of content, faith or belief, parallels in distorted fashion the effects of both the urban context (its sexual licence, cinemas and celebrity-star actors in ape suits) and the other gospels touted on the streets. Obsessed by a preacher who is supposed to have blinded himself for the Lord, he discovers him to be sighted and already an imposter. Another preacher, dressed in the same bright blue suit is employed by a con-man to proclaim the 'Holy Church of Christ without Christ'. Re-doubling fraudulence through blatant mimicry, this imposter is brutally crushed under the wheels of his automobile. With nothing left to do, this outsider from nowhere blinds himself with a bucket of quicklime to live out the rest of his days in self-inflicted discomfort.

Spectres abound in Southern gothic fiction. In Faulkner's *Light in August* (1932), a middle-aged woman who lives, as she has done her entire life, in an old house outside an isolated town is still considered a 'foreigner'. Her family were Yankees from the North, her father and brother killed sixty years before by former local slave owner: 'the descendants of both in their relationship to one another ghosts, with between them the phantom of the old spilled blood and the horror and anger and fear' (p. 37). Ghosts articulate past and present. The spilled blood they recall threatens to spill some more. The first pages of Faulkner's *Absalom, Absalom!* (1936) have 'garrulous, outraged, baffled ghosts', 'ghosts which had refused to lie still', 'old ghost-times', 'stubborn backlooking ghosts', ladies made into ghosts, and 'the invoked ghost of a man whom she could neither forgive nor revenge herself upon'. The novel begins in a dark, dusty, hot airless room on a 'dead September afternoon' in the South with an old lady dressed in black, her vanishing ghostly voice haunted by the ghosts of other voices and fading among the spectral sounds within and without the 'dim coffin-smelling gloom' (pp. 5–6). Her interlocutor and the book's central character, his mind drifting from her words to recollections and associations of his own, is a student closely tied to the complicated, painful family history she relates, and is already familiar with the many names she mentions. But the story of a man, repeatedly described as a 'demon', who bursts into the small town with a band of slaves and a French architect intent on establishing himself with all the accoutrements of a Southern gentleman (estates, mansion, wife and heirs), unravels as a complicated history of secret marriages and offspring, possible incest, spilled blood, and in civil war. Secrets and violent consequences are revealed, the past still living, like one character, locked in the decaying family mansion's attic. At the end it burns down, like the mansion itself. Stories are told, and told again from different perspectives and in different locations. A sense of ghostliness is enhanced by the modernist mode of narration: its stream of consciousness, temporal movements and spatial shifts drift between various figures in reported speech and thought and loose associations. As an entangled family history unravels and entwines, memories are recollected in the present, with an assortment of new observations, or directly relayed as if the past had returned to life. Recapitulations of and commentaries on events are subsequently made by university roommates at another time and in the North. Whereas ghostliness cushions the return of shocking pasts in *Absalom, Absalom!*, the more sensational *Sanctuary* (1931) brings violence and horror to the fore. Here a 'gaunt ruin', 'lightless, desolate and profound', is not inhabited by broken Southern gentility but by a group of bootleggers whose crimes are more mundane yet no less horrific (p. 18). Their leader, whose villainy is described as a 'presence in black and nameless threat' (p. 96), murders one of his gang and rapes a young middle-class white woman before taking her to a brothel in a neighbouring city. Another gang member, too scared to tell the truth, is convicted of both crimes while the woman, traumatised by abuse and urban corruption, is returned to her father. From the wilderness of a decaying rural setting to the moral darkness of urban corruption, the novel tracks a new form of evil and degeneration.

Women in Faulkner's fiction, as decorous ladies and bearers of lineages, abused wives and daughters, long-suffering domestic slaves, are more than figures of idealisation for whom the manners, charm and eloquence of gentlemen are enacted. They bear witness to, and feel the brunt of, transformation and decline. 'A Rose for Emily' (1930) follows this mode. The life of its main female character is lived out under a powerful paternal shadow. The story begins with her death, an event in the community that displays the dusty residues of Southern character: old men pay respect to a 'fallen monument' and women curiously inspect the decayed house shut to society for years (Baldick, *Gothic Tales*, p. 322). The house, her only legacy, embodies decline as a physical reminder of paternal power over her, a place where, whip in hand, he would see off suitors while she, 'a slender figure in white', already almost a ghost, remained behind (p. 325). Her older physical form sees her 'small and spare' skeleton become fat and dressed in black. The contrast of pale frame and excessive flesh makes her appear 'bloated' like a long-drowned body (p. 323). Slender whiteness and obscene corpulence, both associated with death, with mortified excesses of spirit and body, suggest a symptomatic counter-reaction to the extreme restraint of female desire and conjure up a grotesque image of Southern values. It is an aspect – distorted and distorting – that later and horrifically reappears. Stubbornly she holds to the values of her father, refusing to pay taxes on the basis of an old, undocumented gentleman's agreement with a long-dead city elder. The council are unable to deal with a nasty smell from her house on similar archaic grounds, unable to 'accuse a lady to her face of smelling bad' (p. 324). Articulating old and new times, the smell relates to the second major event in her life, her relationship with a Northerner and foreman for the company providing the community with the conveniences of modern, organised life: paved sidewalks. They begin a courtship that causes gossip to circulate, first about marriage and then of scandal when he suddenly disappears. She spends the rest of her life shut away, sometimes glimpsed sitting at night in an upper window 'like the carven torso of an idol in a niche' (p. 329). The truth is more horrific, but again an effect of the 'virulent and furious' quality of paternal values. After she has died a bedroom is discovered still decorated as a bridal chamber. Its dust-covered contents include her fiancé's clothes and possessions; his remains lie, rotted, on the bridal bed in manner that indicates they had once been 'in the attitude of an embrace' (p. 330). What is perhaps more shocking than the discovery that she had killed and kept his corpse as a permanent reminder of marriage in death if not in love is the small indentation on the other pillow and a strand of her grey hair. She continued, for forty years, to lie in a bridal tomb enduring the malodorous decay of flesh, with the corpse of her lover on a bier of mortified desire! It suggests that his death is more than a matter of honour slighted and insult avenged, but an image of love preserved in death, or of the twisted ideals of romance being played out through associations between marriage, sexuality, death in a grotesque and horrifying kind of necrophilia. With its images of decline and displacement, its distorted perspective interweaving house, body, family and paternal honour with the clash of romantic South and modern North, and with its disturbing associations and climax, the story condenses the features that give Southern writing its distinctive gothic form.

PULP MODERNISMS

While modernism brings gothic forms into closer contact with literary ghosts and new popular generic and medial diffusions refract them through the lenses of fantasy, horror, romance and science fiction, not everything is change and innovation. The ghost tales of M.R. James display a deliberate reluctance to engage with anything suggestive of modernity. The horrors that appear, usually unexplained and supernatural, are linked to the distant past, to ancient lore and rites. Their revenance makes it clear that there is more to life and the universe than discoveries being made in the present. James' stories involve mostly unmarried, middle-aged and male collectors, academics, historians, researchers of archaeological, occult and mythological writings, relics and rituals who inhabit college rooms, museums, libraries and isolated archives. Even before strange events occur, their world is already dusty and obscure, haunted by histories and texts whose import is difficult to divine. With an antiquarian atmosphere and a world already isolated from everyday reality, supernatural disruptions impinge in a limited fashion. 'The Mezzotint' (1904) tells of an old engraving of a country house that changes at regular intervals to show a dark figure crawling steadily towards the building with malicious intent. When the house is identified an old tale of injustice and child-murder confirms the story told by the magically moving image. In 'Count Magnus' (1904) a writer travels to an estate in Denmark to investigate the obscure history of its eponymous villain: he finds a mausoleum and sarcophagus with intricate carvings, including images of a fleeing man being pursued by a monstrous shape. His return trip to England is fraught with paranoia and culminates in his sudden death. In 'Oh, Whistle, And I'll Come to You, My Lad' (1904), an academic with no time for ideas of the supernatural finds an ancient bronze whistle with Latin inscriptions on it while on a quiet golfing holiday. He blows it, and later is attacked by an invisible shape draped in sheets. Saved by a friend, he leaves. There is little explanation and no rationalisation. Like the pursuers in dark cloaks or hideous barely human forms, the attacker is just another of James' strangers in the night.

Understated and gently suggestive of terror in stories that detail brief incursions of one world upon another, James' use of an antiquarian gothic atmosphere of old buildings and spaces sustains an arcane sense of supernaturalism. The mystical world of occult lore, popular in the nineteenth century with writers like Bulwer-Lytton and Machen, develops in two directions that, like the gothic, either rationalise or mythologise occult powers. Algernon Blackwood, in 'Ancient Sorceries' (1908), does the former. A story of an English tourist's visit to a sleepy French village whose population are really witches, turning into cats on their sabbath, its events are explained by the psychic doctor, John Silence, to whom the case is related, as an effect of ancestral memory, since the tourist's family once lived in the place. W.W. Jacobs' 'The Monkey's Paw' (1912) offers a kind of cautionary tale with a background in which colonial fantasies of Indian curses return to haunt an English family. In *The House on the Borderland* (1908), William Hope Hodgson moves from gothic settings like ruinous houses in isolated countrysides to take horror into fantastic otherworldly dimensions: beneath the house great underground chasms are populated by hideous, alien creatures able to cross between worlds. In Mervyn Peake's fantastic Gormenghast trilogy – *Titus Groan* (1946), *Gormenghast* (1950) and *Titus Alone* (1959) – the gothic forms, like the castle and its lord, and a Dickensian gothic colouring of industrial and pedagogical horrors, counter-balance fantasy with a grotesque glance at the nightmares of the twentieth century.

Combining European and US gothic traditions with disturbing elements of fantasy, recurrent moments of violent horror and extensive scientific detail, the 'weird fiction' of H.P. Lovecraft occupies a key crossing-point of the different generic forms that develop beyond gothic forms in popular fiction of the twentieth century: horror, fantasy and science fiction. Very much aware of the gothic genre, many of Lovecraft's stories are set amid older towns or isolated farms, forests and mountains of New England

and Massachusetts, involve archaic rites, old manuscripts and occult rituals, and disclose ancestral secrets, sometimes to do with diabolical experimentation and revolting cross-species breeding. Gothic forms and effects are too limiting for Lovecraft's mode of writing. His essay on 'Supernatural Horror in Literature', written in 1927, notes how Walpole's first gothic story constitutes the foundation of the literary horror story, although he finds its supernaturalism 'unconvincing and mediocre' and – crucially – 'altogether devoid of the true cosmic horror which makes weird literature' (p. 1,048). Cosmic horror stems from a dread of 'outer, unknown forces', material, alien powers exceeding human experience and the physical laws of nature, space and time. These 'laws' are the boundaries weird fiction crosses as it brings out 'hidden and fathomless worlds of strange life' that expose the horror, futility and insignificance of human existence when faced with the 'assaults of chaos and the daemons of unplumbed space' (pp. 1,043). Stories that begin in gothic guise escalate into fantastic and extreme horrors: secret witchcraft rituals let loose a gigantic monster with footprints the size of tree trunks ('The Dunwich Horror', 1928); strange noises in a New England Priory lead to an underground city in which creatures feed on human flesh ('Rats in the Walls', 1924); medical experiments reanimating corpses lead to a host of tortured dead souls returning to wreak revenge ('Herbert West – Reanimator', 1922). Modes converge: seventeenth-century witchcraft delivers, via dream-like delirium, the same multidimensional knowledge as advanced mathematics and physics ('Dreams in the Witch House', 1933); quiet Vermont communities notice strange pink hybrid bodies in streams and ditches, aliens able to fly through space ('Whisperer in the Darkness', 1930). In its portrayal of cults, relics, a re-emergent island city and monstrous alien creatures, 'The Call of the Chthulu' (1928) sketches an entire mythology of earth's pre-historic colonisation which is pursued, in 'At the Mountains of Madness' (1936), with Antarctic explorers uncovering an enormous alien civilisation and life hidden amid ice and snow. Fantasy, science and gothic fictions, along with folklore, mythology and occult knowledge, all conspire to tell the same, horrifying story in Lovecraft: humans are both insignificant in a very material and extremely dangerous cosmos and are barely able to imagine the multiple dimensions of space and time or the beings and possibilities they contain. It is an inhuman cosmos, for sure, but one furnished with extensive material powers and energies rather than supernatural or spiritual or phantasmatic forces.

Little of a gothic mode is left after cosmic horror has taken hold. In popular terms, the genre that develops the long engagement of gothic writing with questions of gender, a genre marketed in the USA as 'modern gothic', is the romance. Daphne du Maurier's *Rebecca* (1938), drawing on earlier romance patterns, notably those of Radcliffe's writing and *Jane Eyre*, provides one of the key templates. Rebecca begins with a naïve, young, impoverished heroine falling for an older, reserved and wounded, widowed man. They marry quickly and return to his impressive ancestral home on the Cornish coast. There, and uncomfortable with class customs and expectations, she has to deal with the legacy of his first, highly accomplished, wife, and the revelation of disturbing secrets. Self-consciously attentive to romance formulas in its retrospective narration and in comments in the text by bride and groom, the novel also engages with the power of social form and the expectations and anxieties it engenders; the spectre condensing these anxieties and turning romance into psychomachia between a living wife's self-image and the reputation of a dead wife is Rebecca, the novel's eponymous heroine and villain.

Enchanted by the ancestral home at which she arrives as the new mistress, the novel's unnamed female narrator finds her social discomfort to be an increasing problem when compared to the all-too evident capacities and qualities of her predecessor. Rebecca, whose name, initials, monogram or signature are everywhere, whose exquisite taste is imprinted throughout the house's decoration and furnishing, whose charm, wit, beauty, grace have enchanted everyone she has met. Though dead, Rebecca's power appears as strong as ever, a spectral presence that oppresses the heroine with constant reminders of her own inadequacy. The feeling of being an interloper in what is now her own home intensifies, exacerbated by a malicious housekeeper who is also the self-appointed keeper of Rebecca's flame. Internalised as a figure of self-reproach, self-doubt

and negative comparison that comes from imagining the judgement of others, Rebecca becomes a succubus draining life and sense
of self from the living wife: in Rebecca's old room, which has been
preserved in her memory, the heroine looks in the dressing-table
mirror to observe 'how white and thin my face looked in the glass,
my hair hanging lank and straight' (p. 133). Under the phantom
power of other Mrs de Winter, the unnamed heroine is reduced to
ghostliness.

Although constantly repeating names ('de Winter' and 'Manderley' are, after 'Rebecca', most frequently mentioned) and
thereby suggesting a social and domestic world ordered by masculine predominance, the novel does not simply locate power
among men. Though revealed to be a wife murderer, the husband
is not, however, directly presented as an agent of persecution,
oppression and mental torture. Indeed, since this is a romance,
the heroine's main concern is that he never loved his first wife.
The dynamic of oppression is experienced at the hands, or rather
under the eyes, of women: Lady Cowan, the grandmother, and,
above all, Mrs Danvers bring a feminised critical gaze to the fore.
It is powerfully, and painfully, internalised by the heroine and
associated with all the signs of Rebecca's superiority. A male
world of professions and institutions, marriage and the law most
obviously are rendered fragile by the excesses of Rebecca's life.
Her strength, sense of liberation and sexual ferocity make her
monstrous; her selfishness, callousness or immorality lead beyond
the prescribed, subordinate place allotted to women. However,
what is worse, is the way she performs perfectly in the idealised
role of woman (as wife, hostess, beauty), to the extent that, flagrantly exceeding that role, she treats social forms and rules as
nothing but a masquerade, like the annual ball that made Manderley so famous. Hence Rebecca herself is already double: angel
and monster, she embraces both extremes of conventional femininity and displays them as no more than conventions, empty
superficial forms, effects of style and appearance, like portraits,
dresses and social demeanour. If the heroine mirrors Rebecca at all
in terms of femininity and its doubles, it is as an image of the
disturbing emptiness of social forms that Rebecca's masquerade
reveals: she has been reduced to a ghostly state signifying that she

has almost no substance or identity of her own. Manderley, too, already a ruin from the start of the narrative, is another 'empty shell' (p. 3). Like Rebecca, who recreated the family house as an image of social status, class comfort and English heritage, Manderley is another romantic fiction that is reduced to nothing but a dream, pushed aside by a culture being transformed by mass production and political change. The novel appeared in 1938, on the brink of another World War.

9

CONSUMING MONSTERS

Our monsters are all manic autists. As products of a chimerical combination (even where this is genetic), deprived of hereditary otherness, afflicted with hereditary sterility, they have no other destiny than desperately to seek out an otherness by eliminating all the Others one by one (whereas 'vertical' madness suffered, by contrast, from a dizzying excess of otherness). The problem of Frankenstein, for example, is that he has no Other and craves otherness.

(Jean Baudrillard, *The Illusion of the End*, p. 109)

In the wake of the global social, political and economic reconstructions that followed the destruction of World War II, and in the face of the terrors and horrors accompanying the emergence of a new world order, gothic monsters seemed neither adequate nor useful figures. Yet, they proliferated in and across popular forms, genres and media, old shapes awakening fears or assuming new significance in screening off unbearable horrors. They reiterated shocks to anaesthetise or stimulate excesses of feeling in a culture numbed with repetition; provided distractions from realities and histories; or constructed images of freedom and possibility attainable through acts of subversion or transgression. There were many sources of terror: space exploration, state power, nuclear and Communist threats; scientific discoveries in technology, medicine, cybernetics, genetics; corporate capitalism's freedoms, consumption and exploitation; post-colonial and anti-imperialist democratic and national freedom movements; civil challenges to oppressive social and sexual norms. Global political and economic realignment, cultural, familial and individual transformation, biotechnological research all changed the categories establishing value, identity and meaning. They mounted a challenge to those rational, moral and ideological frameworks which, in modernity, had shaped the world: freedoms, anxieties, monstrosities associated with otherness, power, bodies, sexuality. Genres such as horror, science fiction, fantasy and romance now overlap in their registration of mutations; television, comics, cartoons, music and computer games absorb and develop techniques for the production and screening of terrors and anxieties. As social hierarchies are challenged, so are the aesthetic categories that supported them; judgement is liberated into a range of partial, political and personal interpretations often linked to freedoms of the market or the choices it demands. High art and popular culture collide in an aesthetic context in which personal taste and consumption come to the fore. Transformation is experienced ambivalently, even doubly (good and evil; promise and threat; progress and retrogression; fear and desire), and boundaries become increasingly porous. Gothic monsters may look similar but have different connotations, attractive rather than repulsive, desirable rather than disgusting. Oppositions are inverted, polarisations reversed. Gothic monstrosities still register otherness in the policing of cultural norms and boundaries but also give voice to the effects of exclusion. In displaying extremes of confinement, persecution, oppression, the monstrosity of systems and norms associated with pressures of social conformity, the fabrication of monstrous figures also signals an artifice and a cruelty that is neither natural nor legitimate. Monsters come to reflect upon the monstrosity of social or familial institutions that constructed them and, in suffering or defiance, manifest an appeal that sides with marginalised and excluded groups, thereby steadily turning them from negative into positive images. In this 'postmodern condition' the breakdown of modernity's meta-narratives discloses a horror that identity, reality, truth and meaning are not only effects of narratives but also subject to a dispersion and multiplication of meanings, realities and identities that obliterates the possibility of imagining any final human order and unity. Progress, rationality and civilisation, increasingly suspect, cede to new forms of sublimity and excess, new terrors, irrationalities and inhumanities.

ANTI-OEDIPUS

Popular gothic productions proliferate in the post-war period, presenting all forms of patriarchal power impeached by pressures of pleasure, profit, personal and political change. Films made in Hollywood in the 1930s set the tone for popular gothic developments, and the key motifs, stories and faces (Bela Lugosi and Boris Karloff notably) of monstrosity. In James Whale's *Frankenstein* (1931) individual pathology is signalled in the theft of a brain from a laboratory jar marked 'abnormal'. The impressive machines of electrical creation situated in a gothic tower give the scientific significance an archaic and fearful grandeur. While the attempt to win sympathy for a significantly mute monster defers to Shelley's story (the novel and its 1831 introduction providing a frame in Whale's subsequent *Bride of Frankenstein* in 1935), the closing image of a solitary figure pursued by an angry torch-bearing mob hunting down the monster accentuates a sense of individual pathos. It also resonates, in the context of an economically depressed North America of the 1930s, with threats of social unrest. Tod Browning's 1932 version of *Dracula* and Rouben Mamoulian's *Dr Jekyll and Mr Hyde* (1932) complete the trio of texts that have formed the gothic basis of terror and horror cinema in the twentieth century, playing on questions of the doubleness of identity, the threat and thrill of scientific experimentation, and the violence and insanity that threaten from within and without. In 1950s America, dominated by Cold War anti-Communist anxieties, horror became linked to fears about the invasion of both communities and human bodies. Don Spiegel's *The Invasion of the Bodysnatchers* (1956) capitalises on this context, extending the motif of the double to encompass both fears from within and without. Telling the story of a small American town being overtaken by unseen aliens, whose presence is signalled by huge pods, it suggests that the threat of both the Communist enemy outside and infiltrators within are similarly omnipresent and obscure. Engendering disbelief, paranoia and horror among those yet to be taken over, the transformation is almost as complete as it is visually undetectable. In film, visual likeness is paramount, and victims continue to look, act and talk in the same way as the people they have replaced. The community carries on in much the same way as it did, though more cooperative and without emotion. If the threat imagined in the form of bodysnatching speaks to Cold War paranoia, of invasion by ideology as much as by actual red-aliens, the images it presents are also ambivalent. The very pressures to conform which make one less oneself, less human (American), less emotional, less free are also the pressures of small-town conformity, pressures of family, responsibility, work, neighbourliness, which also constrain individuals in the name of group norms and values.

Gothic formulas readily produce laughter as abundantly as emotions of terror or horror. Stock conventions and themes, when too familiar, are eminently susceptible to parody and self-parody. The ambivalence of popular formulas, the familiarity of their plots and figures and the reversibility of their social and political polarities became a source of both comic, camp and critical reflection, as Abbot and Costello happily exploited in their comic encounters with popular monsters and Mel Brooks caricatured in *Young Frankenstein* (1974). In the 1960s comedy provided the cloak for quietly prodding the conformity engendered by small-town and family mores. Television series like *The Addams Family* (1964–66) and *The Munsters* (1964–66), with their comic inversion of everyday American family life, used a composite of figures from literary and visual gothic texts to beam abnormality directly into the home, gently satirising social expectations and familial roles as fantastic, outmoded and oppressive. Hammer studios in Britain, in the 1960s and 1970s, produced a string of formulaic film horrors inflected by concerns with, and titillations of, the social and sexual liberations of the period. The cult camp musical *The Rocky Horror Show* (1975), bringing Dracula, Frankenstein and

the monster together in its collage of stock horror images, parodies both gothic forms and the horrors associated with them in a
celebration of polymorphous sexuality.

In horror fictions and films, disturbances of the values and
norms of reason, morality, useful production and reproduction
sustaining the family as a model of the wider society for which it
was an essential ideological form multiply in the 1960s and
1970s. *The Texas Chainsaw Massacre* (Tobe Hooper, 1974), *The
Amityville Horror* (Stuart Rosenberg, 1979), *Poltergeist* (Tobe
Hooper, 1982) situated young people as objects of fear, threatening and threatened by cannibalism, traumatic violence, sexual
freedom, television and satanic possession. Turning on the same
violent energies of rebellion, sex and murder that are imagined as
threats, horror films and fictions suggest that a collapse of family
bonds and values is symptomatic of a decline of paternal authority
caused by its own repressive and abusive tendencies. Monstrosity
is within, a family affair. Enacting the repressive imperatives of
wider society, families make their own monsters: psychopaths,
serial killers, abusers. Robert Bloch's *Psycho* (1959) brings family
disintegration, sexuality and mental disorder together in a novel
in which 'filthy' psychology (psychoanalysis) serves to explain the
conflicts and frustrations that lead to hallucination, schizophrenia
and murder (p. 6). Norman Bates comes from a broken home, his
life shaped by paternal desertion and maternal possessiveness,
school bullying and sexual frustration. His surrogate father is a
con-man whom he poisons, along with his mother. Guilt leads to
a psychic fusing with a maternal spectre. He exhumes her, stuffs
her (he likes taxidermy), dresses up as her and acts out his rage on
independent single women staying at the family motel. Cannibalism, incest, transvestism, homosexuality, hysteria, necrophilia
are lumped together in a popular horror imagination to construct
a modern American Freudian hinterland of new sexual and psychological disorders with Oedipus at their root. Told in part from
Norman's perspective, the reader is forced to share his delusion, to
read his apparently real conversations with his mother and believe
her to be living, insane and homicidal. Alfred Hitchcock's version
of *Psycho* (1960) reworks gothic extravagance visually in the creation of mystery, absurdity and menace within the world of family

tensions. It draws a linear narrative of transgression and punishment of a sexually attractive and independent single woman drawn into the gloom of a decaying family house and isolated motel; it also draws the spectator's eye into the psychotic vortex of voyeurism: the famous shower scene slashes through a gothic veil of suspense, linking hallucination and literary imagination with the unseen, and spins, with blood and water, into a visual spectacle of psychosis in which the stare of the peeping-tom-serial-killer-spectator is sucked into the abyss of plughole and eye, eliding camera and gaze in a grotesque mirror of uncertainty. In the film, the psychopath is an object of fear and visual hallucination casting a dark shadow over the limits and effects of family, normal society and reality, with camera, serial killer and spectator rendered complicit and prurient. The disturbance of the novel, its shifting and misleading perspectives in which, as for Norman, the maternal figure is felt to be oppressively alive, attempts a degree of understanding: the killer is also a victim.

There is less opportunity for sympathy in Bloch's *American Gothic* (1974) where a historical serial killing is rendered both gothic and modernised. Based on Herman Webster Mudgett's (alias H.H. Holmes) 1893 construction of a Chicago building specially designed for the efficient dispatch of victims, the principal setting is outwardly gothic in its decorative flourishes (and known as 'Holmes Castle') while its interior is a labyrinth of guest rooms, secret doors, walls and corridors, chutes, cellars and pits for the efficient disposal of victims. Bloch's version, on the one hand, plays upon the 'castle' image to present the terrors of a heroine pursued through dungeons by a murderous villain. The other aspect, however, is very much an image of commercial America: the nearby site of the 'World's Fair', an international exhibition of trade, is a source of victims; the villain is a cool and business-like pharmacist for whom murder is a part of an insurance fraud and a practical means of raising capital. There is more, however: his collection of eyes in chemical preserving jars suggests a perverse scientism underlying his compulsion, not instinct or emotion but a mirror of rational economic practices and values dominating the world around him. The serial killer is a modern monster, a product of collection, consumption, accumulation and codification. He mirrors the bureaucracies, banks and businesses that run mechanically and efficiently in their rational execution of enterprise.

Shirley Jackson's *The Haunting of Hill House* (1959) stages tensions between older forms of haunting and modern gender roles. Ghosts and reason overlap in uneasy co-existence in the account of a research team's investigations of an old house. All the investigators experience the unexplained manifestations of what is described as a diseased and ill-willed edifice: noises, cold presences, feelings of being watched, the oddness of its architectural construction, unexplained writing on walls and curious visions. New inhabitants repeat violent scenes of its macabre past, such as death by hanging, crashing vehicles. The central character is particularly sensitive to spectral effects. Having just escaped a life of domestic confinement caring for a mother she hated, she begins with romantic hopes for an independent life and, like the other inhabitants, constructs a colourful past for herself. But neither scientific research nor modern values frees them: the house, a space of virulent and possessive domesticity, is monstrous in the way that it wants to consume them. The story refuses to distinguish psychological suggestibility or female hysteria from a more disturbing supernatural possession, and the heroine, like a daughter over-powered by maternal demands and never allowed to differentiate herself, succumbs to the retrogressive demands of the house's dark domestic ideology. Female freedom and independence, psychologically as much as socially, was not an easy option in a period in which familial norms were loosening and social freedoms expanding.

The breakdown of familial, social and economic structures has implications for male as well as female characters, and not only in material and psychological terms: the turmoil and disruption of changing familial and social values are seen to unleash supernatural terrors beyond the reach of reason or understanding. In the first novels of one of the most prolific horror writers of the century, telekinesis, diabolical possession and vampires disturb small American towns. Stephen King's third novel, *The Shining* (1977), focuses intensely on the family and paternal monstrosity. Set in a large, snowbound hotel in the Rocky Mountains that is a place of 'shinings' (telepathic projections of violent disturbances in the past or future), the father becomes more and more psychotic while his son glimpses spectral scenes. Flashes from the hotel's history accompany the return of personal memories to reveal recurrent patterns of cross-generational abuse: the father, a writer and a recently sacked teacher, is an alcoholic, a victim of abuse at the hands of his father, with an uncontrollable temper. His derangement is, so the history of the haunted and diabolical hotel suggests, linked to evidence of a wider decline, not only of family values but also of the contemporary values of a nation. Corporate owners conceal the hotel's criminal associations with the Mafia, a more material but equally disturbing other side to the American dream. Maintaining uncertainty between historical, psychological and supernatural origins characterises King's approach – a deliberate equivocation, it leaves open the question of material or spectral causes, equating 'undead people' (actual ghosts) with 'undead memories' (persistent, powerful, traumatic recollections). In the tension between matter and spirit, reality and value, monstrosity cuts two ways: 'we create unreal monsters and bogies to stand in for all the things we fear in our real lives' (p. xii). These include parental abuse, violence, accident and trauma. Imaginary worlds and diabolical horrors return, it seems, as attempts to give form to or filter out the real fears faced by a person or a culture at a particular time.

LUDOGOTHIC

Part of the challenge to the structures, hierarchies, values and exclusions of modernity was manifested in fictions that juxtaposed and reorganised narrative styles and relationships. Piecing together elements of texts from different periods, mimicking forms, subverting assignations of aesthetic value between high and low culture rendered interpretation and meanings plural, partial and political. This fragmentation enacted a form of playful inventiveness and subversion that, in its self-aware reflection on the constitutive dimension of language in forming texts and realities, discloses how ideas and fantasies about self and the world are inscribed in and between the different narratives composing cultural order. Angela Carter's fiction, self-consciously mixing different forms, including fairytale, legend, magical realism, science fiction and gothic, shows how metaphors, conventions and narratives shape reality and identity, particularly in relation to the construction of sexuality. In her novel *The Infernal Desire Machines of Dr Hoffman* (1972), Carter interrogates the play of reality and fantasy by using the idea that the uncanny is inscribed in the entire social formation and all perceptions follow paths of desire rather than physical laws. The narrator's picaresque journey traverses worlds in which conventional distinctions of space and time, matter and spirit, reality and fantasy engage different modes and genres to suggest that the world is fictional in its broadest sense, an effect of narratives, identifications, fantasies and desires that no longer bow to the grand narrative dominated by the reality principle.

'The Bloody Chamber' (1979), like the other stories in the collection of the same name, plays with the way fairytales, legends and gothic fictions police gendered identities. A nameless young female narrates the romance that leads her from poverty to wealth, marrying an old aristocratic libertine and voluptuary in the Sadeian mould. She receives dresses and jewels, becomes mistress of his remote and picturesque castle by the sea but the three-time widowed Marquis treats her as a decorative commodity to be bought and disposed of as he wishes. Using Francois Perrault's tale of the uxoricidal Bluebeard, Carter's story is told from the perspective of the naïve heroine to outline a history of fantastic constructions of femininity. In echoes of *Rebecca*, the heroine discovers letters of the Marquis' first wife. She, a beautiful Romanian countess who was regularly celebrated in fashion magazines, turns out to have been a relation of Dracula. His former wives all display conventionally valued characteristics of femininity, one an artist's model, another, an opera singer. This 'gallery' of beauty and his pornographic library and collection of fine jewels associate femininity with images and objects to be possessed and consumed. Tricking her into disobeying his wishes and thereby drawing out the conjunction between prohibition and desire, the Marquis encourages her to explore his castle. Her explorations lead to Radcliffean terrors in dark vaults full of torture instruments and corpses. Threatened by imminent death at the hands of her husband, a spectral and knightly figure rides to her rescue on a carthorse: the romantic hero is her mother. The heroine escapes to live out a sober existence with her mother and a blind piano tuner, the illusions of romance, despite the blindness that echoes *Jane Eyre*, dispelled by the playful reversal of narrative conventions in which women become agents of their own destiny rather than victims of patriarchal power and ideology. Gothic figures are very much associated with Victorian sexual values. 'Lady of the House of Love', from the same anthology, reworks all the clichés of the vampire tale. An eternally young, attractively wasted female vampire inhabits a ruined castle in a deserted eastern European village. Her disinclination to live up to the demands of her ancestors and her insatiable hunger introduce the idea of a reluctant vampire who dreams of being human. When her next victim, an English army officer on a cycling holiday, appears things change; she does not feed on him and, modern, rational and reserved, he treats her decently rather than as a sexual object by planning her treatment for hysteria at a Swiss clinic. Her condition is not diabolical, but psychological in that Victorian fears of sexual excess cede here to modern medical controls. Neither terrifying nor sensational but, told from the perspective of the exhausted female vampire, the story is reflective: the days of vampires and their horrifying sexual associations are on the wane. However, horrors that are more modern and devastating await: as the officer returns to duty the reader is informed of the date – 1914. A different kind of horror, the story suggests, will displace the world of the Victorian vampire.

Modern concerns and values, however, do not simply displace older literary and social conventions. History, its texts and terrors disturb orders of rationality and progress. A diabolical character in Peter Ackroyd's *Hawksmoor* (1985) declaims against the 'Rationall and mechanicall' Age (p. 101). A story paralleling the rebuilding of London in the early eighteenth century with the reconstructions of the 1980s, the novel sets satanic mysticism against rational materialism in telling the story of ritual murders being committed nearly three centuries apart. Part urban gothic, part contemporary crime fiction and part supernatural mystery, the novel leaves open the questions it raises for its contemporary, rational, commercial and materialistic culture. It ends with an air of uncertainty and unease that not only relives the darkness of past superstitions but also implies that, buried in the foundations of the city, such darkness is prone to repetition.

Encouraging superstitious interpretation, gothic texts interpose fictional and social expectations. In the assemblage of different stories within early gothic novels, labyrinthine complexity ultimately discloses secrets and evokes the horror that expels the object of fear, restoring properly conventional boundaries. Ambivalence and duplicity remain. In gothic fictions and films duplicity emerges as a distinctly reflexive form of narrative anxiety. It involves a pervasive cultural concern, characterised as postmodernist, that things are not only not what they seem: what they seem is what they are, not a unity of word or image and thing, but words and images without things or as things themselves, effects of narrative form and nothing more. Unstable, unfixed and ungrounded in any reality, truth or identity other than those that narratives provide, there emerges a threat of sublime excess, of a new darkness of multiple and labyrinthine narratives.

The horror of textuality is linked to fears of anarchic disintegration and dizzying multiplicity. In an impressive example of gothic fiction, *The Name of the Rose* (1980), Umberto Eco displays the textual form of postmodern gothic: the narrative rearticulates distinctions between Enlightenment rationality and religious superstition, and includes the discovery of a medieval manuscript, labyrinthine spaces, mysterious deaths and medieval architecture and history. The arrival of a monk, William of Baskerville, and his novice, the narrator, Adso, at a fourteenth-century abbey dominated by a great octagonal library coincides with a series of deaths. Interpreted as signs of divine apocalypse or diabolical machination, the deaths engage Baskerville's skills in detection, the allusion to Sherlock Holmes underlining his rational and empirical outlook. The gothic device of a counterfeit 'editor's' preface, though stating its absolute distance from contemporary concerns, ironically focuses attention on the relation between history and the present. Full of modern as well as historical allusions, literary and theoretical references, the intertextuality of the novel highlights the writings of Jorge Luis Borges. Centred on a library constructed in the form of a labyrinth, the novel's mystery extends to mysteries in and about texts, its object and cause being a text, a missing philosophical work whose knowledge and power is feared and desired. Baskerville, monk and detective, is also slightly different from his conventional fictional forebears. His rational and detective skills are presented as critical and analytic abilities in that he is an excellent reader of signs and narrative conventions (pp. 24–25). Superstition appears as an effect of misreading, of the misapprehension of signifying codes. Following the clues through the dark corridors and vaults of the abbey, Baskerville uncovers the trail of textual fragments that conceal and cause the crimes, arriving at the horrifying answer in a hidden chamber of the labyrinthine library. Horror, neither bloody spectre nor corpse, takes the form of Baskerville's double, an old librarian named Jorge, possessed of religious dogmatism and callous and diabolical cunning, which function as a perfect foil for the former's intellectual pride: he has orchestrated murder to prevent monks reading a book that was believed lost, Aristotle's second book of the *Poetics*, on comedy. For Jorge, to Baskerville's horror, a book by so authoritative a philosopher would undermine the power of ecclesiastical order by legitimating the refusal of laughter to respect any law and authority, its rebellious energy threatening the 'dismantling and upsetting of every holy and venerable image' (p. 476). Laughter, anarchically irreverent, activates a diabolical play of insubordination, signs and energies.

For the order that Jorge represents, laughter is reviled as the enemy of truth and power: revulsion produces its own acts of irrational and intolerant suppression. The violence and murder that Jorge's dogmatic order employs is, from narrative identification with Baskerville's position, shown to be the true object of horror: the superstitious and tyrannical oppression of the Catholic Inquisition. Arbitrary, irrational power is opposed by Baskerville's enlightened and rational humanism. The invocation of Enlightenment values that are produced and contested throughout gothic fiction is made with a significant difference: truth and reason are no longer seen as absolutes but are ways of reading in which texts are left open and plural, their play no longer generating a single, authorised meaning. Adso's concluding reflections remain uncertain about his mentor's motivations as well as the message that his own manuscript holds. Adso's subsequent return to the abbey and the ruins of the library, destroyed by the great conflagration that results from Jorge's and Baskerville's confrontation, sees him collecting some of the tiny fragments of scattered books: 'at the end of my reconstruction, I had before me a kind of lesser library, a symbol of the greater, vanished one: a library made up of fragments, quotations, unfinished sentences, amputated stumps of books' (p. 500).

While *The Name of the Rose* advances its vision of the fragmentary forms of textual, individual and social bodies whose meanings and identities are effects of patient and partial reconstruction, the image of flaming disintegration and ruin that shadows it is shocking to viewpoints fostered by ideas of natural unity, homogeneity and totality. Shadows of narrative duplicity split open ideas of reality. Alan Parker's film *Angel Heart* (1986) begins, in the manner of a 1950s detective thriller, with a corpse and a down-at-heel private eye, Harry Angel, being hired to find a missing person by a mysterious client called Louis Cyphre. The investigation leads Angel away from a grubbily realistic New York to Southern states dominated by religious ritual and voodoo. Punctuated by flashbacks of mysterious shrouded figures, blood-filled bowls and blood-stained walls, the film turns one narrative, the detective story, into a Faustian tale of diabolical repossession. It requires a twist that shatters unity: Angel discovers he is double, detective and murderer, perpetrator and victim, deceiver and dupe of an arcane ritual that is alluded to in flashback fragments in which the heart of another was ripped out and consumed in order to escape the terms of a contract with the devil. 'Lucifer', in the shape and name of 'Louis Cyphre', returns to claim his due. The word-play reveals the secret of the film. New flashbacks, replicating scenes from earlier in the film, rewrite the first narrative as a fake: like the shots of mirrors, identity cards and dog tags, it is also duplicitous. Bodies, souls, identities and roles can all be substituted for each other, a movement between genres and reading that diabolically multiplies meanings and identities to the point where nothing is anything more than narrative appearance. The play is also a game of signs: Louis Cyphre is not only Lucifer, but also Lu-cipher, the name that cracks the Faustian narrative's code.

Enmeshed in processes of doubling, *Angel Heart*, as a film, as a set of narrative images, suggests that identity, meaning and unity are spectral effects of signs. It cannot expunge this horror, just as it cannot exempt itself from the play. The invocation of evil, however, signals a return attempting to structure meaning in binary and opposed terms. In the films of David Lynch a similar interplay of good and evil, light and dark, is manifested as an uncanny and unavoidable duplicity. In *Blue Velvet* (1986), visual allusions absorb the American gothic tradition in which the proximity of good and evil is internal to home and community. Lynch's television series, *Twin Peaks* (1990–92), uses similar gothic contrasts in a visual text whose network of allusions, quotations, stylistic parodies and pastiches was as broad as it was self-conscious. Playing with various narrative conventions the series followed the investigation of a terrible murder of a girl in the small-town community to uncover evil's multiplying sources in primordial, individual, cultural and narrative locations: deep in the woods, in human fears, selfish desires and sexual repressions, in the community and within the family. The evil in the woods alludes to Hawthorne; the evil father resonates throughout gothic, as does the identification with psychopathology, distorted faces in the mirror parodies of Southern gothic freaks, the monster-image no longer humanising but playing beyond all frames, laws, norms. The figure of evil, the vagrant face of Bob, appears as the mirror image of the paternal perpetrator, a reflection that haunts the series. Evil, also, is located in outer space, an echo of the Cold War threat of Communism that had just disappeared with the collapse of the Soviet Union. The locations of evil multiply in the dense network of cultural and narrative allusion that extends to popular media, films and fictions themselves. The final battle of good and evil is staged when the detective enters the deceptive Black Lodge, a place of reversals and evil double, in order to save the woman he loves. They both return. But the romantic happy ending is undermined by the final scene. Washing in his hotel bathroom, the detective looks in a mirror.

Staring from it is the dishevelled face of Bob, the evil image and sign of diabolical possession. The turning of one into the other, good into evil, forms a doubly self-conscious and banal inversion of the conventional romantic ending. The camera returns from the mirror to focus on the detective's features, now distorted in a malevolent grin that is itself a reflection of the mirror image's evil face. Not so much a conventional display of the truth of interiority, of the evil within, the double reflection presents evil as an effect of images and narrative surfaces, another device of diabolical duplicity.

Another darkness underlies American gothic fiction as it extends from the backwoods and small towns to Southern cities. Toni Morrison's lecture 'Romancing the Shadow' (1990) traces the 'strong affinity' between the American novel, European gothic romance and the history of slavery underwriting US culture. Recording (European) diabolism, she argues, occurs 'so as to prevent their repetition' (p. 36). The terror of human freedom meets the darkness of others and the self and 'internal conflicts' are transferred to a 'blank darkness' of silenced histories and sufferings: otherness remains a troubling category (p. 38). Morrison's *Beloved* (1987) draws on fictions of ghosts and haunted houses, and on Southern gothic's multiple perspectives, to examine the specificity of historical horror that can only be recorded with difficulty, if at all. Haunting, associated with white and Western literary forms, is powerfully recast in relation to real sufferings whose record is less stable, living in oral histories, transcribed narratives of slaves, traumatised memory and in scars on bodies. Beginning in a house inhabited by three generations of escaped or freed slave women (their husbands, sons and brothers have fled) *Beloved* recounts stories, memories and events in the past and present that move from the immediate aftermath of the American Civil War to the twentieth century. The house is haunted by the enraged ghost of a baby girl, the dead daughter of Sethe, the novel's protagonist, killed by her mother so that she would not be taken into slavery. When another ex-slave arrives, more memories of the past are stirred up. But the man, it seems, drives off the ghost. As if in her place, a young black woman arrives, apparently from nowhere, who is the same age and who has the same name as the dead daughter. She assumes, in bodily form, the function of the ghost, a haunting testament of inconsolable grief and painful self-doubt, a figure from whom Sethe seeks forgiveness that is not forthcoming. Embodied, the psychological projections of haunting, the almost material return of an unspeakably painful past into the present, show that such an oppressive history is still, like the elaborate tree-shaped scars on her back, alive. It is not just the physical effects of slavery, but the psychological devastation that persists. Unable to find forgiveness or to forgive herself, she becomes almost fully absorbed in the ghost. The interplay of literary forms and perspectives does more than realign monstrosity with obvious and brutal manifestations, from constructions of otherness, to systematic terror and persistent haunting. Its examination of psychological effects played out in images of haunting deploys ghosts to embody traumas deeper than memory, which are barely expressible in compound gothic conventions because they are lived painfully and palpably as real. In Morrison's replaying of the motifs of haunting, the gothic conventions that usually cover up or displace guilt, trauma and transgression, come to announce its painful and unspeakable reality: 'this is not a story to pass on' (p. 324). It is too painful to be adequately communicated yet remains a story that cannot be avoided.

In other fictions in which the narratives of history, cultural identity and sexuality are subjected to techniques of play, gothic figures and forms are more readily associated with fabrication and artifice. No novel of recent years engages so critically with and alludes so playfully to as many gothic romances as Alasdair Gray's *Poor Things* (1992). Formally, its composition acknowledges the self-consciousness of many gothic texts: an editor who has also provided extensive scholarly annotations introduces a discovered manuscript made up of letters, illustrations, postcards and illegible scrawls, the veracity of which is rebuffed by a long posthumous letter offering a 'true' version. Discovered in the late 1980s the self-printed manuscript composing the sensational story of *Poor Things* is set in nineteenth-century Glasgow, with industry and prosperity the backdrop for scientific experimentation and medical progress. It is a world, chapter titles declare, of 'making': manufacturing goods, making discoveries, constructing identities. When the body of a pregnant woman is discovered in the River Clyde, a doctor manages to save her by means of an extravagant experiment, he replaces her dead brain with that of her unborn child and then brings her up in his own home without the usual prejudices regarding gender, class or morality. Her education and outlook is thus free, generous and open. To conventional outsiders her character is viewed as both innocent angel and sexual demon, while a tour of Europe and North Africa allows her to develop an open and critical view of capitalism, imperialism and patriarchy. Innocent and monstrous, her brain that of the baby conceived in the body the head of which it now occupies, her self is impossibly divided. She cannot be constrained by laws of identity, norm or morality and, significantly, cannot be owned by the men who claim her: her father, first husband, new 'father', current fiancé, or lovers. Wonderful and challenging, her innocent monstrosity is also fantastic. Her story, written by the man who becomes her second husband, reflects on the fabrication of femininity by men. The 'real' woman appends a posthumous letter to this fiction, one that is critical of male fantasy and offering a realistic (but equally wonderful) account of a woman in late Victorian Scotland who flees an abusive first marriage, trains as a doctor, helps establish socialism and loses her sons in World War I. Her criticism castigates all the gothic trappings of her husband's fantasy image of her. Linked to the Revival architecture that dominates Glasgow and other Scottish and English cities, the 'sham-Gothic' of Victorian Culture is subjected to a particularly devastating materialist attack: the gloomy, dark surfaces of buildings, like darkly fantastic romances, are built upon and conceal a reality of exploitation and profit that is even more horrific in that poverty, filth and human suffering could, at the time, have been ameliorated (p. 275). In the 1980s and early 1990s, of course, a similar set of moral and economic attitudes persisted in the 'Victorian values' championed by successive Conservative governments.

REVAMP

In the second of Anne Rice's Vampire Chronicles, *The Vampire Lestat* (1985), the eponymous hero awakes in a new world: 1980s

America is very different from the stiff nineteenth century he left behind (in *Interview with the Vampire*, 1976). Happy that 'the dark and dreary industrial world that I'd gone to sleep in had burnt itself out finally, and the old bourgeois prudery and conformity had lost their hold on the American mind', he observes that people were 'adventurous and erotic again' and 'had a right to love and luxury and to graceful things' (p. 14). These are not the rights of a modern progressive humanity but the new values of a species, like vampires, given over to consumption. At home, Lestat restyles himself and vampire mythology, remaking himself as rock star and celebrity. Lestat's account acknowledges that conventional vampire connotations have been reversed: romantic rather than revolting, a figure of identification rather than abhorrence, vampires are welcome in a world of shopping and consumer luxury. Where the vampire existed in the shadows of modernity as a destructive, exotic, threatening excess, it now signifies a creature at the heart of the lifestyles and identities of consumer culture. Moving back through diverse cultures, folklore and histories, the novel furnishes vampires with a powerful new mythology. Rice's first novel romanticised vampires in a nineteenth-century context as aesthetic, dandified figures, exciting shadows opposed to the regularity and repetition of bourgeois, urban and economic organisation. Moving from New Orleans to Paris in a novel told in the form of an interview to an aspiring radio journalist, the first-person perspective of *Interview with the Vampire* encouraged identification with vampires engaged in their own search for origins and identity. Suffused with Romantic individualism, Symbolist ennui, and *fin-de-siècle* decadence, the nocturnal existence of vampires is associated with a theatrical performance and easy consumerism in which a range of sexual and aesthetic freedoms are enjoyed alongside a quest for belonging and indulgent and affected questioning of the mores and meanings of life. The pleasures of eternal life and youth, the opportunity to satisfy desires and consume luxuriously and freely, are all shadowed by feelings of despair, anguish and alienation. The glamour is further enhanced by a cast of stars in Neil Jordan's 1994 film version. That, as much as the popular existentialism and the fashionable postures on the issues of sexual freedom and identity, establishes Rice's vampires as models for new and positive associations of vampirism with consumer and youth culture. Where issues of aesthetic sensibility, immortality and aging were explored in the contemporary New York of Tony Scott's *The Hunger* (1983), notable for its staging of Goth music alongside a refined classical score, questions of identity, belonging, adolescent individualism and youth culture are further explored, and more violently, in Poppy Z. Brite's reworking of vampire mythology. *Lost Souls* (1992) presents vampires and humans as separate species occupying a night world of hedonistic consumption, music, occult powers and rituals. With graphic violence and a range of supernatural figures, Brite's fiction drew out a long-standing gothic potential for exploring the fears and excitements surrounding different sexual identities, celebrating homoerotic and bisexual identifications as part of a general experimentation beyond cultural norms. With the appearance of *True Blood* (2008–), an expensively produced television version of Charlaine Harris' *The Southern Vampire Mysteries*, the connection between consumerism (the sale of synthetic blood allows vampires to come out of the cultural shadows), diverse sexual orientation and identity politics had become as established a trope as the association between vampires and the powerful conspiracies of corporate culture in films like *Blade* (Stephen Norrington, 1998). Popular teenage associations of gothic and youth culture are exploited in Hollywood film with a story of vampire gangs haunting the boardwalks, clubs, malls and arcades of suburban California (*Lost Boys*, Joel Schumacher, 1987). In the highly self-conscious, stylised and popular television series, *Buffy the Vampire Slayer* (1997–2003), monsters prowled high school corridors and sleepy small-town streets of Sunnydale. Unfortunately situated above a 'Hellmouth', the town is prone to all sorts of supernatural manifestations which a 'Slayer' and a group of schoolfriends are required to dispatch on a weekly basis. Dressing up a youth culture that had, in comic books, on vinyl and in clubs, already worn black for several decades, the popular emergence of gothic and Goth on screens reworked older motifs to negotiate the gloom and darkness of growing up and negotiating the alienating institutions of high school, peer pressure, family values and sexual awakening. But Goth had already undergone many musical, cultural and aesthetic mutations by the late 1990s. Appropriately enough for a subculture that takes, among its various origins, a song that proclaims 'Bela Lugosi is dead ... Undead, undead, undead', Goth has proved to be an enduring, adaptable and global entity. From the 'punk gothique' of the late 1970s and early 1980s British musical underground, where a ragged, be-zipped, safety-pinned and spit-befouled anti-sensibility met an extravagantly attired New Romanticism, Goth has flowered diabolically and diversely. Retaining a penchant for often elaborately and deca-dently styled dark clothes and cosmetics, maintaining interest in its fictional forebears, and celebrating sexual ambivalence, it con-tinues, in clubs, on disk, in bedrooms, online and at long-running festivals, to develop and embrace 'dark' and often extravagant new inflections of music, design and adornment. If its endurance speaks to a resilient if curiously individualistic sociality and tolerance among its members, Goth's peacefully independent but visible difference in style is not always allowed to proceed along its own path. Popular targets for media attacks whenever a high school shooting occurs on the North American continent, the imagined threats of darkness, immortality and otherness so visibly displayed seem reason enough for occasional violent attacks, and sometimes murder, in countries around the world.

Nostalgia, consumption and sexual freedom are brought toge-ther in Francis Ford Coppola's lush remake of Dracula, where the romanticisation of vampires occurs alongside a cinematic nos-talgia for the undead medium of cinema. For all its claims to authenticity, *Bram Stoker's Dracula* (1992) does not evoke sacrifi-cial horror. Its simulation of authenticity is signalled in the reconstruction of Victorian decadence in Dracula's dress, the London settings, the lurid sexual images, the luxuriousness of the Westenra's house and ornamental garden, and in Dr Seward's drug habit. In the film's magnified shots of blood cells seen through a microscope, the novel's link to diseases of the blood is prominently displayed. The 1990s, like the 1890s, saw terrors linking sex and death, syphilis becoming AIDS. Sexuality, again, confronts humanity with a threat both global and microscopic, internal and external, crossing all borders with impunity and disturbing the security of body, home and culture. Invading from without and destroying from within, the AIDS virus breaks the cellular defences of individual organisms and leaves its sufferers in an emaciated limbo.

In the frame story to the film, the novel's narrative is supplanted by a pseudo-historical account of Vlad the Impaler's tragic love. Dracula is not simply an object of sublime horror. The film also plays down the male bonding so prominent in Stoker's novel and climaxes, not with a hunt delivering the purgative sacrificial violence which restores a patriarchal and domestic order, but where it started, with Mina standing in for Dracula's dead wife in the chapel of the castle. And it is she, rather than Jonathan and Quincey, who delivers the cleansing blow that kills him. In Coppola's version Dracula is no consistent figure of evil, despite the melodramatically demonic dress and a creature costume that seems to be inherited from Batman. Not entirely an antichrist, vicious aristocrat, bad father or beast, Dracula is less tyrannical and demonic and more victim and sufferer, less libertine and more sentimental romantic hero, his passion and violence almost sympathetic when explained as a tragic loss of true love. His anger and anguish and the curse he casts on all holy forms cause him to become undead. Bereft of an object of love he preys upon humanity until he sees Harker's miniature of Mina, the very image of his lost love, and in this role she enjoys secret trysts and dinner. In the final scene Mina kills Dracula in an act of humanitarian mercy and redemption rather than sacrificial violence, the event taking place in the chapel where, centuries earlier, 'they' were married.

The additional frame emphasises how vampire horror has turned into sentimental romance. 'Love never dies' was the epigraph to posters advertising the film. 'Bram Stoker's' *Dracula* is merged with another popular romanticisation of a nineteenth-century novel, *Wuthering Heights*, as a tale of excessive individual passions, of a love enduring beyond all social forms and history, beyond the grave. Coppola's film mourns a lost object, a lost story of passion and human, secular love. The film does not affirm a unified set of values in a moment of sacred horror and sacrifice like Dracula. In the movement between the 1890s and the 1990s, between horror and love, expulsion and tolerance, contradictory and ambivalent impulses disclose radical differences in the relation of one and other, past and present and in the incommensurable narratives in which meaning becomes multiple rather than singular. Human identity and humanist narratives again emerge as duplicitous. Mina, the double of Dracula's wife, assumes that role at the end and thus becomes an adulteress, unfaithful to her other husband, Harker, a strange call to monogamy in an age of safe sex. Dracula, as victim and villain, inhuman yet human, is also divided. His love and the love which he inspires in Mina are also violent and passionate and the cause of the other's suffering. The doublings of narrative make human stories empty repositories: in the chapel, the last act of love is surrounded by sacred icons that have become empty symbols, their imaginary power and unity, like Dracula's horror, decomposing in the gap between two narratives. The closure of the film is also emptied of gothic effect, there is no climax, no solution, no sacred or rational expulsion of mystery, terror or duplicity. The film's grand themes of individual love and death are haunted by a pervasive sense of loss, the sacred nature of humanity trickling away in empty images and hollow signs: one of modernity's most powerful myths fading like a drawn human face in the sand. In not repeating the sacrificial violence by which gothic forms reconstitute a sacred sense of self from the undead and spectral figures of humanist narratives, Coppola's film mourns an object that is too diffuse and uncertain to be recuperated. Rather, it remains, reluctantly, within a play of narratives, between past and present, one and other. With Coppola's Dracula, then, gothic, divested of its excesses, of its transgressions, horrors and diabolical laughter, of its brilliant gloom and rich darkness, of its artificial and suggestive forms, is caught up in the hallucinatory effects of texts, images and media that are on the point of becoming digital.

CYBERGOTHIC

'Raygun Gothic' is a term used in William Gibson's short story, 'The Gernsback Continuum' (1981), for outdated images of a future that continue to haunt a present which has superseded them. With its title referring to the magazine publisher, Hugo

Gernsback, who, in starting *Amazing Stories* (1926), popularised science fiction writing, the story discusses the persistence of old imaginings of architectural, transport and commodity designs for the future. These images of space travel or new gadgets presented in advertising, television and movies are 'semiotic ghosts', images that do not stay in archives but, unlike the shared hallucination offered by 'cyberspace', pop up as dissensual autonomous phantasms in a real world already suffering from an over-saturation of images, signs and information and a general sense of spatial and temporal disorder (p. 48). Fiction and film associated with cyberculture engage with the artificial forms that are given life and consciousness and project anxieties about disintegrating Western cultural and social formations on to a nightmarish vision of the future. Consciousness is transformed as science fiction implodes on the present. Prostheses enhance and develop bodies beyond human capacities, inaugurating a post-human vision of the world in which identity is enmeshed with flows of digital data presented as a shared unreal space which is inhabited on a daily basis. Gibson's *Neuromancer* (1984) is set in a future run by large corporations and controlled by computers. The homogenised corporate and silicon order is maintained in relation to the diasporic proliferation of subcultures centred on drugs, violence and terror. Humans are little more than adjuncts to machines, cast aside as economically unproductive detritus or rebuilt in accordance with technological needs and capacities, leaving nature and humanity supplemented to the point of extinction. However, the 'romance' signalled in the title is far from insignificant. For all the prosthetic implants, the 'jackings in' of individuals' neural networks into the cyberspace of computerised matrices, the novel retains a distinctly romantic plot populated by dark-clad female assassins, uncanny psycho-technologies able to vividly project dreams and fantasy, holographic ghosts generated by machine, and the consciousness of dead people stored and animated on disk. One supercomputer describes itself as a necromancer of the nervous system: 'I call up the dead' (p. 141). The hero, a 'cyberspace cowboy' named Case, is enjoined to participate in an attempt, by an odd collection of misfits, to penetrate the defences of the castle-like home of a corporate family dynasty controlling the two most powerful Artificial Intelligences in the world, Neuromancer and Wintermute, and to prohibit their fusion into a new, monstrous entity. This place, the Villa Straylight, is a 'Gothic folly' (p. 206). In the labyrinth of this building and, for Case, in the labyrinthine networks of cyberspace, the denouement is achieved. The two computers synthesise, creating an absolutely new form of life.

Looking, with excitement and trepidation, towards the imminent biotechnological transformation of the world through binary codes and digital media, cyberpunk also recycles and rewrites the past, inventing another sub-genre, 'steampunk', that transforms the Victorian period from an age of industrial and scientific progress into one dominated by information and technology. Inaugurating the appeal of neo-Victorianism in stylised dress, morals and inventions, Gibson and Bruce Sterling's *The Difference Engine* (1990) constructs a new, virtual history on the premiss that Charles Babbage, credited as the forerunner of computing for designing a calculating machine powered by steam and fed data with punch cards (a 'difference engine'), managed to realise his blueprint. Not only is Babbage very much at the centre of a Victorian world powered by ubiquitous calculating machines and steam engines, his colleague, Ada Lovelace, assumes a central role in the scientific and political meritocracy, as does her father Lord Byron. Byron is brought back from an actual early death to become a leading radical. Rewriting history, imperial power and global geopolitics from the perspective of a thoroughly informatic late twentieth century, the novel ends with a curious vision of a dehumanised 1990s London in which 'ghosts of history' populate a shining 'necropolis' of mirrored crystals, 'hot inhuman dark' of data flows and 'electric phantoms' (pp. 382–83). It suggests another romance, this time of a new, dark and post-human age.

The fusion of old and new forms of romance recurs throughout science fiction. In the modernising of earlier terrors and horrified encounters with life that virtually replicates human existence, the nature and essence associated with the human figure are rendered uncertain, if not obsolete. Instead, robotic doubles signal only mechanism and artificiality, the lack of any human essence. In Ridley Scott's *Blade Runner* (1982), the undertones of nineteenth-century gothic are never far from the surface of this futuristic dark detective film. Set in a gloomy, ruinous and alienating Los Angeles of the near future, the film follows the fortunes of a group of renegade 'replicants', artificial creations virtually indistinguishable from humans, as they try, like Frankenstein's monster, to make their creator, the scientist controlling the Tyrell Corporation, accede to their demands for a more human lifespan. The disaffected blade runner, Deckard, whose task is to identify and terminate the replicants, is the parallel subject of the film as it divides sympathies between pursuer and pursued. Caught between blade runner and replicant, human and android, the narrative gradually erodes the differences that distinguish the one from the other, leaving doubts that haunt the properly simulated romantic ending of the first version of the film.

Film narratives that establish the Romantic differences between strong, self-sufficient and autonomous individuality and destructive, mechanical and programmed simulations are legion. In the impressive image of Arnold Schwarzenegger, however, the two strands are neatly embodied. In *Conan the Barbarian* (John Milius, 1982) the physique is the vehicle for a romance fantasy of the dark ages in which a primordial human bodily and psychological power is imagined; in contrast, the *Terminator* (James Cameron, 1984) generates human fears of obliteration by a relentlessly determined machinic power. The images of strength and power that are established through the opposition of human and machine draw on the masculine elements of gothic fiction, with paternal associations drawn out in the relationship between a boy, his mother and a killing machine (*Terminator 2*, James Cameron, 1991). In *Alien* (Ridley Scott, 1979) other gothic associations are brought to the fore. The wrecked alien spaceship and the bleak planet on which it has crashed suggest the gloom, ruin and awful desolation of gothic architecture and landscape. The coded message the spaceship transmits is not a distress signal, but a warning which goes unheeded by the human cargo ship that attends the call. Unaware of the dangers that their employers, another sinister and powerful corporation, have put them in, the crew are unwitting victims of their attempt to secure the power and profit of possessing such an efficient and utterly inhuman killing machine.

The horror of the alien lies not only in its lethal power; its parasitical mode of procreation, using human bodies as hosts, means that it is a threat that emerges from within. Indeed, brought aboard inside a member of crew, the alien runs amok. In the cavernous and labyrinthine cargo ship the atmosphere of terror and suspense sustained by the reversible dynamic of hunters and hunted follows gothic patterns. This is reinforced by the film's focus on a woman, Ripley, who becomes a science fiction gothic heroine. The strength and self-possession of the heroine, however, distinguishes her from earlier figures, whose faintings and flight signalled the powerlessness of persecuted femininity. Sexual differences, moreover, are presented in the maternal images suggested by the design of the alien 'mother' ship. The vessel is a giant womb, the repository of the eggs that turn into monstrous and destructive progeny. Associations with the conflicting emotions evoked by the mother in 'female gothic', however, are complicated by the irony of the corporate computer's name, 'Mother', which suggests the matrix of technology and artificial intelligence has supplanted human figures. As the *Alien* franchise develops, resurrecting dead characters through a matrix of genetic and digital codes, heroine and monster mutate to the point that differences between human and alien are eroded. The dark settings of a hostile future, too, are realigned in accordance with the popular adoption of new media in the two decades separating the first and fourth films in the series. With a range of disturbing environments and claustrophobic spaces, *Alien Resurrection* (Jean-Pierre Jeunet, 1997), in common with many films where franchising involves new media as much as cinematic and commodity spin-offs, already looks like a video game. Indeed, there are few of the staple texts of gothic writing or horror cinema that have not been adapted as computer games that use conventional sets and techniques of terror, suspense and shock to produce powerfully visceral effects on players' bodies. The design of games not only allows the visualisation of gothic spaces and monsters, but also enables a virtual immersion and active engagement in worlds of fear. The haunting spaces, sounds and figures in games conjoin with the haunting effects of games, interacting with, reacting to and acting out unreal events and monstrous identifications so that the screens imagined in cybergothic fiction's near futures become present, actual and everyday sites playing out darkly dissensual hallucinations.

HOUSE OF BITS/TWILIGHT OF GOTH

Disorientation: multiple interlinked networks of signs, images, bits, flows. Disruption: all spatial, temporal, physical and subjective coordinates diffuse, conflate, expand and enmesh. Where does it begin and end? How is it animated? What can it mean? In digital and virtual contexts, what are its frames, anchors, material supports? Who – or what – writes, reads, projects, imagines, perceives? Are the ghosts it generates actual, hallucinatory or medial? Are they effects of unconscious, textual or technical processes? Mark Z. Danielewski's *House of Leaves* (2000) is a densely layered text about a house with very strange properties: it may be haunted, or worse. Much of what is said to happen is enveloped in mystery and uncertainty, accompanied by an atmosphere of paranoia. Just as its central location attends to variations on haunted houses, its composition is ludogothic in the extreme, using an array of different texts, forms and media. Purporting to be a discovered heavily annotated dead man's manuscript about a lost documentary film, the novel includes letters, photographs, descriptions of film, multiple quotations from numerous cultural and critical sources, further annotations, index and a range of fonts, colours, typographic settings and spacings, all of which draw attention to a highly wrought composite of texts. House and form mirror each other: the former, disobeying the laws of physics in that its internal and external geometry of walls does not add up. In the novel this is extensively documented on poor-quality film as having a new, interstitial void emerging within it. A huge staircase, as in nightmare, descends into an unfathomable darkness of interior space whose dimensions change inexplicably and at random. Neither camera nor sonar can plumb its depths and trained explorers disappear in its expanse. Unmappable, glimpsed in obscure fragments of a handheld horror-style camerawork, heard as a persistent but unlocatable low groaning, and sensed, vaguely, as malevolent, the house not only generates various investigations, it satirically engenders a host of critical, historical, anthropological and psychological commentaries. The labyrinth that unravels in dark sublimity within the house is reiterated in the dense textual labyrinth that is spun around the house – notes, references and criticism extending a playful, frustrating and diverse web of uncertainty vainly searching for answers, origins, causes, all, like exploration itself, disappearing in detours, dead-ends and dark passages. Significantly no monster is discovered at the centre of the labyrinth. Nor is the existence of the house's interstitial void, or the film supposed to document its reality, ever substantiated. All remains immaterial, endlessly reiterated, mysterious, elusive. None-the-less, an existence seems to be maintained in the iterations of texts that interrogate the house, an existence sustained virtually in the many writings on and interpretations of it. The novel finds ghostliness in the reiteration of texts, moving from a space between story and reader to spaces between multiple and entangled readings and interpretations, all displaced among an array of supplementary spacings, texts and allusions. Despite the absence of monsters in the empty and dark heart of novel, there remains a pervasive sense of monstrosity sustained in its movement and assemblage of textual fragments, citations and typefaces. Without form or object except the text itself, monstrosity circulates freely. Like information, however, this circulation seems to dispense with the anchors of reality, body, matter or history, anchors that secure meaning, value or identity in a relatively stable context. Displaying a new demand for active, even interactive, participation in the production of playful fictions, the novel performs the artifices and processes of construction through which readers or users piece together their texts. As a printed, and hence perverse, remediation of hypertextual design, an intricate weave of a deconstructive text interlaced with the partial image of a dense but insubstantial web of information, the haunted house-text involves a different order of unreality, one that engages the palpable immateriality of digital mediation in analogue form. It manifests a retrogressive gesture that, in moving back rather than forward in terms of formal and medial innovation, discloses a virtual and ghostly aspect to all modes of mediation. In refusing the depiction of monsters as objects to be identified, excluded or destroyed, *House of Leaves* introduces a significant shift in horror, ghost and gothic genres. It locates monstrosity elsewhere, unseen, an elsewhere associated with, but not confined by, an allusive, ludic and elusive movement of texts, forms and media.

Familiar monsters, none-the-less, continue throughout popular fiction, culture and media, repetitively recycled in novels, films, magazines, games, cartoons, comics, clothes and commodities with occasional minor alterations of their status, capacities and abilities, all of which constitute small but unique selling points in a competitive market. Unreal, insofar as they are without referents other than long literary and cultural histories, gothic figures, always responsive to changing times, continue to serve as sites of projection and fantasy, metaphors of form and medium, screens of anxiety and desire operating at the limits of norm and meaning. While their appearance remains familiar their significance and value can shift, becoming increasingly attractive images of once negative states. The price of such cultural visibility and ubiquity, however, can be over-familiarity. As a result scary figures, when invested with positive associations, lose the very features and effects that once, negatively in fear or horror, charged them with significance. Werewolves, too hairy, animal, sexual in their associations to assimilate to a slick corporate and post-human context, are generally given supporting and antagonist roles or, hidden away in the wilds of Scotland (*Dog Soldiers*, Neil Marshall, 2002), they remain provincial throwbacks. Glen Duncan's *The Last Werewolf* (2011), a very civilised, witty and reflective voice amid expensive hotel rooms and exclusive London clubs, narrates his own story and comments on the role of monsters in genre fiction. Here vampires consider themselves more refined and are part of a corporate elite; werewolves still enjoy sex and are hunted by a quasi-corporate agency dedicated to monster management called 'WOCOP' ('World Organisation for the Control of Occult Phenomena') (p. 28). The narrator is the last of his kind and is relieved that his time has come because, after two centuries of killing, he is exhausted. An encounter with another of his species, a female, changes his mind. The novel changes, too, from horror to action, romance and adventure. Werewolves live on, and a new series is born (*Talullah Rising*, 2012). In a fiction and film market dependent on identification and branding, seriality is one route to avoid extinction. Generic variation and crossing is another. Indeed, slight variations of formula and convention sustain novelty in a culture saturated with familiar and heroic monsters, mixing the modes and moods in which they develop, spicing romance, fantasy, thriller, science fiction, adventure with a touch of horror and darkness.

Hybrid, self-aware forms manifest an implosion of reflexive, reversible yet readerly entanglements of conventions and cultural mores. Why develop a crush on the rebellious biker boy when there is a vampire sitting at the next canteen table? He drives more quickly, dresses as coolly, is as alienated, moody, poetic and sensitive as any teen rebel but is also impossibly beautiful, incredibly strong, deeply caring, loyal and thoughtful, and a lot more dangerous. Yet it is because he is so bad, as the cliché goes, that he is suffused with goodness. He is both a nocturnal bloodsucker hiding in the shadows and a figure of loveliness who sparkles more brightly in the light of the sun. His difference is redoubled, supplementary, rather than oppositional. It emerges, not in the way that positive and negative have tended to be revalued, the former rendered bland and normal as the latter's darkness becomes charged with depth and erotic possibility, but through a heightened awareness of the very dangerous and monstrous capacities that make his care, restraint and consideration all the more impressive. Of course, he does not want to be a monster or inflict monstrosity on others, but, knowing that he is one, he exercises all possible precaution. He remains like, but better and worse than, other boys. Their adolescent gaze, he disapprovingly notes, sees young women as 'something to eat'. In contrast, he really, really does want to eat them (p. 194). Curiously, *Twilight* (2005), Stephanie Meyer's teen vampire romance, uses traditional forms of monstrosity in the negotiation of desire and prohibition. For the teenager who arrives in an unfamiliar school worrying about belonging, peer pressure and parental expectations, the appeal of the beautiful blood-drinking outsider is only enhanced by obstacles in the path of true love. Aware of his feelings, and unsure of his ability to control himself, he takes great pains to avoid her, not wanting to hurt her despite the almost irresistible urge to drink her blood. A demon who knows himself as such, his restraint is all the more admirable. His attitude is ethical and self-sacrificing: he warns her off, speaks of what he 'should' do, instinct, desire and conscience painfully at odds in his suffering being. As intimacy approaches, he impresses himself with his own powers of self-control, becoming a model of propriety, moderation and good behaviour despite the temptation she embodies. Temptation arises from within, a 'demon' languishing in a 'personal hell' that threatens 'ruin' (p. 236). Held at bay, however, desire becomes all the more meaningful. She is glad, as love blossoms, that she has never really dated before. For her, unconsummated desire makes it all the more consuming while, like a proper heroine, she faints at the sight of blood or the merest hint of passion realised.

The language of restraint and abstinence is equated with vegetarianism, addiction, alcoholism. Good vampires, and, it seems, teenagers, manage their issues. In a context that encourages pledge rings, premarital sexual abstention and virginity vows, the novel's emphasis on waiting and abstinence has strong religious, social and ideological connotations, responding conservatively to a culture that is seen to give too much licence to the expression of young female sexuality. Returning to a traditional association of vampirism, the novel invokes the prohibition that equates (premarital) sex and death. Except, undead, vampirism also summons up the contrary: eternal life and love in pleasure and consummation. Marriage, too, is another sacrifice, symbolic as much as corporeal. The dilemmas thrown up in the novel by the abstinence of vampires raise other questions of adolescence and sexuality that almost replicate the uses of romance in the eighteenth century as guides to conduct, moderations of excess and warnings against immodesty. In *Twilight*, however, the vampire is neither other nor an object of execration, but an agent of conservative morality, having internalised and dramatised the conflicts of a self split between respect and desire, temptation and control. Contemporary lures like sex, drugs and consumption are so powerful that contemporary self-control must be monstrously virtuous to match them. The sparkle is almost saintly. Playing out a mythical and mostly internal struggle also especially requires sensitivity to and compensation for parental inadequacy, envisaged as a divorced mother's problems with her boyfriend and a father's inability to manage a household. Thus, the young lovers' romance is not only with each other, but with individual desire, conscience and prohibition. Indeed, the need to compensate for a lack of parental guidance rather than subvert parental prohibitions and restrictions places the struggle in a curiously vacuous cultural zone that recognises the absence of symbolic and moral authority while, at the same, craving such authority. The division between absence and desire becomes a site of individual rather than familial or social responsibility. In a world organised around the construction, consumption, competition and gratification of individual desires (neo-liberalism), it is up to the individual to manifest the necessary virtues of restraint, responsibility and self control (neo-conservatism).

FURTHER READING

CHAPTER 1

Edwards, Justin D. (2005), *Gothic Canada*, Edmonton: University of Alberta Press.

Halberstam, Judith (1995), *Skin Shows*, Durham, NC and London: Duke University Press.

Ng, Andrew Hock Soon ed. (2008), *Asian Gothic*, Jefferson: McFarland.

Moers, Ellen (1978), *Literary Women*, London: W.H. Allen.

Moretti, Franco (1983), *Signs Taken for Wonders: Essays on the Sociology of Literary Forms*, trans. Susan Fischer, David Forgacs and David Miller, London: Verso.

Summers, Montague (1964), *The Gothic Quest: A History of the Gothic Novel*, New York: Russell & Russell.

CHAPTER 2

Kliger, Samuel (1952), *The Goths in England: A Study in Seventeenth and Eighteenth Century Thought*, Cambridge, MA: Harvard University Press.

Lovejoy, Arthur O. (1948), *Essays in the History of Ideas*, Baltimore and London: Johns Hopkins University Press.

Monk, Samuel Holt (1960), *The Sublime: A Study of Critical Theories in XVIII-Century England*, Ann Arbor: University of Michigan Press.

Tompkins, J.M.S. (1969), *The Popular Novel in England 1770–1800* (1932), London: Methuen.

CHAPTER 3

Castle, Terry (1995), *The Female Thermometer: Eighteenth-century Culture and the Invention of the Uncanny*, New York and Oxford: Oxford University Press.

Clery, E.J. (1995), *The Rise of Supernatural Fiction 1762–1800*, Cambridge: Cambridge University Press.

Napier, Elizabeth (1987), *The Failure of Gothic: Problems of Disjunction in an Eighteenth-Century Literary Form*, Oxford: Clarendon.

Sedgwick, Eve Kosofsky (1986), *The Coherence of Gothic Conventions*, London: Methuen.

CHAPTER 4

Ellis, Kate Ferguson (1987), *The Contested Castle: Gothic Novels and the Subversion of Domestic Ideology*, Urbana and Chicago: University of Illinois Press.

Miles, Robert (1995), *Ann Radcliffe: The Great Enchantress*, Manchester: Manchester University Press.

Townshend, Dale (2007), *The Orders of Gothic*, New York: AMS Press.

Williams, Anne (1995), *Art of Darkness*, Chicago: University of Chicago Press.

CHAPTER 5

Bruhm, Steven (1994), *Gothic Bodies*, Philadelphia: University of Pennsylvania Press.

Gamer, Michael (2000), *Romanticism and the Gothic*, Cambridge: Cambridge University Press.

Goddu, Teresa (1997), *Gothic America*, New York: Columbia University Press.

Miles, Robert (2002), *Gothic Writing 1750–1820*, Manchester: Manchester University Press.

CHAPTER 6

DeLamotte, Eugenia (1990), *Perils of the Night*, Oxford: Oxford University Press.

Fiedler, Leslie (1966), *Love and Death in the American Novel*, New York: Stein & Day.

Schmitt, Cannon (1997), *Alien Nation*, Philadelphia: University of Pennsylvania Press.

Showalter, Elaine (1991), 'American Female Gothic', in *Sister's Choice*, Oxford: Clarendon.

Wolfreys, Julian (2002), *Victorian Hauntings*, Basingstoke: Palgrave.

CHAPTER 7

Dijkstra, Bram (1986), *Idols of Perversity: Fantasies of Feminine Evil in Fin-de-Siecle Culture*, Oxford: Oxford University Press.

Hurley, Kelly (1996), *The Gothic Body*, Cambridge: Cambridge University Press.

Mighall, Robert (1999), *A Geography of Victorian Gothic Fiction*, Oxford: Oxford University Press.

Showalter, Elaine (1992), *Sexual Anarchy: Gender and Culture at the Fin de Siècle*, London: Virago.

CHAPTER 8

Lloyd-Smith, Allan (2004), *American Gothic Fiction*, New York and London: Continuum.

Riquelme, John Paul ed. (2008), *Gothic and Modernism*, Baltimore: Johns Hopkins University Press.

Smith, Andrew and Wallace, Jeff eds (2001), *Gothic Modernisms*, Manchester: Manchester University Press.

Wilt, Judith (1980), *Ghosts of the Gothic: Austen, Eliot and Lawrence*, Princeton: Princeton University Press.

CHAPTER 9

Botting, Fred (2008), *Gothic Romanced*, London: Routledge.

Botting, Fred (2008), *Limits of Horror*, Manchester: Manchester University Press.

Gordon, Joan and Hollinger, Veronica eds (1997), *Blood Read: The Vampire as Metaphor in Contemporary Culture*, Philadelphia: University of Pennsylvania Press.

Martin, Robert K. and Savoy, Eric eds (1998), *American Gothic: New Interventions in National Perspective*, Iowa City: University of Iowa Press.

BIBLIOGRAPHY

TEXTS

Ackroyd, Peter (1986), *Hawksmoor*, London: Sphere Books.

Ainsworth, William Harrison (1980), *The Lancashire Witches* (1849), London: Granada.

Anonymous (1797), 'Terrorist Novel Writing', *Spirit of the Public Journals* 1: 227–29.

Austen, Jane (1985), *Northanger Abbey* (1818), ed. Henry Ehrenpreis, Harmondsworth: Penguin.

Baillie, John (1953), *An Essay on the Sublime* (1747), Augustan Reprint Society 43, University of California.

Baldick, Chris ed. (1992), *The Oxford Book of Gothic Tales*, Oxford: Oxford University Press.

Barbauld, Anna Laetitia (1825), *The Works of Anna Laetitia Barbauld*, 2 vols, London: Longman.

Beckford, William (1983), *Vathek* (1786), ed. Roger Lonsdale, Oxford: Oxford University Press.

Bierce, Ambrose (1926), *Can Such Things Be?*, London: Jonathan Cape.

Blackwood, Algernon (1968), *Ancient Sorceries and Other Stories*, Harmondsworth: Penguin.

Blair, Hugh (1796), *Lectures on Rhetoric and Belles Lettres* (1783), 6th edn, 3 vols, London: Strachan & Cadell.

Blair, Robert (1973), *The Grave* (1743), Los Angeles: Augustan Reprint Society.

Bloch, Robert (1997), *Psycho* (1960), London: Bloomsbury.

——(1975), *American Gothic*, London: W.H. Allen.

Braddon, Mary Elizabeth (1896), 'Good Lady Ducayne', *Strand Magazine* 11: 185–99.

Brontë, Charlotte (1966), *Jane Eyre* (1847), ed. Q.D. Leavis, Harmondsworth: Penguin.

——(1966), *Villette* (1853), ed. Sandra Kemp, London: Dent.

Brontë, Emily (1981), *Wuthering Heights* (1847), ed. Ian Jack, Oxford: Oxford University Press.

Brown, Charles Brockden (1991), *Wieland and Memoirs of Carwin the Biloquist* (1798), ed. Jay Fliegelman, Harmondsworth: Penguin.

Brite, Poppy Z. (1994), *Lost Souls*, London: Penguin.

Bulwer-Lytton, Edward (1970), *Zanoni: A Rosicrucian Tale* (1842), New York: Garland, pp. 273–311.

——(1947), 'The Haunters and the Haunted: or the House and the Brain' (1859), in *Great Tales of Terror and the Supernatural*, eds Herbert A. Wise and Phyllis Fraser, New York: Random House.

Burke, Edmund (1990), *A Philosophical Enquiry into the Origin of Our Ideas of the Sublime and the Beautiful* (1757), ed. Adam Phillips, Oxford: Oxford University Press.

——(1969), *Reflections on the Revolution in France* (1790), ed. Conor Cruise O'Brien, Harmondsworth: Penguin.

Carpenter, Edward (1889), *Civilisation*, London: Swan Sonnenschein.

Carter, Angela (1972), *Heroes and Villains* (1969), Harmondsworth: Penguin.

——(1982), *The Infernal Desire Machines of Dr Hoffman* (1972), Harmondsworth: Penguin.

——(2006), *Burning Your Boats: Collected Stories*, London: Vintage.

Cobbe, Frances Power (1870), 'Unconscious Cerebration', *Macmillan's Magazine* 23 (Nov.): 24–37.

Coleridge, S.T. (1794), 'Review of *The Mysteries of Udolpho*', *Critical Review* (Second Series) 11 (Aug.): 361–72.

——(1796), 'Review of *The Monk*', *Critical Review* (Second Series) 19 (Feb.): 194–200.

Collins, Wilkie (1980), *The Woman in White* (1860), ed. Harvey Peter Sucksmith, Oxford: Oxford University Press.

Conrad, Joseph (1973), *Heart of Darkness* (1902), ed. Paul O'Prey, Harmondsworth: Penguin.

——(1963), *The Secret Agent: A Simple Tale* (1907), ed. Martin Seymour-Smith, Harmondsworth: Penguin.

Cox, Jeffrey N. ed. (1992), *Seven Gothic Dramas 1789–1825*, Athens: Ohio University Press.

Cox, Michael and Gilbert, R.A. eds (1992), *Victorian Ghost Stories*, Oxford: Oxford University Press.

Dacre, Charlotte (1974), *Zofoya; or, the Moor* (1806), 3 vols, New York: Arno Press.

Danielewski, Mark Z. (2001), *House of Leaves*, London and New York: Doubleday.

Dickens, Charles (1966), *Oliver Twist* (1838), ed. Peter Fairclough, Harmondsworth: Penguin.

——(1982) *Dombey and Son* (1848), ed. Peter Fairclough, Harmondsworth: Penguin.

——(1985), *Bleak House* (1853), ed. Norman Page, Harmondsworth: Penguin.

——(1969), *Hard Times* (1854), ed. David Craig, Harmondsworth: Penguin.

——(1967), *Little Dorrit* (1855), ed. John Holloway, Harmondsworth: Penguin.

——(1985), *Great Expectations* (1860–61), ed. Angus Calder, Harmondsworth: Penguin.

Du Maurier, Daphne (1948), *Rebecca* (1938), New York: Doubleday.

Duncan, Glen (2011), *The Last Werewolf*, Edinburgh: Canongate.

Eco, Umberto (1984), *The Name of the Rose* (1980), trans. William Weaver, London: Pan.

Eliot, George (1940), 'The Lifted Veil' (1859), in *Silas Marner, The Lifted Veil and Brother Jacob*, Oxford: Oxford University Press.

Eliot, T.S. (1976), *Selected Poems*, London: Faber and Faber.

Faulkner, William (1957), *Sanctuary* (1931), Harmondsworth: Penguin.

——(2005), *Light in August* (1932), London: Vintage.

——(1971), *Absalom, Absalom!* (1936), Harmondsworth: Penguin.

Flammenberg, Lawrence (1968), *The Necromancer, or the Tale of the Black Forest* (1794), trans. Peter Teuthold, London: Folio Press.

Franklin, Caroline ed. (2011) *The Longman Anthology of Gothic Verse*, Harlow: Pearson Education.

Frayling, Christopher ed. (1991), *Vampyres: Lord Byron to Count Dracula*, London: Faber and Faber.

Gaskell, Elizabeth (1978), *Mrs Gaskell's Tales of Mystery and Horror*, ed. Michael Ashley, London: Victor Gollancz.

Gibson, William (1986), *Neuromancer* (1984), London: Grafton.

——(1986), 'The Gernsback Continuum', in *Burning Chrome*, London: HarperCollins, pp. 37–50.

Gibson, William and Sterling, Bruce (1992), *The Difference Engine*, London: Victor Gollancz Science Fiction.

Glasgow, Ellen (1935), 'Heroes and Monsters', *The Saturday Review of Literature*, May 4: 3–4.

Godwin, William (1985), *Enquiry Concerning Political Justice* (1793), ed. Isaac Kramnick, Harmondsworth: Penguin.

——(1988), *Caleb Williams* (1794), ed. Maurice Hindle, Harmondsworth: Penguin.

——(1992), *St Leon* (1799), in *Collected Novels and Memoirs of William Godwin*, vol. 4, ed. Pamela Clemit, London: Pickering.

Gray, Alasdair (1992), *Poor Things*, London: Bloomsbury.

Grosse, Carl (1968), *Horrid Mysteries: A Story* (1797), trans. Peter Will, London: Folio Press.

Hale, Terry ed. (1992), *Tales of the Dead* (1813), Chislehurst: Gothic Society.

Hawthorne, Nathaniel (1987), *Young Goodman Brown and Other Tales*, ed. Brian Harding, Oxford: Oxford University Press.

——(1906) *The Scarlet Letter* (1850), London: Dent.

——(1991), *The House of Seven Gables* (1851), ed. Michael Davitt Bell, Oxford: Oxford University Press.

——(1958), *The Marble Faun* (1860), New York: Pocket Books.

Hodgson, William Hope (2002), *The House on the Borderland and Other Novels*, London: Gollancz.

Hoffman, E.T.A. (1992), *The Golden Pot and Other Tales*, trans. Ritchie Robertson, Oxford: Oxford University Press.

Hogg, James (1947), *The Private Memoirs and Confessions of a Justified Sinner* (1824), London: Cresset Press.

Horsley-Curties, T.J. (1977), *The Monk of Udolpho: A Romance* (1807), 4 vols, New York: Arno Press.

Hurd, Richard (1963), *Letters on Chivalry and Romance* (1762), Augustan Reprint Society 101–2: University of California.

Jackson, Shirley (2005), *The Haunting of Hill House* (1959), London: Penguin.

James, Henry (1948), *The Ghostly Tales of Henry James*, ed. Leon Edel, New Brunswick, NJ: Rutgers University Press.

——(1984), 'Mary Elizabeth Braddon' (1865), in *Literary Criticism*, ed. Leon Edel, New York: The Library of America.

James, M.R. (1987), *Casting the Runes and other Ghost Stories*, ed. Michael Cox, Oxford: Oxford University Press.

Johnson, Samuel (1986), *The Rambler* 4 (1750), in *Samuel Johnson,* ed. Donald Greene, Oxford: Oxford University Press, pp. 175–79.

Kafka, Franz (1957), *The Castle* (1926), trans. Willa and Edwin Muir, Harmondsworth: Penguin.

——(1959), *Letters to Milena*, ed. Willy Haas, trans. Tania and James Stern, New York: Schocken Books.

——(1961), *Metamorphosis and Other Stories*, trans. Willa and Edwin Muir, Harmondsworth: Penguin.

——(1968), *The Trial* (1925), trans. Willa and Edwin Muir, London: Heron.

Kames, Henry Home (1839), *Elements of Criticism* (1762), 11th edn, London: B. Blake.

Kant, Immanuel (1952), *The Aesthetic of Judgement* (1790), ed. James Creed Meredith, Oxford: Oxford University Press.

Khair, Tabish (2009), *The Gothic, Postcolonialism and Otherness*, Basingstoke: Palgrave Macmillan.

King, Stephen (1978), *The Shining*, London: Hodder and Stoughton.

Le Fanu, J. Sheridan (1990), *In a Glass Darkly* (1872), Gloucester: Alan Sutton Publishing.

Lee, Sophia (1972), *The Recess: or, A Tale of Other Times* (1783–85), 3 vols, New York: Arno Press.

Lewis, Matthew Gregory (1980), *The Monk* (1796), ed. Howard Anderson, Oxford: Oxford University Press.

——(1990), *The Castle Spectre: A Drama* (1797), Oxford: Woodstock Books.

Lovecraft, H.P. (2011), *The Complete Fiction*, ed. S.T. Joshi, New York: Barnes and Noble.

Luckhurst, Roger ed. (2005), *Late Victorian Gothic Tales*, Oxford: Oxford University Press.

McCullers, Carson (1961), *The Heart is a Lonely Hunter* (1940), Harmondsworth: Penguin.

——(1953), *The Ballad of the Sad Café* (1943), London: Cresset.

Machen, Arthur (1894), *The Great God Pan*, London: John Lane.

——(1895), *The Three Imposters*, London: John Lane.

McNutt, D.J. (1975) *The Eighteenth-Century Gothic Novel*, New York: Garland.

Macpherson, James (1896), *The Poems of Ossian* (1762), Edinburgh: Geddes.

Mallett, Paul-Henri (1847), *Northern Antiquities* (1770), trans. Thomas Percy, ed. I.A. Blackwell, London: Bohn's Library.

Marinetti, F.T. (2005), 'The Founding and Manifesto of Futurism' (1909), in *Modernism*, ed. Lawrence Rainey, Oxford: Blackwell, pp. 3–6.

Marsh, Richard (2004), *The Beetle* (1897), ed. Julian Wolfreys, Peterborough, Ontario Broadview Press.

Matthias, T.J. (1805), *The Pursuits of Literature* (1796), 13th edn, London: T. Becket.

Maturin, Charles Robert (1979), *The Milesian Chief* (1812), ed. Robert Lee Worff, New York: Garland.

——(1992), *Bertram, or, the Castle of Aldobrand* (1816), Oxford: Woodstock Books.

——(1989), *Melmoth the Wanderer: A Tale* (1820), ed. Douglas Grant, Oxford: Oxford University Press.

Melville, Herman (1967), 'Benito Cereno', in *Billy Budd, Sailor and Other Stories,* ed. Harold Beaver, Harmondsworth: Penguin, pp. 215–308.

Meyer, Stephanie (2007), *Twilight*, London: Atom.

Morris, William (1907), *The Early Romances of William Morris in Prose and Verse*, London: Dent.

Morrison, Toni (1988), *Beloved*, London: Picador.

——(1993), *Playing in the Dark*, London: Picador.

O'Connor, Flannery (1988), *Collected Works*, New York: The Library of America.

——(2008), *Wise Blood* (1952), London: Faber and Faber.

Paine, Thomas (1987), *The Rights of Man* (1791–92), in *The Thomas Paine Reader,* eds Michael Foot and Isaac Kramnick, Harmondsworth: Penguin, pp. 201–364.

Peacock, Thomas Love (1986), *Nightmare Abbey* (1817–18) and *Crotchet Castle* (1831), ed. Raymond Wright, Harmondsworth: Penguin.

Peake, Mervyn (1969), *Gormenghast* (1950), Harmondsworth: Penguin.

Peake, R.B. (1990), *Presumption; or, The Fate of Frankenstein* (1823), in Steven Earl Forry, *Hideous Progenies,* Philadelphia: University of Pennsylvania Press.

Percy, Thomas (1966), *Reliques of Ancient English Poetry* (1765), 3 vols, ed. Henry B. Wheatley, New York: Dover Publications.

Poe, Edgar Allan (1986), *The Fall of the House of Usher and Other Writings*, ed. David Galloway, London: Penguin.

Polidori, John (1966), 'The Vampyre: A Tale', in *Three Gothic Novels,* ed. E.F. Bleiler, New York: Dover Publications, pp. 255–84.

Radcliffe, Ann (1993), *A Sicilian Romance* (1790), ed. Alison Milbank, Oxford: Oxford University Press.

——(1986), *The Romance of the Forest* (1791), ed. Chloe Chard, Oxford: Oxford University Press.

——(1980), *The Mysteries of Udolpho* (1794), ed. Bonamy Dobree, Oxford: Oxford University Press.

——(1981), *The Italian, or the Confessional of the Black Penitents* (1797), ed. Frederick Garber, Oxford: Oxford University Press.

——(1826), 'On the Supernatural in Poetry', *New Monthly Magazine* 16: 145–52.

Reeve, Clara (1977), *The Old English Baron: A Gothic Story* (1778), ed. James Trainer, Oxford: Oxford University Press.

——(1970), *The Progress of Romance* (1785), 2 vols, New York: Garland.

Review of *Frankenstein, Edinburgh (Scot's) Magazine* (Second Series) 2 (Mar. 1818): 249–53.

——*Melmoth, Monthly Review* XCIV (1821): 81–90.

——*The Monk, British Critic* 7 (Jun. 1796): 677.

——*The Monk, Analytical Review* 24 (Oct. 1796): 403–4.

——*The Monk, Monthly Review* (New Series) 23 (Aug. 1797): 451.

——*The Mysteries of Udolpho, European Magazine* 25 (Jun. 1794): 433–40.

——*The Mysteries of Udolpho, British Critic* 4 (Aug. 1794): 110–21.

——*The Mysteries of Udolpho, Gentleman's Magazine* 64 (Sept. 1794): 834.

Reynolds, G.W. (1989), *The Mysteries of London* (1848), 2 vols, New York: AMS Press.

Rice, Anne (1977), *Interview with the Vampire*, London: Futura Publications.

——(1995), *The Vampire Lestat* (1985), New York: Warner Books.

Rider Haggard, H. (1991), *She* (1886), Oxford: Oxford University Press.

Roche, Regina Maria (1810), *The Children of the Abbey: A Tale* (1794), 4 vols, London: Minerva.

——(1968), *Clermont: A Tale* (1798), 4 vols, London: Folio Press.

Ruskin, John (1905), *The Stones of Venice*, 3 vols, London: George Allen.

Sade, D.A.F., Marquis de (1989), 'Reflections on the Novel', in *One Hundred and Twenty Days of Sodom*, trans. Austryn Wainhouse and Richard Seaver, London: Arrow Books, pp. 91–116.

Scott, Walter (1981), *Waverley* (1814), ed. Claire Lamont, Oxford: Clarendon.

——(1818), 'Review of Frankenstein', *Blackwood's Edinburgh Magazine* 2: 613–20.

——(1991), *The Bride of Lammermoor* (1819), ed. Fiona Robertson, Oxford: Oxford University Press.

Shelley, Mary (1968), *Frankenstein; or, the Modern Prometheus* (1831), ed. M.K. Joseph, Oxford: Oxford University Press.

Shelley, Percy Bysshe (1986), *Zastrozzi* (1810) and *St Irvyne* (1811), ed. Stephen C. Behrendt, Oxford: Oxford University Press.

Sinclair, May (2006), *Uncanny Stories*, Ware: Wordsworth Editions.

Stevenson, Robert Louis (1979), *The Strange Case of Dr Jekyll and Mr Hyde and Other Stories* (1886), ed. Jenni Calder, Harmondsworth: Penguin.

Stoker, Bram (1998), *Dracula* (1897), ed. Maurice Hindle, Harmondsworth: Penguin.

Summers, Montague ed. (1949), *The Supernatural Omnibus*, London: Victor Gollancz.

Twain, Mark (1981), *Life on the Mississippi*, New York: Bantam Books.

Walpole, Horace (1982), *The Castle of Otranto: A Gothic Story* (1764), ed. W.S. Lewis, Oxford: Oxford University Press.

——(1937), *The Yale Edition of Horace Walpole's Correspondence*, eds W.S. Lewis and A. Dayle Wallace, New Haven, CT and London: Yale University Press.

Warton, Thomas (1979), *History of English Poetry from the Twelfth to the Close of the Sixteenth Century* (1774–81), 4 vols, ed. W. Carew Hazlitt (1871), New York: Haskell House Publishers.

Wells, H.G. (1921), *The Island of Dr Moreau* (1896), London: Heinemann.

——(1951), *The War of the Worlds* (1898), London: Heinemann.

Wilde, Oscar (1985), *The Picture of Dorian Gray* (1891), ed. Peter Ackroyd, Harmondsworth: Penguin.

Williams, Ioan, ed. (1970) *Novel and Romance: A Documentary Record 1700–1800*, London: Routledge & Kegan Paul.

Wollstonecraft, Mary (1989), *A Vindication of the Rights of Men* (1790), in *The Works of Mary Wollstonecraft*, vol. 5, eds Janet Todd and Marilyn Butler, London: Pickering.

Woolf, Virginia (1961), 'Street Haunting: A London Adventure', *The Death of the Moth and Other Essays*, Harmondsworth: Penguin, pp. 23–36.

——(1966), 'The Cinema' (1926), *Collected Essays*, vol. 2, London: Hogarth Press, pp. 368–72.

——(1988), 'Henry James's Ghost Stories' (1921), in *The Essays of Virginia Woolf*, vol. 3, ed. Andrew McNeillie, London: Hogarth Press, pp. 319–26.

——(2003), *A Haunted House: The Complete Shorter Fiction*, London: Vintage.

Young, Edward (1989), *Night Thoughts* (1749–51), ed. Stephen Cornford, Cambridge: Cambridge University Press.

CRITICISM

Abraham, N. (1987), 'Notes on the Phantom: A Complement to Freud's Metapsychology', *Critical Inquiry* 13: 287–92.

Alexander, Christine (1993), '"That Kingdom of Gloom": Charlotte Brontë, the Annuals and the Gothic', *Nineteenth-Century Literature* 47: 409–38.

Ames, Dianne S. (1979), 'Strawberry Hill: Architecture of the "as if"', *Studies in Eighteenth-Century Culture* 8: 351–63.

Arata, Stephen D. (1990), 'The Occidental Tourist: *Dracula* and the Anxiety of Reverse Colonization', *Victorian Studies* 33.4: 621–45.

Badley, Linda C. (1996), *Writing Horror and the Body: The Fiction of Stephen King, Clive Barker, and Anne Rice*, Westport, CT and London: Greenwood Press.

Baldick, Chris (1987), *In Frankenstein's Shadow: Myth Monstrosity and Nineteenth-Century Writing*, Oxford: Clarendon.

Barthes, Roland (1988), 'Textual Analysis of Poe's "Valdemar"', in *Modern Criticism and Theory: A Reader*, ed. David Lodge, London: Longman, pp. 173–95.

Bataille, Georges (1973), *Literature and Evil* (1957), trans. Alastair Hamilton, London: Marion Boyars.

Baudrillard, Jean (1994), *The Illusion of the End*, trans. Chris Turner, London: Polity.

Benjamin, Walter (1999), *The Arcades Project*, trans. Howard Eiland and Kevin McLaughlin, Cambridge, MA and London: Belknap Press.

Bloom, Harold, ed. (2006), *Edgar Allan Poe*, New York: Chelsea House.

Brantlinger, Patrick (1985), 'Imperial Gothic: Atavism and the Occult in the British Adventure Novel, 1880–1914', *English Literature in Transition (1880–1920)* 28: 243–52.

Briggs, Julia (1977), *Night Visitors: The Rise and Fall of the English Ghost Story*, London: Faber and Faber.

Bronfen, Elisabeth (1992), *Over Her Dead Body: Death, Femininity and the Aesthetic*, Manchester: Manchester University Press.

Brooks, Peter (1973), 'Virtue and Terror: *The Monk*', *English Literary History* 40: 249–63.

Brophy, Philip (1987), 'Horrality – the Textuality of Contemporary Horror Films', *Screen* 27: 11–25.

Brown, Marshall (1987), 'A Philosophical View of the Gothic Novel', *Studies in Romanticism* 26: 275–301.

Byron, Glennis ed. (2013), *Globalgothic*, Manchester: Manchester University Press.

Cixous, Hélène (1976), 'Fiction and its Phantoms: A Reading of Freud's *Das Unheimliche* (The "Uncanny")', *New Literary History* 7: 525–48.

Clark, Kenneth (1962), *The Gothic Revival: An Essay in the History of Taste*, 3rd edn, London: John Murray.

Coates, J.D. (1981), 'Techniques of Terror in *The Woman in White*', *Durham University Journal* 73: 177–89.

Cooke, Arthur (1951), 'Some Side Lights on the Theory of Gothic Romance', *Modern Language Quarterly* 12: 429–36.

Craft, Christopher (1984), '"Kiss Me with Those Red Lips": Gender and Inversion in Bram Stoker's Dracula', *Representations* 8: 107–33.

Creed, Barbara (1993), *The Monstrous-Feminine*, London and New York: Routledge.

Dekker, George (1987), *The American Historical Romance*, Cambridge: Cambridge University Press.

Derrida, Jacques (1975), 'The Purveyor of Truth', *Yale French Studies* 52: 31–113.

——(1994), *Specters of Marx*, trans. Peggy Kamuf, London and New York: Routledge.

Dolar, Mladen (1991), '"I Shall Be With You on Your Wedding-night": Lacan and the Uncanny', *October* 58: 5–23.

Drakakis, John and Townshend, Dale eds (2008), *Gothic Shakespeares*, London: Routledge.

Durant, David (1982), 'Ann Radcliffe and the Conservative Gothic', *Studies in English Literature 1500–1900* 22: 519–30.

Eggenschwiler, David (1975), '*Melmoth the Wanderer*. Gothic on Gothic', *Genre* 8: 165–81.

Elsaesser, Thomas (1998), 'Specularity and Engulfment: Francis Ford Coppola and *Bram Stoker's Dracula*', in Steve Neale and Murray White eds, *Contemporary Hollywood Cinema*, New York and London: Routledge, pp. 191–208.

Fletcher, John (1995), 'Primal Scenes and Female Gothic: Rebecca and Gaslight', *Screen* 36.4: 341–70.

Foucault, Michel (1977), *Language, Counter-Memory, Practice*, trans. Donald F. Bouchard and Sherry Simon, Ithaca, NY: Cornell University Press.

Fowler, Kathleen (1986), 'Hieroglyphics of Fire: *Melmoth the Wanderer*', *Studies in Romanticism* 25: 521–39.

Freud, Sigmund (1955), 'The Uncanny' (1919), in *Standard Edition of the Complete Psychological Works*, vol. 17, trans. James Strachey, London: Hogarth Press, pp. 218–56.

——(1984), 'Beyond the Pleasure Principle' (1922), in *The Pelican Freud Library*, vol. 11, trans. James Strachey, Harmondsworth: Pelican, pp. 271–338.

Glover, David (1993), 'Travels in Romania: Myths of Origins, Myths of Blood', *Discourse* 16: 126–44.

Gordon, Jan B. (1983), 'Narrative Enclosure as Textual Ruin: An Archaeology of Gothic Consciousness', *Dickens Studies Annual* 11: 209–38.

Guest, Harriet (1992), 'The Wanton Muse: Politics and Gender in Gothic Theory after 1760', in Stephen Copley and John Whale eds, *Beyond Romanticism*, London: Routledge.

Haggerty, George (2006), *Queer Gothic*, Urbana-Champaign: University of Illinois Press.

Harries, Elizabeth W. (1979), 'Duplication and Duplicity: James Hogg's *Private Memoirs and Confessions of a Justifed Sinner*', *Wordsworth Circle* 10: 187–96.

Heath, Stephen (1986), 'Psychopathia Sexualis: Stevenson's Strange Case', *Critical Quarterly* 28: 93–108.

Heller, Tamar (1992), *Dead Secrets: Wilkie Collins and the Female Gothic*, New Haven, CT and London: Yale University Press.

Hogle, Jerrold E. (1980), 'The Restless Labyrinth: Cryptonomy in the Gothic Novel', *Arizona Quarterly* 36: 330–58.

Horner, Avril and Zlosnik, Sue (1998), *Daphne du Maurier*, Basingstoke: Macmillan.

Howells, Coral Ann (1978), *Love, Mystery and Misery: Feeling in Gothic Fiction*, London: Athlone Press.

Hume, Robert D. (1969), 'Gothic versus Romantic: A Re-evaluation of the Gothic Novel', *PMLA* 84: 282–90.

Huyssen, Andreas (1981–82), 'The Vamp and the Machine: Technology and Sexuality in Fritz Lang's *Metropolis*', *New German Critique* 24–25: 221–37.

Jackson, Rosemary (1981), *Fantasy: The Literature of Subversion*, London: Methuen.

Jarrett, David (1977), 'The Fall of the House of Clennam: Gothic Conventions in Little Dorrit', *Dickensian* 73: 155–61.

Jentsch, Ernst (1995), 'On the Psychology of the Uncanny', trans. Roy Sellars, *Angelaki* 2.1: 7–16.

Kahane, Claire (1980), 'Gothic Mirrors and Feminine Identity', *Centennial Review* 24: 43–64.

Knoff, C.R. (1976), '*Caleb Williams* and the Attack on Romance', *Studies in the Novel* 8: 81–87.

Kristeva, Julia (1982), *Powers of Horror: An Essay on Abjection*, trans. Leon S. Roudiez, New York: Columbia University Press.

Lacan, Jacques (1972), 'Seminar on "The Purloined Letter"', *Yale French Studies* 48: 38–72.

Land, Nick (1998), 'Cybergothic', in Joan Broadhurst Dixon and Eric J. Cassidy eds, *Virtual Futures*, New York and London: Routledge, pp. 79–87.

Leps, Marie-Christine (1992), *Apprehending the Criminal: The Production of Deviance in Nineteenth-Century Discourse*, Durham, NC and London: Duke University Press.

Lévy, Maurice (2004), 'FAQ: What is Gothic?', *Anglophonia* 15: 23–37.

Longueil, Alfred E. (1923), 'The Word "Gothic" in Eighteenth-Century Criticism', *Modern Language Notes* 38: 453–56.

Lyndenburg, Robin (1978), 'Gothic Architecture and Fiction: A Survey of Critical Responses', *Centennial Review* 22: 95–109.

Lyotard, Jean-Francois (1979), *The Postmodern Condition: A Report on Knowledge*, trans. Regis Durand, Manchester: Manchester University Press.

Madoff, Mark (1979), 'The Useful Myth of Gothic Ancestry', *Studies in Eighteenth Century Culture* 8: 337–50.

Marx, Karl (1976), *Capital* (1867), vol. 1, trans. Ben Fowkes, Harmondsworth: Penguin.

Maxwell, Richard C. (1977), 'G.M. Reynolds, Dickens and *The Mysteries of London*', *Nineteenth-Century Fiction* 32: 188–213.

McIntyre, C. (1921), 'Were the "Gothic Novels" Gothic?' *PMLA* 36: 644–47.

Modleski, Tania (1982), *Loving with a Vengeance*, New York and London: Routledge.

Morris, D.B. (1985), 'Gothic Sublimity', *New Literary History* 16: 299–319.

Nelson, Lowry Jr. (1962), 'Night Thoughts on the Gothic Novel', *Yale Review* 52: 236–57.

Nietzsche, Friedrich (1968), *Beyond Good and Evil*, in *Basic Writings of Nietzsche*, trans. Walter Kaufmann, New York: Random House.

Novak, Maximilian E. (1979), 'Gothic Fiction and the Grotesque', *Novel* 13: 50–67.

Paulson, Ronald (1983), *Representations of Revolution (1789–1820)*, New Haven, CT and London: Yale University Press.

Pick, Daniel (1984), '"Terrors of the Night": *Dracula* and "Degeneration" in the Late Nineteenth Century', *Critical Quarterly* 30: 71–87.

Platzner, Robert L. (1971), 'Gothic versus Romantic: A Rejoinder', *PMLA* 86: 266–74

Poovey, Mary (1979), 'Ideology in *The Mysteries of Udolpho*', *Criticism* 21: 307–30.

Poteet, Lewis J. (1971), '*Dorian Gray* and the Gothic Novel', *Modern Fiction Studies* 17: 239–48.

Prawer, S.S. (1980), *Caligari's Children: The Film as Tale of Terror*, Oxford: Oxford University Press.

Punter, David (1996), *The Literature of Terror: A History of Gothic Fiction from 1765 to the Present Day*, 2 vols, London: Longman.

——(1999), 'Heartlands: Contemporary Scottish Gothic', *Gothic Studies* 1.1: 101–18.

Sage, Victor (1988), *Horror Fiction in the Protestant Tradition*, London and Basingstoke: Macmillan.

Saposnik, Irving S. (1971), 'The Anatomy of *Dr Jekyll and Mr Hyde*', *Studies in English Literature* 11: 715–31.

Schroeder, Natalie (1980), '*The Mysteries of Udolpho* and *Clermont:* The Radcliffean Encroachment on the Art of Regina Maria Roche', *Studies in the Novel* 12: 131–43.

Sconce, Jeffrey (2000), *Haunted Media*, Durham, NC and London: Duke University Press.

Spencer, Kathleen L. (1992), 'Purity and Danger: *Dracula,* the Urban Gothic, and the Late Victorian Degeneracy Crisis', *English Literary History* 59: 197–225.

Spivak, Gayatri Chakravorty (1985), 'Three Women's Texts and a Critique of Imperialism', *Critical Inquiry* 12: 243–61.

Thompson, G.R. ed. (1974), *The Gothic Imagination: Essays in Dark Romanticism*, Pullman: Washington University Press.

Twitchell, James B. (1977), 'Heathcliff as Vampire', *Southern Humanities Review* 11: 355–62.

Van Elferen, Isabella (2012), *Gothic Music*, Cardiff: University of Wales Press.

Veeder, William (1980), 'Carmilla: The Arts of Repression', *Texas Studies in Literature and Language* 22: 197–223.

Warner, Marina (2006), *Phantasmagoria*, Oxford: Oxford University Press.

Watkins, Daniel P. (1986), 'Social Hierarchy in Matthew Lewis's *The Monk*', *Studies in the Novel* 18: 115–24.

Wheatley, Helen (2006), *Gothic Television*, Manchester: Manchester University Press.

Wicke, Jennifer (1992), 'Vampiric Typewriting: *Dracula* and its Media', *English Literary History* 59: 467–93.

Wilt, Judith (1981), 'The Imperial Mouth: Imperialism, the Gothic and Science Fiction', *Journal of Popular Culture* 14: 618–28.

INDEX